The Good Life

My Legacy for You

James Klopovic

The Good Life:
My Legacy for You
by James Klopovic

Copyright © 2023 by James Klopovic

All Rights Reserved. No part of this publication may be reproduced, distributed, or transmitted in any form or by any means, including photocopying, recording, or other electronic or mechanical methods, without the prior written permission of the publisher/author, except in the case of brief quotations embodied in reviews and certain other noncommercial uses permitted by copyright law.
Direct requests for permission to *jklopovic@gmail.com,* Affinitas Publishing.

Cover and Interior Design: Nick Zelinger, NZ Graphics
Editing: Peggy Henrikson, Heart and Soul Editing
Virtual Assistance: Kelly Johnson, Cornerstone Virtual Assistance, LLC

Published in the United States by Affinitas Publishing

Library of Congress Control Number: 2023917751

ISBN: 979-8-9850119-3-7 (Paperback)
ISBN: 979-8-9850119-4-4 (eBook)
ISBN: 979-8-9850119-5-1 (Audio)
ISBN: 979-8-9850119-6-8 (Hardcover)

To my children, Nicole and Cindy

Nic, know that you are this father's dream come true.
Not a word herein was written without you in mind.

Cindy, my fondest memories of you course throughout these pages.
May you both find worth in them and the love with which they were written.

*There is nothing that matters more
in the end than love.*[1]

— Steve Leder

About Reading This Memoir

I wrote these reflections separately over time in answer to particular questions. Thus, you will find parts repeated here and there when they are relevant to different answers. You may feel drawn to read the answers to certain questions as they spark your interest, which is fine. However, the sections of this memoir form a more comprehensive and understandable picture of my life, adventures, musings, and philosophy when read in order—and, I hope, in their entirety.

I wish to convey to you, Nicole and Cindy, the magnitude of my efforts to overcome difficulty and yes, tragedy, to achieve a good life. I managed to do well against steep odds, and I wish for you to learn from my experiences so that you, too, can achieve the "Good Life." Please know that in my heartfelt opinion, you are my greatest accomplishments.

Remember: This is more than a memoir; it is a *history* which, now written, exists.

> I believe happiness, as our Founding Fathers wished for us, *can* be pursued—but knowing *how* matters. It's a matter of living the Good Life, respecting our unfathomable natural gifts to be rational, human, and humane and our deep responsibilities to others. We must work continuously, relentlessly, doing those things that are worthwhile; then happiness happens. It is that fleeting moment when we are captured by a sense of well-being, feeling that life is good and worth the work, worry, and wonder of it.
>
> – JK

Contents

Dedication iii
About Reading This Memoir v
Introduction xi

PARENTS, FAMILY, AND GROWING UP 1
What Are Your Earliest Memories of Your Parents, Family,
   and Childhood? 3
More About Parents and Childhood 10
What Hobbies and Other Activities Did You Pursue in Grade School? 17
Were You Ever Teased About Anything As a child? 21
What Lessons Did You Learn from Your Parents? 23
What Were You Like As a Teenager? 27
How Did Farm and Body Shop Work Experiences Affect You? 33
Ahh . . . the Female Sex! 39

THIRTY, MARRIAGE, AND CHILDREN 49
What Were You Like When You Were Thirty-Plus? 51
When Did You Decide to Have Children,
   and What Were Your Earliest Memories of Each Child? 55
Have You Ever Had Your Heart Broken? 59
What Is a Proud Moment for You and How Does It Affect You? 62

THE MILITARY 65
How Do You Feel Your Time in the Military Changed You As a Person? 67
How Was Your Air Force Experience with Combat? 74
How Does Veteran's Day Affect You? 85

TRAVEL 89
What Was Your First Big Trip, and How Did It Affect You? 91
What Later Trips Did You Take with Your Family? 94
What Is the Strangest International Experience You've Had? 98
Where's a Favorite Place You've Traveled and Why? 102
How Has Travel Enriched You? 108

CULINARY UPS AND DOWNS 119
What Was Your Favorite Thing to Eat as a Child and Young Adult
 and the First Thing You Cooked on Your Own? 121
What's the Worst or Most Bizarre Food You've Tried? 127
Do You Have Any Tips on How to Host a Great Dinner Party? 135

VALUES 147
Have You Ever Had to Make a Moral Decision? How Did It Turn Out? 149
If You Could Have as Much Money As You Wanted,
 How Would You Spend It? 154
What Qualities Do You Most Value in Your Friends? 160
Small Things Matter; Which Matter to You Most and Why? 166
How Would You Describe Your Politics? 170

INFLUENCES 173
What Are Your Favorite Books, and Why and How Have
 They Affected You? 175
What Book Really Made a Difference for You as an Adult, and How? 180
What Historical Figure Influenced You Most and How So? 184

AGING 189
Describe One of Your Most Memorable Birthdays 191

How Do You Grow Old Gracefully? 195
How Do You Practice a Philosophy of Good Health? 201

BIG QUESTIONS 209
How Can We Make Up for Lost Time, If Only a Bit? 211
How Did You Get Through Your Greatest Challenge? 215
Do You Have a Big Regret and How Does It Settle With You? 220
Have You Ever Cut Someone Out of Your Life? 224
What Was Your Biggest Failure and How Has It Affected You? 228
How Did You Lead With Your Heart? 231
Are You Spiritual? If Yes, How So? 233
What Makes You Happy and How Does It Do So? 235
What Is Love and What Does It Mean to You? 242

ADVICE 245
What Life Advice Do You Have to Offer? 247
What Advice Would You Give to a Family Member
    About to Go to College? 249
How Do You Face Obstacles Well and Overcome Them? 257
What Makes a Good Person and How Can One Become So? 261
What Is Good Advice to Live Well and How Do You Do It? 268
How Does Good Financial Advice Work? 272

REMEMBRANCE 279
How Do You Wish to Be Remembered? 281
What Will Your Epitaph Say? 283
What Will Your Final Blessing Be? 284

EPILOGUE	289
My Legacy	291
Last Words in Summary: My Ethical Will	293
Bibliography	297
Endnotes	299

Introduction

James Klopovic
Born: December 24, 1948; Euclid, Ohio
Mother: Audrey (Tucker) Klopovic
Father: Joseph Klopovic
Raised my first 18 years in the city of Euclid
and the farming community of Huntsburg, Ohio
Memoir drafted January 2022–September 2023, into my 74th year

This memoir is part of my legacy—my journey and our family history.

With each passing year, I have become more concerned with legacy. I hope those who care will find herein a few gems of wisdom, perhaps profit from some of my experiences, and smile at some of my memories. This remembrance adds to my written and photographic journals.

Thus far, I've written six books, including this one, and three more are drafted. Most importantly, The Nicole and James Klopovic Charitable Foundation grows with monthly contributions. Its purpose is to "Fund permanent answers to permanent problems at the local level of government" with capacity building.

While doing research for this memoir, I read a small and stunning book by Will Durant titled *The Lessons of History*. Dr. Durant is one of our most accomplished and cherished historians. He made the insightful comment that history does not exist unless it is *written*.

Now you have this memoir, which became more than just a remembrance; it is our history—and more. It's formatted to answer questions—some yours, Nicole. You will find at the end my wishes for you and Cindy—an ethical will.

My hope is that these pages, along with my chosen quotations, will motivate you to live well, learn wisely, do good things, and be inspired to write your own history. Your story must be told or be lost to the sands of time. From my experience, just the writing of it is worth the effort, even if you are the only one to read it.

Note that the photographs may not match the sections they introduce, but they mark events in my life and thus merit inclusion. Pause and take in the moment of each one—maybe its message, maybe the memory. They are snapshots of how life took me here and there, to you and beyond. For most of my life, I was led more by events than the other way around. However, in retirement, I am learning to live deliberately, meaningfully. I wish to make memories and leave a legacy that makes you proud to be a Klopovic.

This memoir, this part of our history, will live beyond me because it is *written*. As you peruse these pages, remember me well.

James Klopovic
September 2023

PARENTS, FAMILY, AND GROWING UP

What Are Your Earliest Memories of Your Parents, Family, and Childhood?

Mom, Audrey Tucker Klopovic, with me, firstborn

It may be possible to gild pure gold, but who can make his mother more beautiful?
– Mahatma Gandhi

The older I get, the more I realize Mom was stoic and a saint. Oh yes. She put up with, well, a lot. She was rarely flustered, though she could worry. Her most expressive exclamation for just about any emergency was, "Oh, dear!" If things were particularly bad it was, "Oh dear, oh dear!" She just did not use "colorful" language. She modeled class. She taught us love. She had that British stiff upper lip—and she was there, always there, working, comforting, being a truly great mom. We kids were not easy. She taught us manners and class by example. She wished us success without pushing. Mom could instruct and not punish. She modeled industry so we wouldn't be lazy. She gave us just enough praise. We knew we were special in her eyes.

What guts she had! She showed up in San Francisco in 1947 from Australia with two old-fashioned suitcases in hand, which held all her worldly possessions. All this for Dad, who had one or two dances with her at a USO function in

Sydney. She came to literally do or die, no turning back! A true war bride, leaving all she knew to join an ex-army private on the other side of the world, having written letters to Dad for about four years. Those treasured letters still exist in Aunt Carolyn's keeping.

Don't forget the small army of women who answered a letter or a call to come to America and arrived to . . . nothing—never to see the lads who asked them to come.

Mom came to endure, to have a family, to make it work—and she did. What fortitude, what determination. It proves what it takes to make a family, thus country, strong—one life at a time. Little did she know the drudgery, disappointment, and truly dark days ahead. Nevertheless, she smiled, hugged (in a propah British kind of way), and laughed with us all.

We five kids certainly weren't spoiled. All we had for school were a few shirts and pants—oh, and one pair of shoes for dressing up. I had much more in the way of work-around-the-farm gear than school clothes.

We were happy in Mom's presence, which was vital because we hid from Dad. He was authoritarian, as the order of the day dictated, and he played it to the letter. We would sneak in a little TV after school then scatter like flushed quail when we heard his car roll over the gravel drive. We didn't know it, but we were becoming self-sufficient with a tough upbringing by today's standards. Especially when we got the farm when I was five, about 1953.

Our parents both taught us in their own way. Mom formed my character, and the work Dad required of me on that farm made me confident and capable.

It is never too late to be what you might have been. – George Eliot

Memories? Most of those memories of growing up were carefully saved by Mom in a bookshelf of albums of old-time photos taken by a Kodak camera with a bellows, over which one looked through a small viewfinder. Those hundreds of pictures had to be mailed to the drugstore for developing, the cell phone and internet being 50 years in the future. I can see Mom now, bending over that Kodak. She was our chronicler. She saved boxes of stuff for each of us. Her photos are stored in about 36 albums, which Aunt Carolyn now keeps in a bookcase. They're a treasure.

I always looked forward to going shopping with Mom to hang out at the drugstore, parking myself by the classic illustrated comic books. I needed lots of pictures in my books then. My real love affair with books—being totally entranced by a good read—began with Mom reading to us, even from infancy, even though she had five very demanding children, with four little more than a year apart. I was the first-born, then came David the tempest, then John, who had polio from infancy and needed constant care. He couldn't dress himself for years. My first sister, Jennifa, craved attention in the midst of the melee. Then came Carolyn, nine years behind me, all "cogs and gears," according to Mom.

Memories from childhood are skimpy when I try to remember. Then, as if lurking, a memory comes to mind as vivid as I lived it. Thank goodness Mom kept this and that from my growing up. I now have those boxes in my attic. They're mostly random bric-a-brac, but together—from the pictures of me in her arms as the first born to military records, my letters home, and random pictures of my siblings and the farm—it forms a bit of family history.

Before I was five and we got the farm in Huntsburg, Dad and Uncle Ed built our house of about 1,000 square feet for the seven of us in Euclid, 29 road miles away. Nothing special, a cracker box, but it did the job. Mom made our house a home, but Dad was distant. He expected to be served and obeyed, and he was. Mom had a hot breakfast ready for all of us—every day. She packed all our lunches and a lunch pail for Dad and served a hot supper—every day. Dad would eat then watch the news and take a nap every evening. Many evenings he devoted to Masonic business. At 11 p.m. Mom had tea and a graham cracker ready for him. Mom kept everything clean and in order, right down to sewing various colors into our sock tops to identify them. My color was blue, and it's still my color, maybe because it goes with my eyes.

A mother's love is peace. It need not be acquired; it need not be deserved.
– Erich Fromm

Then, in 1953, the farm "happened," and the world changed for the whole family—but especially me as the eldest. The previous owner sold the farmhouse separately, so we had no place to live, no running water, no toilet, no nothing. But the farm had the old oak barn, built before the Civil War, according to city records. It was an Amish auction barn. It leaned precariously to one side, threatening to fall at any moment. Dad and Uncle Ed righted it with railroad locomotive jacks and braced it so well it still stands today. The initial work on the farm had to be devoted to plumbing mobile homes for us to live in. Before that, we had a two-hole outhouse. My Aunt Jeanette would walk me to it in the night. At five years old, perhaps she feared I might fall in.

Dad put real effort into making it work. It was his therapy, he said. A great part of being on the farm was working and being with Uncle Ed, the second of six of the first U.S.-Croatian generation after Dad, the oldest. (One boy died in childbirth.) This beneficial association with Uncle Ed ended shockingly. Our dear uncle committed suicide when I was 16, a .22 to his forehead. He had crushing WWII PTSD and kept it from us.

Uncle Ed was a poet, carpenter, patriot, war hero, and my hero. Imagine, he was a machine gunner at the Battle of the Bulge. He left us too soon, a casualty of WWII. We never knew how this gentle man carried the physical and especially mental wounds of war for two decades after being gut shot, left for dead, and then evacuated. His telegraph to Dad from the hospital in Germany said he was "cracked up." His state wouldn't be called PTSD for a few more decades. He finally succumbed to the horror of what he had to do for duty, honor, and country. He would barricade himself in Grandma's attic, unbeknownst to us children, to keep the Germans at bay. Dad would talk him down.

Thank the heavens for this man, my Uncle Ed. I can still see him, even hear him, now.

Following is perhaps one of two or three pictures of Uncle Ed Klopovic.

Uncle Ed at the spillway for the two-acre pond on the farm

Parental roles reflected those common at the time. Dad was the breadwinner, and therein ended his interaction with us. Never picked any of us up, but he was quick with the discipline. This progressed as we grew, from an ear pinch to a bop on the head to kneeling in the corner, nose stuck into the crevasse. Then it was the wooden spoon, the long handle applied to the back of the fingers. The spoon head made a handy grip. Oh, and a lot of name calling. We were alternately a "sleeping Moses" (whatever that meant) or a "Dumb Wroblesky," inspired by our Polish neighbors, who provided a steady stream of fodder and grist for the name mill.

I remember a Wroblesky instance when brother David and I met the Wroblesky boys at the back of the farm near one of their cows at pasture. They avowed as how their cows gave chocolate milk—and proved it with a few squirts in a tin cup layered with Nestle's chocolate powder mix. Another time, the Wroblesky boys and I bound David, arms to his sides, and left him hanging from the rafters in their barn for a while like a cocoon on a string. Such were "Dumb Wroblesky" shenanigans.

Even from my first days on the farm at five years old, work was constant. I was put to rolling seed spuds off the little green wagon so they could be covered and stomped into the ground by the adults. That wagon still exists in working order, and work it does.

Agriculture is the most healthful, most useful and most noble employment of man. – George Washington

We were no longer city kids, even though we spent winters at the Euclid home to attend primary and secondary school. Weekends and summers we spent on the farm with the never ending to-do list. We all worked, though most of it fell on me and David. For example, picking rocks from the fields was an annual job. John, even with severe polio, figured out how to run the tractor and wagon while we fanned out picking up the rocks that magically appeared after a winter of frosts working the ground. We all pitched in. The massive gardens produced freezers full of veggies. Everyone planted, hoed, watered, weeded, picked and collected "tons" of veggies and fruit. Mom learned to put up preserves and applesauce to die for.

The farm was an extension of Dad; it was a strict taskmaster. We learned its lessons of hard work and the realities of it. Such was Dad's way of raising us. Looking back, it was a good baptism for life.

Mom then had to keep two households, making her responsibilities even more daunting: one in the town of Euclid, Ohio, the other on the farm, in the farming community of Huntsburg. We considered it all normal, and Mom made it bearable. She was forever busy but always had time for us. First one up, last one to bed.

My relationship with Mom was one of comfort in the storm. I remember, as a child of perhaps seven or eight, I once woke from sleep, slipped over the side of the upper bunk, and padded to the top of the stairs. Then quietly, but with ever increasing volume until Mom heard me, I'd call, "Mom, I don' wanna die." She would come to the foot of the stairs and simply say, "Don't worry; that won't happen for a long, long time. Now back to bed." She would turn back to her chores and I to my bed, reassured.

Our greatest strength lies in the gentleness and tenderness of our heart. – Rumi

She got a chuckle whenever she found me getting my night's sleep in the bathtub, the coolest place I could find. No air conditioning in that house. That "costs money."

For the yuletide and my birthday, December 24th, she decorated the house with lights and a tree. Everyone got birthday cake and gifts. Christmas day, a blazing tree was magically surrounded by a sea of gifts. Somehow, she kept them hidden until then. She always cooked a nice dinner and made it fun. She made it family.

If at first you don't succeed, try doing it the way Mom
told you to in the beginning.
– Unknown

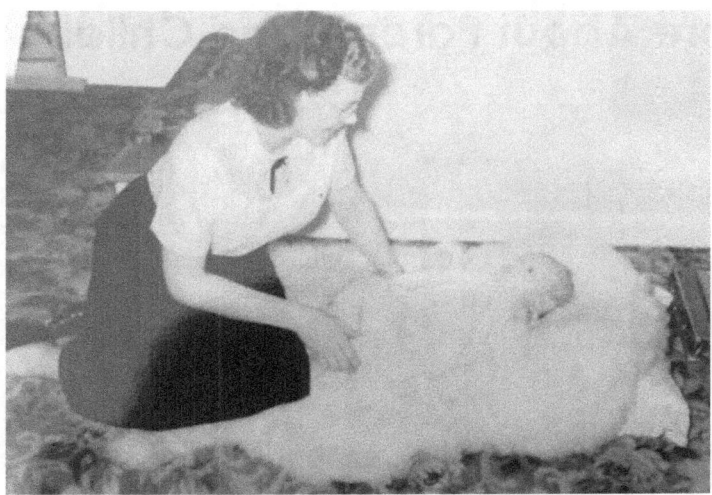

I still remember that Marino wool blanket from Australia.

Mom loved us all; see the smile.

More About Parents and Childhood

Mom, Dad, and me at about two months old, February 1949

Mother is the name for God in the lips and hearts of little children.
— William Makepeace Thackeray

Mom, Audrey (nee Tucker) Klopovic, grows in stature and grace as I remember her with the passing years. More and more, I thank the stars we had our mother. I think about her often and thus gather strength to face the day. She, quietly and with a mother's love and determination, kept the family together and provided us with an example of how to be a good person and live well with purpose. She's the reason I can eat chicken with a knife and fork and not waste a morsel.

A vignette stays with me: We were having lunch in the old red trailer, the five of us kids and Mom. I was cutting up and happened to glance at Mom, leaning against the kitchen sink, silently giggling to herself, her well-earned tummy just jiggling away. I hopped over to her to give her a hug from behind and jiggled her tummy with my hand saying. "Mom, why are you laughing? Mom, it's not funny. Mom, stop laughing!" First, she leaned on the counter, then she slumped on it, breathlessly begging me to stop—and on we laughed.

Dad constructed a hierarchy and division of labor to suit his purposes. Top down, my way or the highway. Draconian in retrospect by the evolution of parenting—even a throwback to bygone agrarian eras. He brought home the paycheck, and once we had the farm, Mom did everything to run the two households of five difficult children and a husband who expected to be served and obeyed. She even laid out the monthly bills, envelopes addressed and stamped, and checks made out for Dad to sign.

Dad left much in a state of incompletion. For example, the gravel drive remained forever waiting to be paved. But, recall, he did build our house with Uncle Ed's help. Dad could do just about anything. If a thing broke down, he fixed it—whether it was an overused bulldozer he bought for $600 with our farm neighbor to clear land or a worn out water heater. I never saw a repairman come to the house that I can remember.

When Dad was a teenager (he was born in 1919 just after WWI) and during the Depression, he built a race car (#35) from found parts. I have a framed picture of him sitting in it with his handwritten description of it. The car frame was a junked Ford, J Model I think, as was the engine, running gear, and a hundred other junked bits and pieces. How in the world did he do it as a teenager during the Depression? During that time, he and his brothers Ed and John were jumping trains to throw coal off and gather it in grain sacks for a little fuel. My goodness, Ford was still inventing cars and establishing the assembly line and factory.

He taught himself to fix, weld, and shape tin, paint, and a hundred other tasks. Ol' #35 was skinned with repurposed street signs. Then neighbors asked him to fix dents in their cars for five dollars, which birthed Goller Body, named for Grandma's street. He fed and clothed us with the shop, which he kept with his high school buddy Harold Sirk till his death at 60 years in 1979. The funeral was the last time the rest of the family were all together.

He took the same attitude to the farm. No place to live?—get a mobile home. No sewer? Dig the trenches, lay the crockery tile, and put in the septic. No tractor? Get a steel-wheeled beater for a song and fix it up. Barter with the neighbors for bailing hay and combining. Try just about anything for money.

Thus, we went into the fruit business with 750 fruit trees, including two trellises of grapes and blackberries. This occasioned a ghastly amount of work, especially the day 450 whips (small young trees), the bulk of the 750-tree orchard, arrived in a wood and wire crate. Try planting anything in mud. The only fun for young teens was using dynamite to dig the holes. We rigged a series of half stick charges so it went *whump, whump, whump* down the line. It loosened the dirt which smoked of dragon's breath. Cool.

The orchard never worked. Carolyn yanked all the trees out years later and put in hay for horse boarding. The farm had to pay, so we dug monstrous gardens to fill three chest freezers with endless boxes of veggies, along with our pork and beef. Golly, we grew 3,000 broccoli plants one year to sell to a roadside vegetable vendor. I'm sure it didn't pay, as we never did it again. I can't eat broccoli today without picking a few heads in my memory.

Dad was tough, and by today's standards, even abusive. Discipline of us kids was corporeal and progressive, getting tougher as we got older. Somehow, though, he was beloved in the community. I suppose that was because he did a lot for other people personally and via the Masons, in which he eventually became president. Plus, he was personable, talkative, and outgoing. He did like a joke.

One time he sat, slumped over, on the toilet in the body shop with a sharp drift-pin pointed to his stomach and lying over his leg. Then he spilled a small puddle of blood-red paint on the floor at his feet just before the hired hand wandered by. The poor fella ran from the scene wailing, "He did it, he did it! Joe finely did it!"

Believe it or not, Dad also loved his hi-fi and Tchaikovsky. Go figure.

Dad's mother's (your great grandmother's) house was a refuge. There we enjoyed TV, caring, Snap (a card game capturing doubles with a snap of the hand), laughing, and food. I would walk there even at five years old. A knock on the porch door to announce myself and in I went. Grandma was concerned I needed to eat; I obliged her. She had a rough, rough life as many did in the early 20th century, especially Slavic immigrants.

All of Grandma's children were delivered at home by Dr. Rosen, who became my doctor. His first house calls were by horse and buggy. My grandma smiled and giggled her way through the day. In my teens, I would visit to get to the phone and call a *girl*, to no end of ribbing from the aunts.

Dad was Grandma's firstborn, and he took command early on. I was at Grandma's house when he unexpectedly popped through the kitchen door from the rear porch. His sister, Aunt Francis, was putting something in the "icebox" as it was called even though it was electric. She glanced toward the footfalls and uttered a startled then withering "Oooah!" Then she stuck her head farther into the icebox and not a word passed between them. That was the only time in the 18 years of my youth that Dad visited Grandma's house, and we lived literally a stone's throw away, just five houses 'round the corner. The stories that rattled through the walls of that house were never told. However, I did hide behind a door when Aunts Amelia, Jeanette, and Francis were arguing . . . loudly. They doted on me and were fun. They tried to teach me to waltz, riding on their toes.

Dad, however, was profane, prejudiced, and critical—not unusual for northern Ohio, peopled by ethnic Europeans who set up their own neighborhoods with a ferocious work ethic and ethnic pride. That manner was tough stuff for children. I suppose he wanted us tough to survive the world. We spent summers on the farm, working the endless to-do list. I *still* have a to-do list, which will no doubt continue to grow even after I hoe that last row of beans. I, the oldest, would lead my intrepid band of brothers and sisters to accomplish the to-do list—only to be berated because I didn't search all 56 acres, the barn, outbuildings, and three well-used house trailers for *more* to do. At 16, I effectively ran the place during the week after Uncle Ed passed.

I remember Dad crying at Uncle Ed's funeral. Ed was a good, good man. Dad cried one more time that I know of, probably because my brothers and sisters were being difficult. He called me in the Air Force then to order me to tell my siblings to mind him, "even if you have to lie." I didn't call them, thus lying was not necessary.

Dad seemed to know the whole of Euclid and was a presence in and around the Huntsburg farming community. Therein lay the problem, always outwardly focused, not minding the family other than our subsistence and discipline. I know he accomplished much philanthropy via the Masons, but he never talked about it. There's something there about reaping and sowing, I suppose. His funeral ceremony was Masonic and appropriate for a past president, complete with Masonic members laying pine sprigs on him in his flag-draped casket of a WWII vet. The ceremony was reverent and beautiful, and the procession seemed to go on for miles.

Don't judge each day by the harvest you reap but by the seeds that you plant.
– Robert Louis Stevenson

I started to have a relationship with Dad when I visited home while in the Air Force. True to form, he would introduce me as Lieutenant Klopovic. He was proud, yes. But he enjoyed taking more than a bit of credit, too. Plus, back then and for a WWII vet, being an officer was something.

On one such visit home, I saw him sitting in his tall-boy chair, his face displaying a death-like pallor, shirt buttoned to the top as he was always cold. I wanted to take him fishing. But then he was gone. He died at 60, before the budding truce between us could mature . . . perhaps with that fishing trip. What a lesson. Cardiac disease had come-a-calling, fed by Type A stress and good kielbasa.

I don't want to denigrate kielbasa, as I kinda like the stuff a little too much myself, though only when I visit the farm. Easter breakfast was scrambled eggs with kielbasa and green onions plus toast with heavenly homemade peach jam (and plum jam and apple sauce too—excuse me while I swoon), which Mom had mastered. Yes, kielbasa is in my blood, bones, brain, and heart—but I trust my modest, periodic consumption of it won't be the death of me as it contributed to my dad's. One of my life's philosophies is, "The body won't follow a discontented soul." Yes, a good kielbasa is balm for the soul. I do love Croatian foods.

Mom brought us English manners and poise, and so much more we couldn't recognize as children in an environment that was "Old World." She was religious and tried to bring us up in the church. She had us go to the Church of the Epiphany for a year, complete with Bible study. I liked the singing. That ended when we began to do real work on the farm, which started early. Dad may have tilted toward the trappings of religion as would befit a 33-degree Mason, but he didn't practice a religion. He never came to church except to be married and buried—and for Uncle Ed's funeral.

Aside from being the first one up and last one to bed, Mom carried a monstrous, 16-hour day-long workload. Three meals a day for seven. A hot breakfast daily, five lunch bags and a lunch box lined up ready to go every school day morning. She spent the day keeping house and getting the evening meal ready. Dad installed an ancient powered washing machine, but we had no dryer. That could come "later," another day that never came, with so many other stillborn projects.

Laundry for seven was strung from corner to corner on clotheslines that webbed the tiny utility room. We had to come home through the side door, knocking through a phalanx of drying clothes. The room housed the washing machine, a cabinet, the water and space heaters, and Dad's changing room, which was tucked under the staircase to the second floor. The whole house could not have been more than about 1,000 square feet—the epitome of post-Depression, WWII sparsity and stability. Every fraction of that house was used. The attic had stuff organized in rows. Dad even hung kielbasa from the rafters to drip fat till they became piston hard.

Mom with me in the backyard garden of the Euclid house

Stability? I graduated with most of the kindergarteners with whom I began school. Mom made our life work, so we didn't realize what we didn't have. Much to the envy of my friends, I had the farm, a tractor at my disposal, and . . . *dynamite.*

After supper, Dad watched the news on a 13-inch black-and-white tubed TV screen in a petite cabinet, with three main channels—ABC, CBS, and NBC, and WEWS-TV with Dorothy Fuldheim—whom Dad called "ol' hatchet-face." Then he took a nap before attending Mason meetings. I recall Mom was still at work in the kitchen. Her day ended at 11 p.m., the last to bed, and she rose about 6 a.m., the first up to do it all over again . . . for decades. Hour upon hour, day after day, year after year, your Grandma Audrey Klopovic did what great moms do.

In her stoic way, she was proud of us all (except David who was, well, a problem even early on, rebelling from Dad's iron fist). They were proud of me, though, as I progressed. A milestone for us all was the first Klopovic to finish a college education. Both Mom and Dad drove all the way to Stillwell, Oklahoma, for my graduation from Oklahoma State University—an unheard-of excursion for folks from the farm, shop, and homestead. I was number two in my college class. Dad's remark was, "Who's number one?" I knew it was a joke that time. He was overtly proud. Mom was elegantly delighted. She did have class, even in her cotton dresses.

I know Mom was proud as she followed my career from afar in time and distance. Yet, when I finally did resurface, she was just glad to get a hug. As I wrapped her up in my arms—she was all of about five feet then and frail—she would say, "Ooooh, be careful! You will break my riblets."

What a woman, what a neighbor and friend, what a mom.

When Carolyn and her husband Tom took on all the work around the farm, Mom volunteered at church and the county hospital. Her picture is still there, as she put in over 8,000 hours at the front desk, greeting the lame and loathsome, the malcontent and misaligned. Imagine being greeted with a smile and perfect English, if with a truly lilting Australian inflection. I can hear her now.

Her funeral was simple and well attended enough. So I reflect on her 80th birthday party, three years before her death. Aunt Carolyn, ever the keeper of family traditions organized an evening at Mary Yoder's Amish restaurant. There had to be dozens of people there. She smiled elegantly the whole evening as friends surrounded her. I was asked to say "a few words," which after weeks of agonizing and practicing went well. I remember a neighbor wished her a happy birthday with many more. Mom's answer: "Well I *hope* not." She was ready, with her wish granted three years later at 83, a nondescript but great life ended by Alzheimer's. Still, what an evening. She was quite happy.

Yes, I am the product of strong Klopovic (Tucker) women—and so are you, Nicole and Cindy.

How did any of us know as our parents passed that we would see the mobile phone enabling us to talk to the other side of the world, DNA and RNA cures, rockets to the moon, cars that drive themselves, and computers that are nearly human. This all would have fascinated Dad, as he was a bit of an engineer. Mom would have taken it all in stride, perhaps with a giggle and a smile.

The meaning of life is to find your gift. The purpose of life is to give it away.
– William Shakespeare

What Hobbies and Other Activities Did You Pursue in Grade School?

Jimmy sittin' proud

The least of things with a meaning are worth more in life than the greatest of things without it. – Carl Jung

The only hobby I remember was stamp collecting—because Mom thought it would be a good thing to do. I remember getting packets of stamps to be placed in collections in an album. It didn't take.

So, when I got home from school, out I went to friends' homes and did what all children of the 1950s did—play—baseball in summers and snowball fights in winter. This was short lived as time was increasingly devoted to the farm, with weekends and summers there. We even made trips during the week for the odd job. That wasn't all. I also began working at Dad's body shop, Goller Body. At first it was sweeping floors then little jobs on a car. Just before I left for the Air Force, I could take a minor fender bender from dent to perfect finished paint in a day.

Nobody locked their homes back then, and keys stayed in cars, maybe under the floor mat. The key to the house hung on a nail in the laundry closet by the inner kitchen door.

Homes were going up all around us, so it was an adventure to explore the construction. I remember finding a few square feet of wire mesh used to plaster the walls. Back then a home was well constructed. Drywall was years in the future. Anyway, this piece of mesh was the perfect net for trapping pollywogs. The best way I could get the mesh out of the building was to toss it out a window. Well, a razor-sharp bit of wire caught the back of my hand, and I still have the scar, the first of too many to count. It was worth it, though. I'd just lay it in a bit of water, the 'wogs would come and rest there, and we could pick them out—then put them back in the water. What does one do with a frog in the making anyway?

We went with the seasons. Naturally, baseball was big, even in elementary school. One of the neighbors, Mr. Guttman, saw potential. He built a diamond—just cut the grass in a diamond shape—in an unused field quite close to home. We would gather and choose two of the older players to pick sides. The first pick went to the guy who, when a bat was thrown to him, could catch it closest to the flared end. I was always one of the last chosen as I was smaller and younger than the others. I still remember getting a guy out as he hit a fly nearly over my head in right field. I jumped with all I could give it and came down with the ball.

When a game wasn't going on, we played Three Dollars. Two guys would hit a ball, one to the other. A fly was worth a dollar, a catch on the first bounce was 50 cents, and a grounder was 25 cents. At three dollars we switched batters. Mom got me my first glove, a bat that was way too big, and a big-league ball. I loved baseball.

Then they built a pool near that ball field. I would spend hours there, only getting out of the water when the lifeguard emptied the pool for swimmers to "rest." Mom took me to Euclid High for my "water proofing." Still, I didn't really learn to swim until my 50s. Till then, I did some sort of floundering as I had to keep my head up all the time. Now it's a different story. I'm so glad I learned, as now swimming is one of my main modes of exercise. I recommend learning it very early and keeping it up. Make sure you learn a flip turn as a basic skill. It's worth the agony.

Grade school was at Roosevelt Elementary. That's where my dad went to school. I'm told it's still standing but is for storage only. So many memories there. Mom was a dance teacher in Australia, so she got me in a ballet class. You know, holding onto a chair and picking up a leg. That didn't take either.

The winter came early and stayed late. It brought snowball fights, building snow forts, and shoveling. Snow gave me my first "big" money. I'd shovel a drive, walkway, and sidewalk with a foot of snow for 25 cents! I didn't know I could have gotten 50 cents. Some customers threw in a cup of hot chocolate. No snow days from school. The girls wore pants under their dresses to get through the snow and below-zero temperatures. The pants came off when they got there, as dresses were the code. It was unheard of to be driven to school. I never was.

The two-acre pond was built by Clinton Piers Excavation shortly after we got the farm in 1953. There was a natural ravine which was fed by an artesian well, ideal for a pond. As an aside, that water was probably why prehistoric Native Americans had a village there. Uncle Ed found artifacts—arrowheads and a skinning stone.

Back to the pond. All it took was to dam the ravine, put in an overflow, hollow it out a bit, and there it was, soon to be complete with muskrats and wild geese. Dad immediately stocked it with bass and bluegill, a balanced population. When I was about 10, I sold seeds door to door, motivated to get a spinning rod, which otherwise I couldn't afford. It was the essence of cheap, but that rod caught bass on a yellow jitterbug. I loved that old green piece of junk. I couldn't wait for a lull in the work and a little rain, when the fish would strike. I still like to fish.

It didn't take long before the farm precluded all extracurricular activities. There was so much to do, even for a child—including driving tractor, when all that was required was to hold to a row.

I was not the best student, but I got by. Showing my report card to Dad was a minor trauma. Math is *still* baffling. I was average in all the classes. I needed classes such as choir to almost approach a C average. A few rare teachers saw a spark in me.

I took choir beginning in the 5th grade right through the 12th grade. Performances were nerve racking, including the time my throat itched and the itch became an uncontrollable cough. I had to leave in front of the whole student body. Mortification.

In high school, I became one of only two boys who could hit the base notes. Got into the Choral Masters, a subgroup of the better voices, to do Christmas gigs for restaurants and local organizations. We sounded pretty good, thanks to Mr. Taylor, our choral master. Singing with the Choral Masters made many good memories, which I recall even now. Loved it—and still love music but have little talent to pursue it. Maybe as a last-ditch flirtation with music I can sing the "three cords and the truth" of country music. "Sixteen Tons" by Tennessee Ernie Ford—yeah, that's the way to go.

Where words fail, music speaks. – Hans Christian Anderson

Despite my lackluster academic results, I was punctual and rarely missed a day of school. In 12 years, I think I was sick for only a few days. Dad didn't permit us to complain of sickness or ask to go to the nurse. We had to look bad enough to be sent to the nurse. However, I remember one time I had poison ivy so bad in unspeakable places I had no trouble being the picture of misery.

How did this happen? David and I had prepared a tree to be blasted out of the way of Dad turning the tractor at the end of the field. It was covered by ivy vines as big around as your wrist, which we hacked away with machetes. We thought nothing of providing a little liquid fertilizer to the field. Big mistake. The ivy essence was everywhere. A day later I could barely walk. Still had to go to school. Finally, off to the nurse I waddled. She asked what the problem was, and I said I had poison ivy on my legs. "Well, let me see," she said, demanding to see the evidence.

"I have it all the way *up* my legs," I replied. She sent me home. Still no ride, so I waddled my way back. All I could do was lie in bed, feet in the air, swathed in calamine lotion to await death or a miraculous recovery to save me from the afterlife.

You have no idea what farming is like unless you do it.

Can't remember *ever* getting a ride to school. We had a bit of a hike to get to the bus stop for Shore Junior High and to trudge to Euclid Senior High. It's just what we did—snow, wind, rain, sickness, and all. For years, I would walk to Roosevelt Elementary with Danny Hoffman. We would talk about Ms. Chachi, our fifth grade teacher, our first crush. Besides Pamela Warmald, that is (how do I remember that?!). She looked like a Heidi with pigtails. Danny and I would sing Beatles tunes . . . ah me.

My biggest achievement in grade school was getting my one-page book report on Old Yeller posted on the bulletin board.

To help people believe they can achieve victory, put them in a position to experience small successes.
– John C. Maxwell

Were You Ever Teased About Anything As a Child?

Eight-year-old Jimmy, the Tin Man, October 31, 1957
Aunt Jeanette loved to dress up her nephews and nieces.

I am an American; free born and free bred, where I acknowledge no man as my superior, except for his own worth, or as my inferior, except for his own demerit.
– Theodore Roosevelt

Being the first born, I was the lead experiment. If you have read thus far, you know Dad was dictatorial and Mom kept the peace and set the example for character. Dad did all the "teasing," if you could call it teasing, in that he called us names—not very nice. As I've mentioned earlier, the truly unique torment from Dad, the one to put me in my place, was to call me a "sleeping Moses." Don't know to this day what or who that was, even upon contemplation. (Sure, Moses had to sleep, but he wasn't that bad of a guy!) Then, as I've also mentioned, he would call me a "stupid Wroblesky," coined from the Polish neighbors whose many children were always pulling stunts. For example, after being told to prune a beautiful tree when their parents went on vacation, they lopped off every main limb nearly next to the trunk. Took nearly 20 years, but it grew back beautifully.

At school, I can't remember being out-and-out teased, unless it was that dunking of my head in the toilet by fellow wrestlers. Luckily, the porcelain convenience was in a compact stall so I could free a hand to flush it ahead (excuse the pun) of the "rinse."

However, I do remember in elementary school the class bully, Skeeter, self-appointed by being from the meaner part of Euclid—the "projects." He took off after me during recess, I know not why. Maybe it was because I was always smaller than others in my class, having started school when I was four, as my birthday was in December, in the middle of the school year. Anyway, he would tear after me around the playground, and just as he was about to grab my collar—timing had to be perfect—I would fall to the ground in a ball. He would go sprawling, giving me time to leap like a rabbit in the other direction. I can't remember ever getting caught in a sprint, but he did eventually waylay me.

One time he chased me along the entire length of the school. It had to be payback for tripping him. Well, he got me nose to snotty nose, breathing hard. I did the only thing I could do. I opened my lunchbox and took out the paring knife Mom had there for my orange and pointed it at him. That was the end of that. Good thing it wasn't reported, because then I would have been considered the bully. I think his bullying was a matter of keeping up appearances. In retrospect, he wasn't mean.

Harkening back to middle school, a group of us congregated to see a segment of a full-length movie—20 minutes at a time for a nickel. Well, a rude noise erupted; yes, from me. It was quite appropriate for 13-year-old boys to also erupt in screams of laughter. We were sent to the principal's office for disturbing the peace. No doubt he had a hard time keeping a straight face. Other than that, there's not much to report. Everyone was the same—mostly lower-middle-class kids from working families, though we didn't know we were middle-class; never thought about it.

Somehow, I managed to get through my courses. Who could have even deliriously predicted that statistics, mathematical modeling, calculus, economics, honors, a dissertation, and authorship lay ahead for me.

I was kind of a nerdy, geeky type. And I loved math. People teased me about it.
I felt pretty much like an outcast.
– Jennifer Doudna (Nobel Laureate in Chemistry,
who developed genetic scissors, CRISPR)

What Lessons Did You Learn from Your Parents?

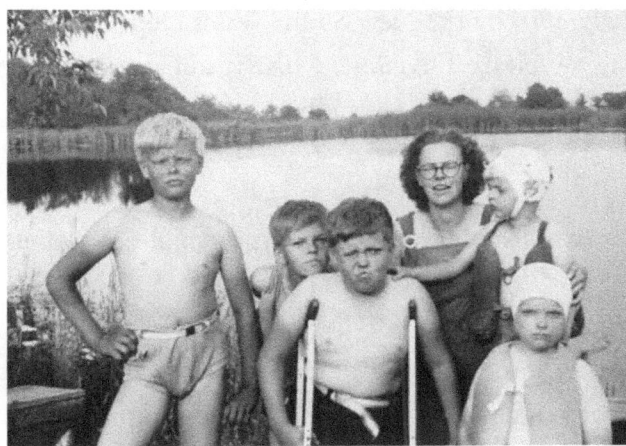

Me, David, John, Mom, Jennifa, and Carolyn: Ready for a swim after working, June 1960. We came by our farmer tans honestly.

Children learn more from what you are than what you teach.
– Unknown

Growing up in the '50s and '60s, we functioned with a division of labor inherited from eons of human survival, a real concern. It was a vestige of colonial/pioneer days. Only later, in the second half of the 20th century, did running a family and parenting bring sharing of roles, duties, and responsibilities.

Mom and Dad were children of hard, hard times—worldwide depression, world war and rationing. I've mentioned before that Dad was the king of the castle and Mom kept the home and hearth, raised the children, and made the castle function for the king. The children were expected to obey, be quiet and mannerly, do well in school, and respect the king. Dad had that model down pat.

Regarding parenting, how did my parents, or for that matter *any* parent, figure out how to do those things they were least qualified for, least knowledgeable about, and occasionally the most horrified of doing? There's no practice for parenthood and no manual (except perhaps for Dr. Benjamin Spock's book), and no real training for parenting. Oftentimes, their own parents aren't the best role models. But in spite of the odds, Mom did parenting well. She was the chief nurse, pharmacist, psychologist, psychiatrist, even doctor. For all matters health, she had a volume of *Gray's Anatomy* and one other I can't recall. For child rearing, she did use *Baby and Child Care* by Dr. Spock. Her child-raising how-to library was filled out with *Our Babies* by the New South Wales Department of Public Health, Maternal and Baby Welfare Division. Mostly, her duties involved loving care and concern and doing what had to be done, which she did with poise and grace, always grace.

> *A mother's love is peace. It need not be acquired; it need not be deserved.*
> – Erich Fromm

Dad, on the other hand, was quite aloof. He never held us or did anything associated with a baby or child except the discipline and putting us to work. (I refer you again to the picture above: Dad's behind the camera; look at our faces.) A compliment once in a while would have done wonders. Oh yes, I do remember once when David and I came into the utility room, grimy nose to toes, to dump our clothes in piles on the floor for Mom to pick up and wash. Dad mentioned to Mom that "the boys worked hard today." That was as far as his compliments went.

Although I may sound critical of him, I have to say he did the best he could. He worked hard, provided for us, never drank, didn't smoke, co-ran a business for 35 years—no frills, no philandering. And he was well-known and well-respected throughout the communities of East Cleveland and Geauga County, where the farm is located.

He purchased the farm when I was five, in about 1953. Yes, land was the Old-World way. But boy, did we learn from hard work! I suspect I was one of the most "educated" graduates of Euclid Senior High, 1967, practically speaking. I can blast a stump, milk a cow, and slaughter a chicken. Later life, with its tough and desperate days, did not defeat me because the farm and Dad gave me a spine; Mom gave me determination. Unknowingly, I was learning Stoicism from back then. I survived and thrived from parental strengths, especially from Mom and that farm. One can do anything after digging 100 feet of drainage ditch in the iron-hard Ohio clay.

As I've mentioned, Dad brought home a paycheck for 35 years by being co-owner and co-body mechanic in Goller Body. He owned the shop with a childhood chum, Harold Sirk, whom we called Uncle Harold. These two men were remarkably talented, steeped in Old World folkways, shaped by the Depression and war. Nothing daunted them. Truly.

While Dad built a functioning racecar from repurposed Depression era junk, Uncle Harold wanted to fly. He got a pilot's license then rebuilt a crashed single-engine Cessna. He would fly it back and forth from Key Largo, Florida, where I helped him build a vacation home. He'd poured the foundational 16 pillars the previous year, and I helped him dry it in within two months. That means we built the house from the ground up to a roof. We went much further by raising the walls and framing the rooms, hand-building the roof trusses, then "skinning" the trusses with plywood and tarpapering (drying in) the roof, ready for the next year's work of finishing the interior. He even laid the cast iron water drains. An old fella passed by every morning to say hello and commented he never saw two guys do so much in so little time. We lived in the camper trailer I'd built. Only took Sunday off. We knew how to work . . . together.

Uncle Harold always had late-model cars, all rebuilt from wrecks. He got two junked Plymouth Bonneville convertibles, one with a demolished front end, the other with a walloped rear end. He essentially sliced off the good halves and welded them together. I can see him now, figuring things out, folded arms, chin in hand, staring at those two junked halves held aloft by a chain, ready to be pasted together, sparkling new.

An example of "Uncle" Harold's pieced-together Plymouth Bonneville

Amazingly, Dad got well into an electrical engineering degree at John Carrol, a Jesuit university, but he never finished because he made "too much money at the shop." He may have been tough on us kids, but I must have been influenced by his persistence and industry, luckily not by his procrastination. Dad wasn't all bad.

Only years later did I come to realize what Mom did with and for us. Her lessons shape me still: my love of books; my trying to live a good, well-meaning life; my willingness to tackle and accomplish the "impossible"—overcoming the Depression era mentality of beg-borrow-or-steal to get by. I ingested her kindness given without expectation, a sense of noblesse oblige, and pride in doing a job neat and right. If I have any manners, presence, and comportment, it is because of her. She loved gardening, which taught me to appreciate a flower or two here and there around the house. She was and is easy to love. Maybe my mother's love of her children rubbed off on me as well. I have always loved hearing my girls call me "Dad."

Mom's life was one of service to her husband and the five of us. John needed uncountable hours of tending, as he had polio from infancy and was completely helpless for years. David and I would come home from working on the farm, dirty from toenails to eyebrows and many times stinking of manure. We would disrobe in the utility room, dumping our clothes into a fuming pile. The next day, those clothes were like new with Mom's use of an old tub washer (but, as I've said, no dryer).

Both Mom and Dad had a sense of community. Dad did many good works, especially via the Masons. His gruffness and iron discipline for misbehavior was a side he rarely showed outside the confines of the house and farm. Mom made Dad's work in the community possible, and even when she was quite senior, she would insist on delivering meals to the elderly, when she could have been a recipient.

Mom exemplified the best of Stoicism, although I'm sure she didn't know it. She had a high school education and was a child of the Depression and WWII. She made it possible to "see the light" and make some progress toward being good. The example of her unending drudgery displayed to me the value of hard work and determination. And her love was beyond unconditional for us all. I must say she is the reason I have advanced degrees and have completed careers against steep odds.

Spur them [children] to conceive of great things for themselves
but curb them from arrogance.
– Seneca

What Were You Like As a Teenager?

Graduation photo from Euclid Sr. High – 17 years old, 1967

True worth is in being not seeming,
In doing each day that goes by
Some little good—not in dreaming
Of great things to do by and by.
  – Alice Cary

Consider my high school graduation picture. What I see is the clean-cut look of a child of the '60s. I had the "Princeton" haircut, which is still with me except the part is intentionally a bit roughed up. My smile was easy and sincere below those no-frills horn-rimmed glasses, which always slipped forward on my nose. I developed a way to screw my face left to right and pull my ears back to raise them a bit higher on my nose. My teachers thought I had some sort of tic. Luckily, that ended with adjustable nose pads. I was still a boy but ready for the world.

I was, or thought I was, unnoticed. Just part of the crowd. Trying to fit in. Quite timid around my opposites, along with 999 other classmates. I went out for wrestling in junior high, seventh through ninth grades. Began at 110 pudgy pounds from two sandwiches for lunch to a lean 90 pounds in two weeks of practice and half a sandwich. Never missed a workout, but never wrestled in a meet. I did like the physicality of it. I would come to school a little early to learn to climb a rope to the ceiling. Eventually I did—and still can.

I didn't know my life wasn't normal, in that the farm dominated my spare time. I was there weekends, summers, and many times during the week for odd jobs. When I was still little, I would fall asleep, bone tired, my head on Dad's lap, on the 29-mile drive home. How young and small I was to be doing real work! This was the closest Dad and I ever got and oh so rare.

At school, we did little hanging out, unless we did it between classes for a stolen moment with friends or, heaven forbid, a girl. We did have the E (Euclid) Room for socializing, and I did a bit of that. I had friends, but I was not considered one of the "popular" kids. Little did I know that everyone was more than a tad mystified about the opposite sex. It took me ages to hold a girl's hand—and a girl had to kiss *me* to get that first kiss. Ahh . . . I remember Jeanie Price. I walked her home from a football game. At her side door, she kind of grabbed my collar, tugged it a bit, and there it was. I said the only thing that could be said. "Uh, can we do that again?" She obliged.

What was I thinking as a teen? Nothing lofty. My adolescent attitude consisted of the superficiality of making it through the school day, getting my hair right and my shoes gleaming, and accomplishing routines at home amidst the bustle of too many people in too small a house. Imagine me sharing a tiny bedroom with brothers David and John. All our stuff had to fit into one very small clothes closet, one door wide and another door deep, and one chest of five drawers. The room held a bunk bed for David, with me on top, a twin for John, and a tiny, tiny study desk for all three of us. Barely room for a small trash can. We would pile our dirty clothes (except for those that were "farm dirty") by that can for Mom to scoop up and make brand new.

I liked to read, but not enthusiastically. I gained more appreciation for it when I went with Uncle Harold to Key Largo to help build his vacation home. I read in every spare moment, as I turned chestnut brown topped with sun-bleached platinum blonde hair from two months in the Florida sun.

I began to display my adventurism and wanderlust as I investigated and took a SCUBA class and took the bus to Key West, which is another story. Uncle Harold and I worked very well together, six days a week. Having one day off a week was novel to me. The work was very gratifying as Uncle Harold was quiet and not critical. I knew how to work, thanks to the farm and the Old-World agrarian mentality that came with it. I have to believe Uncle Harold appreciated the free labor. Plus, we went together like peas and carrots. With much meaning, the only mistake I made in the hundreds of Skilsaw cuts I made was when Dad showed up and lent a hand for an afternoon.

Back to school. I didn't like school except for a flicker of light from Mr. Aultz in English. I beamed a little at my B. His daughter Jennifer and I were in the school play *Finian's Rainbow*. I played the sheriff. Had one line. Didn't need a costume; just wore my farm clothes and a dazzling pair of clodhoppers (Redwing boots from the Amish store). I was there for the singing and socializing. Jennifer gave me a smooch at the after-play party. Woohoo!

Of course, the elders organized dances for us, a well chaperoned, keep-your-distance exercise in awkward embarrassment. It took several years of such experiences for the separate Gideon knots of girls and boys to untie for a dance. It took nearly the entire time of the affair to screw up the courage to ask for a dance. Dance? Step to the side, step to the other side, maybe venture a step forward over the abyss.

Holy Jiminy, I nearly missed the senior prom for fear of asking a girl out. I delayed so long my choices faded. I finally walked Joanne Brunnell, head majorette, home and asked her. She said yes only because no one else had asked her as she was going with a college guy. Whoa. Of course I didn't know. We had a semi-famous group of singers, the Four Seasons, I think, for the dance at a gathering hall at a local factory. I danced scarecrow-like. However, afterwards I got to drive that canary yellow Chevy Impala station wagon with Danny Hoffman, his future wife Cathey Carpenter, Charles Hrastar and his date, and Joanne to the farm for a picnic and fire by the pond. Dad made sure we had a pile of wood at the ready for a bonfire. Gadzooks! Again I say he wasn't all bad. In his way, he was proud.

THE '65 Chevy wagon—my senior prom chariot.
Bought junked, destroyed really. Dad helped me get it showroom ready.
Here roadside, fixing a bearing that burned out driving home from Florida.
I built that camper trailer from scratch.

Firepit at the farm pond – Memories, memories, memories

I went steady with Carol Bell from the "rich" side of Euclid. Going steady meant getting a cheap ring, which in this case was way too big and had to be sized by wrapping the band in yarn. Anyway, I wangled an afternoon at her house. It took at least "10 years" for me to put my arm behind her as we sat on the couch. There it stayed—my arm, not the couch—until it went numb. It took another "10 years" for me to give her a peck.

I don't think I ever missed school except for the time I had that horrendous case of poison ivy. Oh, one other day: David and I snuck a bottle of alcohol to the farm when Mom and Dad were on vacation. I ventured into the cold and got really sick. I was so afraid of missing that I trudged to school through the freezing cold, quite miserable with a wracking cough, just to tell a teacher I was too sick to be in school.

I had a minimally positive opinion of English, but math was a . . . well, horror. Was that because Dad taught me fifth-grade division by bopping me in the back of the head every time I made a mistake—which I did aplenty? Mom would plead with him to stop, but her risked kindness only got her a snarled, "Stay out of this." Bringing home those written report cards was just not pleasant.

I had to go to summer school for a (civics) class as I recall. My Spanish teacher felt compelled to refer to my IQ test, no doubt to determine if I was a bit "slow." I was not. "Pretty smart" was the verdict, so I got the downgrade. No sympathy for a "bright" boy. I still dislike an IQ test, as it says nothing about potential and grit and especially character.

I was punctual, courteous, even shy. Never a teacher's pet, never a problem, just there—trying to figure out how to pass a class—and the girls. Always on time, in the background.

Fashion plate? Hardly. I had a couple of pairs of school pants with stovepipe pegged legs and a couple of shirts or so for school. One tan dress-up overcoat. One pair of dress loafers that went schlop, schlop when I walked. I had just enough winter clothes and more work clothes than school clothes.

We dressed up as Elvis demonstrated: hair slicked back with Brylcreem, a little curl in the front and a ducktail in the back, if we could manage it. The ensemble was topped off with Canoe cologne and bottomed off with wingtip dress shoes polished to a mirror finish (skill prepping for the military).

Euclid, a relatively small, working-class suburb of Cleveland, bred neatly dressed and largely behaved children, many of Eastern European and European descent. The town boasted one black and one Asian. We were all fairly prejudiced but didn't know it, a reflection of the home. Dad used every slur for every minority. How did we know? Now, Euclid High has only a few white students among the crowd.

Throughout growing up, I showed little potential in school and socially. It was simply about survival at home and school. Oh, I evidenced glimmers of the possible from the practical. I "ran" the farm at 16—but I only had my rag-tag bunch of siblings and Mom there during summers. (I really loved the dynamite.) Academically, though, I was a cypher. Barely maintaining a C average. I was preordained by circumstances and demeanor not to do anything consequential or be anything remarkable. The body shop beckoned. I knew no better.

I picked up autobody work by osmosis by watching then doing enough to take a crumpled fender from pounding to putty to paint to polish and to do most of the rebuild on that Impala. I also picked up enough to follow a template of a small camper trailer made by Uncle Harold and Dad to completely build several others. Then there was framing that vacation cottage in Key Largo.

In the final analysis, though, I knew I had to get away—away from Dad and all.

I still don't know how I ended up at the Air Force recruiting office—but I must say, my upbringing and the farm made my basic training endurable. That's when I began to grow substantially, as I realized I was totally in charge of how things turned out. I genuinely worked hard. I went to tech school at Wichita Falls, Texas, to become an Airplane General (APG) mechanic. On the last day of class, the civilian instructor commented, "Well, boys (we were really all boys), you have just finished 12 hours of college." I fairly levitated from my seat. I was on fire. An honor grad, I was barreling ahead to a college degree, but I didn't know how or where. As it turned out, I didn't stop going to college and professional schools for 30 years. At the time, though, I was about to turn 19, still a teen off the farm in many ways.

Let the American youth never forget that they possess a noble inheritance, bought by the toils, sufferings, and blood of their ancestors; and capacity, if wisely improved, and faithfully guarded, of transmitting to their latest posterity all the substantial blessings of life, the peaceful enjoyment of liberty, property, religion, and independence.
– Joseph Story

How Did Farm and Body Shop Work Experiences Affect You?

A fallen tree from the pasture in the morning, stacked at the pond by afternoon, ready to split when it freezes, 2017

Let us prepare our minds as if we'd come to the very end of life. Let us postpone nothing. Let us balance life's books each day . . . . The one who puts the finishing touches on their life each day is never short of time.
— Seneca

Our lives as Klopovics became unique when we got the farm. Fifty-six acres in Huntsburg, Ohio, Geauga County, just a whisp of wind (20 miles) away from Lake Erie. During the school year, we stayed in Euclid, where Dad had the autobody shop and we could go through the Euclid school system. Summers and many weekends, and even some weekdays, we were on the farm. That farm made me. I sometimes introduce myself as a fella who can milk a cow and blast a stump. True.

Dad had his autobody shop just off Babbit Road for 35 years. Yet another opportunity for work. I began at the shop at about 10. I swept floors and absorbed body work. I learned to straighten a fender with hydraulic jacks and hammers and prep the metal with a pneumatic grinder ready for the Bondo. I got the Bondo just right for succeeding stages of sandpaper. Next, I learned to prime it for more sanding till it was perfect to a factory finish, paint ready. Tape and paper came next to prevent overspray. I sanded successive coats of primer to perfection, then

I'd mix the paint by formula. I had to spray the watery paint carefully—one light, very light coat at a time—so it wouldn't run, then "smoke" or feather-out the margins so it matched the original paint. I remember spending a long day doing such a job on a big green Buick. It turned out quite well. But Dad dressed me down for not greasing the opposite side driver's door that had a small squeak. Ahh . . . his fatherly manner, modes, and methods left something to be desired.

I guess it was the hereditary "plan" that, as the eldest, I would take on the farm and the business. Thank goodness I took that bus ride to the Air Force recruiter at 17! While we're from agrarian, tradesmen stock, I was neither in my soul—although I knew not what I would do.

Back to the farm. No time for mischief. The farm involved endless work, and thus I had many workday experiences. My most memorable workday helps narrow the memories flitting by, almost like a disconnected vignette from a continuous film.

I remember a "workday" when I was probably six or seven. It wasn't work that time. Dad rigged up a rope on a pulley from the roof timbers of the barn to make a Tarzan swing. The pulley came loose, fell from the rafters, and *schklooked* (my Grandma Klopovic's word) me on the head. Gadzooks, what luck—yes, luck. It was a glancing blow. Dead on it would've smashed my skull. That was the first of about 18 visits by the Grim Reaper . . . that I'm aware of. I screamed like an air raid siren. Mom came running, Oh dear, oh dearing. The result, a *boondah,* as my grandma would describe such. It could have been a real *katastrofa* (catastrophe), she would have said in Croatian.

This may be the time to mention a bit about my grandpa Ignatz. He was still alive and around when I was born, but I remember little of him. He was gruff. Smoked a stubby pipe with Prince Edward tobacco and was just there. He may have done a little yard work but that is all I remember of him. Soon he was put in a nursing home, and I was never taken for a visit. In dribs and drabs, I heard he was an abusive alcoholic. Still, he learned to be a master mason and could bring home a paycheck with a diversion to a bar. My grandma was the presence. Cheerful, smiling, laughing, and always busy—cooking, crocheting, gardening, cooking (or did I say that?). She could doily a picture and cook for dozens. She was the force that kept things going—all five feet of plumpness, always in clumpy lace-up boots/shoes with stockings that fell around her ankles. Oh, and that cotton apron.

Well, back to work.

Work experiences, as they stream by in my mind, were such as these:

- We were nearly killed in a dynamite accident. Farming poses real dangers every day. Hopefully one learns preventive safety instead of experiential recuperation.

- I cultivated a field of corn too fast, burying half the crop, facing possible death at the hand of Dad. We had to pick out the buried wispy leaves by hand—a few acres of them. The whole family had to cooperate on that one.

- We hoed endless rows of beans and corn all day in the hot sun.
  The lesson? The end of the row does come.

- We dynamited holes to plant 750 fruit trees over a few years, mostly in mud.

- I had to figure out the most efficient, effective, even expeditious way of getting a job done. These lessons served me through my later 45 years of various other forms of work. Now I continue to figure things out—like designing a striking pergola for my patio and mastering the writing and book publishing morass.

- David and I dug 100 feet of septic line ditch in that Ohio clay.
  I would swing the pick; David would shovel; then we would switch. Cooperation at its finest. If you can dig a ditch in the Ohio prehistoric clay, you can do anything.

- Remember that '65 Impala, my chariot for the senior prom?
  What a confidence builder for a young man. I did most of the work transforming it to showroom shape, smelling of new paint.
  Then it transported the bunch of us to our picnic on the farm the next day. Work is rewarded.

That ol' Chevy was not the only wreck I resurrected from the bone yard. We needed a new pickup truck. Slight problem: The right front fender was pushed out of whack. Actually it was pushed into the driver's side seat. No problem. I had the wrecked parts cut off with a torch and separated with a sledgehammer in a day. Then I put in weeks of work only to have Dad sell it for $400. What the heck. The (slave) labor came at the price of a few bowls of soup and bread, figuratively.

More dribs and drabs. . . . Dad ran out of solder one day and sent me in our 1952 Ford pickup to the Wroblesky's when I was about 12 or 13. I drove on the wrong side of the road. Lucky! No traffic.

A couple of years we made maple syrup. Dave and I remained on the farm to tend the flow of sap to the evaporator pan and stoke the fire. One morning we got into an argument over who was supposed to get up and check the sap flow. "Man, it's too cold to get out of a warm bed." Neither of us budged. Burned up the pan and the syrup. Lesson? That's what happens without cooperation. P.S. Dad fixed the old pan with solder—yes, lead solder!

I began driving the tractor at 10, which provided more and more workdays. I was so small at 10 I had to stand on the clutch and brakes and pull up on the steering wheel to have enough force to stop it.

Soon after that, I could run the front-end manure fork better than Dad. It would take a day to empty the loafing pen of the winter's used hay—scoop by small scoop into the spreader to take to the fields. The small pens had to be done by hand. One of the worst farm jobs. By the time the weather warmed, the Herefords were rubbing their backs on the roof joists. That's a lotta pitching.

I became quite at home and adept with that tractor. One day while plowing a rough, hard patch, Dad told me to pop the clutch when it got bogged down. Tore the transmission main gear right out. Cure? New tractor. A Massey Ferguson 35 diesel. The first one in Huntsburg. My *dream* machine.

Now that I think of it, a good, most pleasant day of work was running the tractor, accomplishing the many tasks of fitting up the soil and taking in crops. Plowing—ah plowing. It was meditative, even though I didn't know the word. I would take pride in making the first furrow as straight as a die cut steel beam by aiming at a tree at the end of the field. Then back again on the other side of that cut, equally straight. Up and down, up and down. I could see the progress of my work. I loved those kinds of jobs—like buzzing up fireplace logs and splitting them to see the pile grow as testament to labor and determination.

Now feel the tractor as you read . . . rumbling, roaring, straining, vibrating down a furrow. Nearly hypnotic until one hits a rock—*blam-a-lama-lama!* Shocked back to awareness. Some of those rocks would stop the tractor. We grew award-winning rocks. We found tons of rocks that way, and a few Indian artifacts. Those rocks now find themselves on the ramp to the barn, on the dam, and in the firepit at the pond. A fitting repose—memories to retell.

Many times, hitting a rock would bend the tip of the plow, one of two plowshares as they were called—all the four-cylinder 1952 Ford farm tractor could handle. Then it was back to the barn for a quick repair. We just lowered the bent plowshare tip by the hydraulic lift onto the hunk of railroad rail Dad made for an anvil. We'd sledgehammer the top of the bend till it was straight again. Then back to the furrow. Things broke, things got fixed.

Still doing manual labor at 74. Did most of the landscaping at my home, 208 Courthouse Dr., Morrisville, North Carolina. Yes, I broke that shovel. – June 2022

Spring planting at the farm: The weather would be just right for plowing and discing for planting. My farmer's tan was award winning. I toasted my arms to a god-worthy hue of bronze to where my T-shirt began. Underneath the shirt was a ghastly white. My hair turned a brighter shade of platinum. No hat, no suntan lotion for the live-long day. We defied the spirits; oh, what we did not know. We poisoned fruit tree bark-eating mice with instructions to burn or bury our gloves afterwards (look up zinc phosphide). I handled mountains of Atrizine, now banned in some places because it created a little problem with birth defects and cancer. Imagine! I dodge yet another handshake by the Grim Reaper.

I was at home on the tractor, and by 13 I was adept. The smells, oh the smells—clean air, scents of grass, trees, and fresh earth—the best. Plowing turns up worms, lots and lots of worms. The birds would follow the furrow to feast. A few (hundred) thanked me, I'm sure. Just me, the wormy pungent dirt, birds feasting, blue skies, all hues of green, and the roaring, vibrating tractor. I could tally the day in black furrows. What a sense of accomplishment. Yeah, those furrows taught me to appreciate a good day's work.

The farm teaches so much, as does a body shop. Even under the hand of a disciplinarian. Little did I know how much I was being prepared for life. Those endless rows kept me at the books for 30 years and four degrees—and so much more. Being sick or tired or both matters little.

Process matters. Heck, I went out for wrestling for three years, never missed a practice—and never wrestled a meet. Hard practice and hard work matter. Climbing a rope to the ceiling matters. I can still put in a good day's work with much younger tradesmen, shoulder to shoulder, though my back delegates the heavy lifting to them. Good sense also matters.

We must all suffer one of two things: the pain of discipline or the pain of regret and disappointment. – Jim Rohn

Ahh . . . the Female Sex!

In my early 20s, about 1971
I thought Mom would like a picture.

*You're still alive. And that means you'll love and be loved . . .
and in the end, nothing else really matters.*
– Nicholas Sparks

With regard to finding a partner: Never has there *ever* been a topic so fraught. Pairing up has the potential to be life affirming, even blissful, a predictor of longevity, a Good Life—or a slow, grinding nightmare. But pair up we must, at least in my book. I wanted a partner and children. I was never meant to be alone. At first, children are the aim. Gadzooks, the instant and mutual love between father and daughters is ethereal, indescribable, enduring. Hopefully the leap into marriage is based on mutual love, real understanding, good give and take, true sharing of the laughter and work. Even better if it matures well.

Let me begin at the beginning and explain my relationship with girls, and then women, as I look back. I will work my way through to marriage. Some of this exposé you've already read, so I'll be brief for those parts. I'll start with grade school.

Grade School

I knew there was something intriguing about girls, but I couldn't figure out just what. It was—and is—an unsettling prospect. I suppose my first infatuation was with the aforementioned pigtailed pixie Pamela Warmald in the fourth grade. I don't think I ever talked to her. I had a crush on Ms. Chachi, our fifth grade teacher, but that probably doesn't count. A more interactive association with girls began with choir practice in fifth grade and continued right through to graduation. I loved to sing the base. Good interaction with the gals.

Middle School or, as We Called It, Junior High

Still intrigue and real fright in approaching a girl. Because I started school nearly a year behind all the others, it seemed I was always behind in size. Imagine me wrestling, or at least going out for the team, in the 93-pound class in the seventh grade. The first stringers used me for practice. Progress with the girls, though. I actually talked to a few! Gasp! I do remember asking Jennifer somebody—or was it JoAnne?—if I could walk her home. We took the bus. That was it. The school had a few "dances," where all the boys lined up on one side of the gym and the girls on the other. Mostly the girls danced with each other. One or two boys screwed up the intestinal fortitude for a dance, which was reciprocated. Ah, envy. Imagine a lot of 13-year-olds chattering, giggling, and speculating about what we could not imagine . . . on both sides.

High School

"Did any girls pursue you in high school?" you ask. I guess you could say so. I walked Jeannie Price home from a dance. When we got to her door, I just stood there, she, parked on the doorstep plate, propping the door open. Then as she took a step into the house, she turned, grabbed me by the shirt, pulled me closer, and kissed me. That thing about guys being opportunists is not exactly right. I'm glad I didn't resist.

I had a number of dates with Carol Bell—you know, the steady. One day we and another couple just took off in the midst of painting the house in Euclid with Mom Oh dear, oh dearing, as we left for Lake Erie beach. Again, quite naïve, we harmlessly strolled on the shore. The house still got painted. Carol and I continued to walk from class to class together. One afternoon I visited her house when her parents were gone. As I've already related, I put my arm around her on the sofa back for so long it went numb—a classic young teen move. The phone kept ringing regularly. Turned out it was her friend asking if I had kissed her yet. (I did give her a little peck, but it took hours to get there.)

I conducted an experiment by observing the so-called popular guys. Detailed analysis, well a pondering or two, anyway. Conclusion? Tell corny jokes and laugh. I was learning to talk to this strange lot who intrigued me and were fun; but they were still most unsettling. Little did I know they were just as "shell shocked" by it all, if not more so. It's part of the pairing business.

Oh yes—the senior prom. I've told you a little about it. Again, terrifying. Fear of rejection. Anyway, I screwed up my courage and asked Joanne Brunell (probably shortened from Brunelchi from her Italian forefathers who immigrated). She said yes. Holy smokes. What to do now? Get a tux fitted and rented, get a corsage and boutonniere. Pretend I know how to dance. Rebuild that '65 canary yellow Chevy Impala station wagon—the one Dad got for junk, a song, and free labor. Turns out it was one of the coolest prom chariots, and the whole event was a good time, even to the picnic we had with other couples by the pond on the farm. Prom was a moment, but I knew I was headed for the Air Force next April.

Reunion

Years later, I went to my 50-year reunion, which was quite an extravaganza as about 1,000 of us had graduated together. Of course not all attended, though. At the reunion, we were made to walk the gauntlet to the dining room past two three-foot-square boards of all our dead classmates. I wondered about the wisdom of that grand flourish by the planning committee. For me, it was especially motivating to stay the course of living with purpose.

Reunion Sidebar: Decades earlier, I had stood up one of the class beauties because I got "trapped" in Indiana with Uncle Harold on a trip to buy materials to build camper trailers. No iPhone then, and who the heck keeps a phone number anyway? That had bugged me for 50 years—a too frequent distraction. I sheepishly confessed my angst, my shame of a half-century, to the offended, who instantly shot back, "What date?" Ah me! That says it all. Allow me an unkind moment. . . . Do I dare say she did not age well? Another life lesson. I heard that many now mature women did not attend as they sheepishly admitted, "I've gained a little weight." Another lesson, for sure.

I was approached by one of the matronly gals, pleasantly plump, immaculately, appropriately dressed, and elegant, and we chatted freely, all mysteries having long since been figured out. Then, out of the blue, she asked, "Did you know how good lookin' you were?"

"Not a clue," was my answer. I wish I would've said, "Whadaya mean, were!" No, I never knew. I was just a guy—and I'm still just a guy.

Ah, it was nice to be remembered well. In truth, the conversation a half-century later was casual and not very extensive or inclusive of meaningful experiences. I realized that my life was a bit beyond imagining for my classmates—almost unbelievable, except that it's not. I've discovered it's important to define and live the "Good Life."

I believe in reunions to keep old friends, if possible. (Look for my Euclid Senior High Graduating Class of 1967 photo album in the little pile of mementos your Grandma Klopovic, my mom, saved for us.)

College

At Oklahoma State University, the Homecoming Queen was my "study buddy." The Strawberry Queen thought she wanted to marry me and I her, but that fizzled, thank goodness. The Buffalo Queen (from Buffalo, Oklahoma) was a good buddy and the best of the lot. There were others, but *studying* came first, foremost, and finally. School was serious business for a guy who barely made it out of high school. I went from a high school GPA just under 2.0 to a 3.8+ GPA in my BS in Management Science—a good start to a lifetime of formal education. Cap that with worldwide travels, extensive reading and writing, and life experiences. My take on living well.

A Bit of Musing

Companionship for the long haul is the aim. I say this as decades spent in continuous education (formal, technical, and professional), work, children, and marriage crowd out the work of building companionship. In the end, I see companionship as the reward of simply surviving it all. I know many in long-term relationships of decades who exemplify the work and accommodations of pairing up, which is proof positive of this reward. Through them, I see that growing old together is a remarkable thing. Now science establishes that it's the determining independent variable to longevity and realistic happiness, which is fleeting *and* remarkable at the same time.

Pairing well is largely luck. Still, choose as wisely as you can. Then commit to the work of it. Passing along your genes by raising a moral child is one of the primary goals, if not the primary goal, of living. Doing parenting well, necessarily strict and concomitantly understanding with abundant demonstrated character and love pays the most and best of dividends—the immeasurable kind.

Growing old, if we are privileged to do so, is better with a partner, if the couple shares character, companionship, commonality, congruency, and conversation (the 6C recipe, if you will). This doesn't just happen; it is nurtured. Know when it is worthy to pursue, push, and prod a healthy relationship along. And know when it is not. Hopefully, any children are off on their own to a good, promising start so you can devote your mature years to the task of grandparenting and life. Best, of course, that they live nearby, visit often, and present grandchildren. Grandpap—moi—is at the standby; continuously in training for the duties. I plan to teach a love of life and books by reading to them. I will begin with books on Stoicism for children, read at bedtime. What a great time of day and of life to teach in a child's language about truth (Socrates), happiness (Aristotle), imagination (Descarte), equality over equity (de Beauvoir)—with plenty of pictures.[2] And of course we will watch *The Princess Bride* movie till we memorize the dialog as we did when you were small. "Stop rhyming, I mean it. Answer: "Anybody wanna peanut?" Return answer: "Dooooh."

I can teach the love of food with a blue-ribbon apple pie. I can teach the love of nature by taking a "hike" 50 feet from the car to "camp" and make s'mores—the little campers complete with smiley-face backpacks. I can teach them to write a paper, a poem, or a book—then produce and publish it. I can teach the respect for guns and how to shoot skeet. We can picnic at the pond on the farm and ponder the four generations who've left their essence there. Then there's fishing. Giving. Teaching responsibility and gratitude . . . and so much more. . . .

But now let's return to the task at hand—the chronology of my life with regard to the "unfathomable" female sex.

The Air Force, 1967-1987

A little prelim: For the first six years in the Air Force, I pursued not women but work and school full time. My 16-hour days continued from enlistment till I was 30. Before I was commissioned, I made all my mechanic upgrades, was a qualified SCUBA diver, got a private pilot and Airframe and Powerplant mechanic license, and earned a BS in Management Science. Just six years from the day I enlisted, I was commissioned a Second Lieutenant. I also had gained about 30 pounds; I was still growing.

I returned from the PI (Philippines) to Carswell Air Force Base (AFB), Texas, to work on FB-111 fighter bombers. I detested being a mechanic crew chief. I was in to get out, so I enrolled in night school on base, an extension of Texas Christian University, where I also enjoyed classes. Enjoyed? Still over-compensating for fear of failure. Got my first real car to commute—an American Motors Ambassador, which ran okay. I think I paid about $600. Then Dad fixed up a 1964 burgundy Mustang, three on the floor, for $400. I polished that thing like a new dime. Loved it—piece of continuously broken glued-together bits and pieces that it was.

All I did was study while I wangled my way into a job as the Maintenance Training NCO (Non-Commissioned Officer) for the squadron. Read: I could study most of the day on the job. Again, I was in the AF to get out.

Back to the gals.

I was introduced to one gal, Margaret Ann Dome from Edmond, Oklahoma. It seemed to get serious, and we were figuring out the mysteries of a remote relationship. She even met Mom and Dad when they visited me at Carswell AFB—on the way to Belize, I believe. (By then, Dad had a little extra money. Both parents were as frugal as any of that generation and probably more so.) Regarding Margaret Ann, no comment from Mom, no enthusiasm from Dad. They recognized a nonstarter. Then she went off to school at Oklahoma State University in Stillwell, Oklahoma, and felt moved to hook up with a "religious" fella. We simply moved in different orbits. She looked me up years later at George AFB, California, looking to reconnect. "Nope" was my easy answer to that request.

I was always most determined, driven, and disciplined. I went to the student union every night after workout and supper and closed it down with fellow AF students. We commandeered quite a bit of that real estate; no one else dared enter the AF bastion. Funny anecdote: One student was in a froth on the first day of class and nearly ran over the prof to drop it. Reason: "Did you see all the briefcase boys [as we were tagged] at the front of the class? There'll be no curve!" We all had Samsonite briefcases, sat in the front of our classes, and stopped the hearts of the long-hairs squeaking by.

College

I kept a little company with several gals in school, but women were never a priority; I was totally focused on doing school right. The Air Force wanted me to graduate quickly.

I dated a bit. Went steady with another Margaret Ann—this time Margaret Ann Couch. Met her parents, got approval. Then, just after commissioning, I let her know it was over—and it was mutual. The search for a mate was, is, and will be fraught. I was getting over the fright but not the caution. I wanted a mate because I always wanted to be a *dad*.

During one of the classes in grad school I met another young woman, Liz. We thought we were in love and played it as such. It was the thing to do during and after college. Then Dad died—and I got an assignment to Iran. Thus endeth another romance.

The Air Force, Iran, and Marriage

During my strange assignment in Iran, the chief of maintenance, Major Keshvad, would actually cross the street to avoid me. The Iranian military was very hierarchical and class conscious. The conscripts on the bottom were actually from the villages and were sent, for example, to sweep the roads with no equipment, not even brooms. They had to hack switches from the trees for the job. Petrodollars by the boatloads built the military, not proper motivation and leadership. Fortunately for me, the U.S. Air Force encouraged, nearly ordered, its advisors to take a mid-tour vacation.

My vacation took me to Russia, and that's when I met your mother. She was beautiful in tight black jeans and a classy, gauzy yet discrete blouse. Captivating. She was the darling of our large tour group—mainly because she's a doctor and treated many of us who had giardia from the Moscow hotel water.

I remember she traveled in sandals, being from the tropics, although it was May, still the Russian winter. We struck up a conversation, literally behind the bust of Lenin just off Red Square. I was taken. She appeared to be quite so as well.

Back in Iran, we pursued a long-distance relationship. I would travel from the Persian Gulf to Tehran for some "business" or "medical" reasons. During an all-too-brief courtship, mostly remote, we decided in naïveté and haste to get married. Still, we pursued a "relationship," and this time it stuck for both of us. Pressed by the urgency of the fact that we were each approaching 30 and would be going our separate ways, we planned a wedding. With the Filipino community, she put together a nice, if small, Filipino ceremony and reception in the U.S. district. She knew many people. A relative of the Shah sent us a bunch of flowers as big as a small garden. She made her own wedding dress, having never done so, and it was lovely.

Unfortunately, this relationship began and remained fraught. Some description of it can be found in my journal of approximately the 1980s and '90s. I kept the journal to record what was happening as history, but writing about my life was no doubt also therapeutic. Cindy would be on the way shortly, and I had said "I do," so I did my best to follow those vows. Besides, I loved—and still love—being a dad, which did much to get me through each day.

I still believe in marriage. Just not the one I lived. It, a marriage, will never be perfect, but the potential of it is worth the leap. (Gadzooks, I have two "golden" daughters!) After the leap, one must endeavor like the possessed to make it work. If the relationship lasts, it is worth the to-ing and fro-ing, especially in the latter years. The companionship carved out by the years is pleasant, even if the two of you are so familiar that few words need be spoken. It's not the best to grow old alone when there's the moment, maturity, and means to be together. So, believe it or not, I would do the marriage thing again—as incredible as that may sound. As I say, one has to roll the dice. "Nothing happens unless something moves." (Thanks, Albert.)

While I was there, you can't imagine what went on behind the scenes. But you children made it worthwhile. And it is fate. Don't trifle with fate. Some things must be endured, even if they can't be understood. There's always something to be thankful for—and you girls were it . . . *are* it. It wasn't all bad.

Always, when one moves in a direction of responsibility—becoming good, being good, and doing good—things must work out. These truths matter. It's yet another reason to work on healthy longevity and living the Good Life.

I hope Cindy comes around, and I cannot think of life without you, Nic. In the end, life IS good. This April, 2023, we went to the Culinary Institute of America, Copia, Napa Valley, learning plant-based cooking, then repacked for 10 days in Bali.

This fall, you, Nicole, will be at basic training, "charm school" for the medical corps, for two months. I hope to be fishing for big game tuna, mostly catch and release, in the Gulf of Mexico with Dustan Taylor. Then Dustan will accompany me to Miami to fish for tarpon with the "Tarponator." By then, he will know if he'll be one of a two-man team going to Paris to represent the U.S. in skeet. If so, I'll be there—with you, Nic. Then we may have our little excursion to Tanzania. I am a lucky dude. Ain't life great!

A good person dyes events with his own color . . . and turns whatever happens to his own benefit.
– Seneca

Captain Klopovic, PA-C, reporting for monthly weekend duty, Travis AFB, California

THIRTY, MARRIAGE, AND CHILDREN

What Were You Like When You Were Thirty-Plus?

Tarpon fishing at 73 off N. Miami Beach, January 2021

Perseverance is the hard work you do after you get tired of doing the hard work you already did. – Newt Gingrich

As I write this, I will be 74 in about two weeks, December 24, 2022. I have no pictures or mementos of me from about 1967 to 2001, as they were destroyed. Hence, this photo of me at 73. It remains my essence. However, at 30, I was busier—in fact, beyond busy. Determined. Organized. A new father. Pressured. Adjusting to married life. Hanging on to the Air Force career. Confronting challenges.

Yes, when I was 30, I was a newlywed, having just returned from Iran with a new wife and assigned to Field Training Detachment 311 at MacDill Air Force Base, Tampa, Florida. I was handling many of life's milestones and challenges and more. New job, new wife, child on the way. New job, and as a commander and still a young captain, I knew I was an Air Force careerist and worked hard.

I was also harried by the demands of marriage. My new wife, Zenaida, had been an MD in the Philippines, quite intelligent and challenging. She wanted to invest, so we bought properties—eight rentals, minimum down, maximum fixing up, including two duplexes for which I did the general contracting and much of the work. I was going seven days a week—hard.

I did everything I knew to do to have a good marriage. Besides my own work, I did the best I could to find an internship match for Zen so she could resume her medical career. That didn't work out. I was unimaginably busy. I did most of the housework as well as extensive landscaping and maintenance to our home (in fact, to every house in which we lived), which we filled with furniture and household goods. Paid cash. I brought $65,000 to the marriage, then we got a loan of $30,000 from Mom and Aunt Carolyn, which they offered readily. For my part, I had two lots in Key Largo, Florida, bought with savings as a teenager, a townhome in Huntington Beach, California, my former paid-for mobile home, and savings. I got a brand-new car for Zen and an old pickup for myself, mainly to do the work on rental houses and commute to work. We bought our first new home and stuffed it with furniture. As is my habit, I landscaped it extensively.

Cindy was born, which meant a quantum leap in responsibilities. For example, I was the one to get up in the middle of the night when needed. I did much of the feeding and tending to Cindy, as it was just neat to have a dream-come-true child. Although wonderful, this was difficult; but I knew that these gestures would cement bonds. I really loved being a dad and still do.

Children are certainly too good to be true. – Robert Louis Stevenson

Zen was obsessed with getting ahead, and that meant investments, mainly real estate, and mainly rental housing. All the money I saved and invested went into buying four houses and building two duplexes. The houses were fixer uppers, which meant we provided minimum down and a ton of work to get them ready to rent. I did the work, with some hired labor. She found two lots, which we had rezoned for the duplexes I built, doing much of the labor myself. The lots were inexpensive because they were in a difficult location, a few doors down from motorcycle gangs.

During that time, Zen also got interested in the stock market and bought precious metals and platinum on margin—highly complex and notoriously risky investments, even the riskiest, as experience tells and will tell again.

On top of my "money-making" labors were my duties as the detachment commander. Need I say more? The responsibilities were what they should be. I was in charge of 39 enlisted men and answered to the base hierarchy and the major command at Sheppard AFB, Texas. My detachment was an island in the middle of all that. It had to run well.

During the week, I would wake early to get things going around the house then head to work for the day. I always made breakfasts, packed my lunch, and did all my own ironing, for example. I took on almost all the housework and certainly all yard work and auto maintenance. Zen did stay with Cindy during the day. Many days I would have to leave to work on, or coordinate work on, the rentals. At home I was generally busy, with a little time for TV. Weekends were jammed with work on our house and rebuilding, building, fixing, managing, and renting the properties. Renters would call about anything. I got a call at the detachment one afternoon. A delivery truck was stuck on a stump by the duplexes. I blasted out the door, rented a chainsaw, and freed the truck. A day in my life.

I barely had a minute to spare, managed it all, and largely kept calm, especially at the detachment, where I was figuring out leadership. The detachment did well, good guys all. For example, I submitted one of the instructors for Instructor of the Year for all 36 worldwide training detachments, and he won. It was a good moment. The detachment, a wooden WWII relic, remained award winning.

I had pressures at home, but I maintained passivity till the storm of the moment passed. It did no good to engage in argument. I made it all work as best I could.

All of this in two years. Then I got assigned to Phoenix, Arizona, to be on the faculty of Arizona State at the ROTC detachment. I was still in my early 30s. A very good assignment.

As absentee landlords with struggling renters, all properties failed quickly. We sold the houses and the duplexes had to be foreclosed. The platinum on margin? The margin calls came nearly immediately, so I had to close the account. All money was gone.

In Arizona, it was hand to mouth. I sold my truck and got a moped to commute. Your mom traded her car in for a Toyota Camry. I got a second job as a bill collector, which I kept for two years. Your mom went back to school as the two internships she applied for never panned out. She gave up on pursuing a U.S. MD.

In the mornings, I would get Cindy ready for daycare, have breakfast, make and pack a lunch and bag supper, pack a set of civilian clothes for after work, then take Cindy to Palo Alto daycare in the seat on the back of my bicycle. I'd come home and was off on my moped to the ROTC detachment at Arizona State University, where I taught Aerospace Science to cadets. I also managed JROTC units for Arizona and New Mexico. I spent the day at the detachment, then *wang, wang, wanged* my Puch moped to Zales Jewelry bill collection agency to earn a few more bucks. Got home at 10 p.m. to begin again at about 6 a.m. . . . But I had two *beautiful* daughters.

I would *putt putt* Cindy around the neighborhood on that moped while she stood on its frame to her pure glee—another joyful memory permanently ready to be called up as I please. Oh yes, I just can't describe what it's like to have two very young daughters race to the door as I came in from work. Each clamped onto a leg, sitting on a shoe, laughing as only children can as I *clump, clumped* Frankenstein style around the house. It just doesn't get better even if for a moment.

When you came along, Nicole, you were another absolute joy—and still are, thank the heavens.

Again, I loved, and do love, being a dad. Yes, we had friction in the family. I leave it there. Another side of the story was and is being told and retold. That's why I kept a journal for many years of the marriage—all in three, three-ring binders in my study. I hope you find some interest in it. It's also why I keep photo journals, write books, and try to live as if you were with me. I want you and Cindy both to be proud of me.

My early 30s were tough beyond description, but understand, I would do it again to have you two—especially you, Nicole, as we have reconnected since the divorce, and I so enjoy you as the remarkable lady you are and continue to become. Cindy, I still have hope that you will reconnect for a good mutual relationship between father and daughter. We have much to gain and time slips away.

You are loved. You make me smile. My world is better with you in it. – Dad

When Did You Decide to Have Children, and What Were Your Earliest Memories of Each Child?

On the farm for your Aunt Jennifa's wedding, April 2017 – A beauty and one very, very lucky *dad*

Anyone who tells you fatherhood is the greatest thing that can happen to you, they are understating it. – Mike Myers

As I mentioned briefly earlier, my thoughts of wanting children occurred when I was still a teenager, and a young teenager at that. It had to be the love we got from Mum (she liked to be called "Mum," very British). I imagined they would be daughters for sure, blonde hair and all. Well, when you brown-eyed bundles came along fully equipped with a couple of inches of dark hair, it was all over for me. No more thoughts of blondes. You two were dreams come true.

I remember distinctly, now over 40 years ago: I was sitting at my desk at Mac-Dill AFB, Tampa, when I got a call from the hospital saying I needed to call my wife. Although I suspected the news, the corpsman spilled it—well, hinted at it. Cindy was on the way! Honest to goodness, I became flushed, actually lightheaded and a bit giddy physically. I fairly floated. I *really* wanted to be a dad and it was happening!

Indeed, both of your births, unequivocally my very first memories of each of you, were dazzling. Cindy, you came along on June 25, 1979. I was about 29, a captain and the commander of Field Training Detachment 311. Nic, you were born at Good Samaritan Hospital, December 3, 1983, in Mesa, Arizona. I was on the faculty of Arizona State, Tempe, with the ROTC detachment. Your mom was studying nursing during that time, because continuing as a foreign MD wasn't to be. She wanted to return to cardiology, which was a bridge too far. She stopped trying after three application letters for residency.

On those first days, in those first moments, you both were perfect in every way. Ten of this, ten of that. Two of this, two of that. Nic, I remember at first you were quite blue and silent, just lying there on the table. The doctor gave your back a firm rub to which you croaked a bit as your lungs filled and then squirmed a little; next you went from quite blue to a mottled purple then pink as a carnation. No wailing, just bubbly. Then we exchanged gazes. It was a marvel—I fail to capture the words.

I was there for both births. Wouldn't have missed them for any reason. The labor was, well, laborious. Many hours. An epidural was administered. We were lucky that the AF allowed us to go to two local, private hospitals that specialized in the entire birthing process. The doc had the forceps ready for a cesarean, which luckily didn't happen. The doctors pronounced each delivery "normal." No extraordinary occurrences or measures were necessary. Everything went as it should, even to me being the first to hold each of you, all wrapped up like little sausages.

With the first birth, Grandma Klopovic waited at our home for our return, though we stayed in the hospital for an extra couple of days. The hospital even had a candlelight dinner to send us off. Grandma stayed for a few days after that. I still see her face as she held you, Cindy. She glowed. I know she would have stayed long and visited often if asked. That would have been my preference.

I always wanted more than one child. I am fond of saying, "One is an only child; two is a family." The third one would have been a boy, I'll bet. But it was not to be.

After a couple of days at the hospital so dad, mom, and baby could get acquainted, we settled into the family business. We were ready. The nursery was a bassinet in our bedroom, and we had prepared an array of clothes and care items. Your mom could shop.

I truly enjoyed feeding you two, which commenced at birth. We kept you each in that bassinette near our bed for quick and easy access. It was reassuring to know you were near. The demands of parenting removed any fear. Also, your mom was most competent about the technical and medical aspects. Luckily, on balance you were both good babies and toddlers. Quite full of life. It was just a marvel to feed you, bathe you, and have you hold a finger. Oh yes, some times were exasperating when you fussed, but they passed. I loved everything from the feeding to the cuddling, even the midnight calls (well, that was tough) to chase away a goblin or two or just to be nearby. I tucked you in at bedtime like mummies and massaged your heads to help you drift off—and you were gone in minutes.

I remember taking you, Cindy, to the Village restaurant in Tampa for our Saturday morning breakfast. We would put a paper napkin on the highchair table, then put Cheerios or bites of this and that on the napkin. We did that for both you and Nicole. I still remember you fisting the food to your mouths, quite content. You both liked to eat and laugh. I don't remember much fussing, though there had to be some when you were infants. I loved those breakfasts together with a beautiful, bubbly baby. I remember one breakfast where you (Cindy) bounced on the bench chair all happy as can be then blasted projectile vomit into my ear. Ah . . . fatherhood. In retrospect, a funny story. There's much more, which is why I took a ton of pictures. I know not where they may be.

The memories even now of the joy of children overtake and overshadow the work of it. Gadzooks, I am sure I could just about change a disposable diaper with one hand, and I did mountains of them. You both loved to be changed and cleaned, and squirmed to prove it.

We had a big time even at that mundane task. I would play the tickle game with you both. The game was to see how close I could get my index finger toward you before you would burst into the best of laughter. I would wiggle and twitch my finger as I moved fraction by fraction closer. Never made it closer than six inches before hysterical giggling consumed you.

Golly, you were both so beautiful. I called you my little China dolls. Nic, the moment you were born, the nurse proclaimed you an "angel baby." I remarked,

"You must say that to all parents of newborns." The answer? "Oh NO; we *don't*." I guess many parents aren't so fortunate.

I also remember at a detachment function one of my fellow instructors saw Cindy and remarked to me and your mom, "Your job should be just to have babies."

I took shoe boxes of pictures; I hope those precious—no priceless—pictures still exist. You both loved to pose for photos. I would be in heaven to tell the story of each one.

Daycare began soon, as we both worked. I sold my car to economize. Cindy, I took you to Palo Alto daycare in Mesa, Arizona, in the infant seat on my bicycle. Your mom usually picked you up, as I worked two jobs to make ends meet. Then I took on more parenting when she went back to school. We managed. When you came, Nic, we found a competent daycare for infants.

Ah me. Those were tough and good days. I'd do it all over again for sure. You, both of you, changed my life profoundly; it's hard to describe all the ways. Again, I say "dad" is probably the best word ever invented.

Children are the hands by which we take hold of heaven. – Henry Ward Beecher

Nicole in Bali on one of our trips and adventures in 2022

Have You Ever Had Your Heart Broken?

At the National WWII Museum, New Orleans, November 17, 2022

Unable are the loved to die. For love is immortality. — Emily Dickinson

Oh, how many times?! The most devastating, and that's a mild word for it, had to be during the process of the divorce. My world was shredded, scattered, trampled; it's hard to find the words. I thought your mom was a great catch—beautiful, accomplished—and it was easy to fall in love with her. The problem began at the very start of our relationship, as we decided to get married after knowing each other only for a few weeks. But it was the time in our lives to get married. We were both professionals, the right age, and it was our next step in life.

Know that no matter how tough it would become and remain so, I always think back on the wisdom of never tempting fate. There was a reason for it, and that reason was to have two beautiful daughters with so much potential—my most important legacy, really.

I'll skip the day-to-day struggle, as we were all culpable, especially in hindsight. Others who know of the situation have told me, "You did more than what could be expected." I'll leave it at that.

The culminating heartbreak came from the process of the divorce. Everything blasted to bits. In moments, you girls were banished from me. You were about 17 and 21 years old. And little did I know it would be a decade before you, Nicole, would come back into my life. I can't even begin to tell you how much that meant, and means, to me.

Our fellowship is very similar to an arch of stones, which would fall apart, if they did not reciprocally support each other. – Seneca

It took three years of legal matters to end the marriage. At the beginning, for who knows how long—months?—I had trouble getting out of bed. My legs were so heavy, my heart had no will, and my head was so fogged. But I did. I had a job, thank goodness, and I'm good, or at least well practiced, at confronting obstacles. This one was the biggest.

My house was gone, my blowup mattress went flat by midnight, and my car was taken in the middle of the night. I had to take a bus to Ohio to get Mom's old Subaru. My money was all but gone. Thankfully, I had a small 401k, a smaller insurance policy, my military paycheck, and a job at the North Carolina Governors Crime Commission (GCC). By the time of the crushingly harsh separation, I had been at the GCC for about 10 years. I was then their Federal Policy Analyst, a policy-making position. This was enough to start all over again; it had to work. But that was just the physical part.

As is a tale, so is life: not how long it is, but how good it is, is what matters.
– Seneca

The matter of the heart remains. Cindy, I miss you as only a father can, and I hope for the day when we have some meaningful communication that leads to a remarkable reunion and a mutually loving relationship. I hope beyond hope nearly daily. As of this moment, March 2023, it has been over 25 years since we have spoken. Quite tragic considering how close we were when you were an infant and child.

Then there's you, Nicole. You know how tough things were. How tough the aftermath. *And your presence in my life makes up for it all.* Never forget that. You are a father's dream. I would go through the hellish parts of life again just to have you. It took 10 years, but one day, you called and said "Dad, ..." Truly, my heart swelled so much I became a little dizzy. I'll say no more. I still believe in family.

The family is the nucleus of civilization. – Will Durant

What Is a Proud Moment for You and How Does It Affect You?

Captain Nicole Klopovic, USAFR, Medical Corps, June 20, 2022

The most splendid achievement of all is the constant striving to surpass yourself and to be worthy of your own approval. – Denis Waitley

On June 20, 2022, I administered the U.S. Air Force Oath of Office to you, Nic, when you entered the Air Force Reserves as a captain in the Medical Corps. *You did it!* What a remarkable moment of moments in the trajectory of your life, of a family. To have a worthy child inherit the name, spirit, and blood of a family; to have that child work hard, beyond endurance, to become a medical provider against so many odds; and to have a father who is a retired Air Force officer empowered to administer the Oath is incredibly remarkable.

I commented just before administering the Oath, that you are the fourth generation of Klopovics to tread those 56 acres that Dad and Uncle Ed bought in 1953 with their GI Bill funds. That pond behind you was built shortly thereafter when I was about five years old.

Uncle Tom and your Aunt Carolyn were there to witness the ceremony . . . simple, profound. You are holding your first set of captain's insignia in the picture above. Had I given you an Aston Martin, you would not have been so pleased. That's why you are worthy. Look at that beautiful smile.

It's unfair that the question above is to mention a proud moment. There are so many! So many as a result of simply being your DAD. Recounting them all is yet another book. You bless the family wherever you lead it.

The two most important days in your life are the day you are born
and the day you find out why.
– Mark Twain

THE MILITARY

How Do You Feel Your Time in the Military Changed You As a Person?

Delivering the Oath of Office to Nicole, June 20, 2022 on the Farm

Successful leaders see the opportunities in every difficulty rather than the difficulty in every opportunity. – Reed Markham

My answer to this question: Beyond profoundly!!

A little recap reveals I already had the mindset and discipline for the military, but it took the Air Force to bring it out and polish it—to give me confidence.

Growing up, I was always in the background, shining in or at nothing. Well, I did like singing base in the Choral Masters in high school and yes, I was good at it. In general, however, school represented adding bits of boredom to what seemed like tads of torture. I didn't know how to study. Classes seemed foreign, especially anything with numbers. I didn't have much encouragement. Again, handing over those handwritten report cards to Dad occasioned real "approach avoidance," to put it mildly. I liked the classes taught by teachers who were dedicated to the profession. I made friends well enough. I did go out for the high school play and had one line, and I loved the singing and occasional choral recital. Went out for wrestling for three years in junior high. My only match was for the school intramurals. I won in my 93-pound weight class. Again, my time went to the farm and the body shop. College seemed a fantasy. No, a distant galaxy, light years away. Was watching Star Wars, and guiding me was Master Yoda, lucky am I:

Secret, shall I tell you? Grand Master of Jedi Order am I. Won this job in a raffle I did, think you? 'How did you know, how did you know, Master Yoda?' Master Yoda knows these things. His job it is. – Yoda

I could not see my potential, even though it was there, popping out: I ran the front-end loader at 12. By 14, I was adept, and safe, with dynamite. I ran the farm at 16 with my crew of four siblings. Picked up body work by osmosis. Did most of the work on a totaled Chevy wagon for the prom, and raised a vacation house with Uncle Harold in Key West, as mentioned. Built camper trailers from the frame up by copying a model, and I could stack a rolling hay wagon with the best of 'em.

Upon reflection, I demonstrated traits over and over that predicted I could be and do better. In wrestling, I never missed a practice or a home meet, observing from somewhere in the crowd. I was first at the gym in the morning to practice climbing rope for strength. I worked out hard. We had an indoor track where we warmed up—*before* warmups and conditioning. I commonly went 48 laps on that track, weaving in and out of most who walked. In the seventh grade, I went from 110 pounds to 90 pounds of lean, and I stayed lean.

I was still growing even into my 20s. I went to the Philippines at about 129 pounds. When I made captain at about 28 years, I was 168 pounds. (Now I'm just a little over that. I maintain a philosophy of staying at an optimal, age-appropriate weight. It's intuitive that it's much harder to lose weight than it is to *maintain* health, fitness, and thus weight. And I find it fun to run upstairs or at least take them two treads at a time . . . while I can.)

No! Try not. Do. Or do not. There is no try. – Yoda

Then the Air Force happened.

Truly, I know not why my feet and the bus took me to the AF recruiter the year before I graduated high school in '67. To get away from Dad? For adventure, travel? Dumb, profoundly silly luck is probably the real reason. What does one know at 17? That bus ride made all the difference—from a life destined to pounding fenders, farming, or working on a factory line to one accomplishing and doing things only imagined by many. Ah, I still remember induction.

How could I forget when we recruits—still no buzz cuts—were all ordered to stand in a line then to "Drop 'em, bend over, and spread 'em" as a doctor walked by inspecting our nether regions, probably for hemorrhoids. True! Civilians will never know.

The Air Force made me responsible—or at least made me realize I *could* be. First, I was given responsibility, then I sought it. I was singled out from the crowd to take a bundle of all our records on the flight to Lackland AFB for basic training. My second plane ride. (The first was to return from Sydney at five with brother John afflicted with polio.) I learned I was captain of my own ship and got serious.

I've mentioned the most profound event after I enlisted, which happened at the end of tech school following basic. On the day of graduation, the instructor gave a farewell pep talk and told us we had just accomplished the equivalent of 12 hours of *college!* I was given "permission" to succeed! Even stand out. I was entranced and obsessed with going to college. It was now a realistic way up and out of my agrarian, mechanic destiny. I became driven.

Just think! With a single sentence, a few words, my life leapt impossibly, unimaginably forward. I had purpose and a path: a college education. My trajectory has allowed me to do a great many things and affect many lives. I sit here as Dr. Klopovic, Major, USAF, Retired, the author of several books, and proud, proud father. Humbling, really. It's another stark lesson of how a life can be changed and thus change the lives of others with the pursuit of being good, better, one's best. Let's continue from that astonishing day.

It was off to the Philippines after tech school. I immediately enrolled in a correspondence course, English 101. Laborious, but I got an A. Then I enrolled in American Government 101 and Psychology 101 through the University of the Philippines extension on Clark Air Force Base. I still remember Dr. Catapusan, who commuted to Clark AFB from Manila to teach us Psych 101. Marvelous. I took notes on my notes and combined them into mnemonics to test well, which I did. I had a drive to succeed, although part of the goad was a fear of failure.

Great warrior. Hmm. Wars not make one great. – Yoda

Little did I know, changing strategies I was. To a commission I was headed.

Early on, the AF taught me that taking responsibility judiciously was and is wise. It's good to be in charge of something, and it's actually rewarding to figure things out. Crewing fighter aircraft anywhere, let alone in the tropics with jungle rotted feet, is most unpleasant. It's hot, cold, sweaty, dirty, boring with long shifts—and one can't study. Not for me, so I had to make a move.

At Clark, I volunteered—oh that shunned word—to take care of non-powered Aerospace Ground Equipment, AGE—Liquid Oxygen (LOX) carts, to be specific. I could study much of the day in an air-conditioned cubby hole in the hangar, out of the monsoon lakes of rain and withering tropical heat. No jungle rot for me. If the birds were LOXed for launch, I could come and go as I pleased. I also studied every weekday to bedtime, before work, and most of the weekends, except when I went SCUBA diving and toured the main island of Luzon.

The guys tut-tutted me as working a job beneath them, and I snickered all the way to my comfy office. Initially, a major problem arose. Most of the LOX carts were condemned. Opportunity! So, I fixed them all for our squadron and our sister squadron. Didn't have to but I did. I had them lined up on the flightline like shiny little soldiers for all to see, ready to do their duty. My little humiliating job got a commendation medal, and I made buck sergeant a little faster, too. Ah, the memories flood back. This only hinted at the things I could and would do.

I was in to get out. Still, I applied to finish my BS at Oklahoma State and become an officer. I began with 48 hours of college, with a good GPA. I finished 18 months later with 135 hours with bypass tests and four semesters a year. More astonishingly, I ranked number one in my colleges as my overall average remained high. Man, and all my time off during the school year, what did I do? Study. Another profound change was afoot as I began new levels of responsibility and learned how to handle them. I could see that one succeeds by persisting.

Who would have thought I'd be writing this after retiring twice, having traveled the world (and still be traveling), and be well educated, well read, broadly experienced, and the product of so many schools of hard knocks. Along the way, I made a sincere effort to develop personally, become interesting, and be interested in life.

Try, you must. Succeed, you will. – Yoda

The AF helped me begin my study of how to live well. To know when enough is enough. To know what it is to be a good person and pursue being so. How to be a good friend to earn friendship. It was a start, yes, but fitful as I worked the AF, got married, had and helped raise two children, got fired, hired, bankrupted, and divorced. After a total of 45 years with the military, work with the Governor's Crime Commission, and four degrees, I now have the time, wherewithal, and especially mentality to be as good a person as I strive to be and pass on a decent legacy.

The Air Force even brought me to a wife. Yes, marriage was tough, and it toughened me. I can truthfully say I did my best, and I'm eternally thankful that marriage brought me fatherhood—having worthy, beautiful children. At least I know how wonderfully you turned out, Nicole—and you would simply not be here if it weren't for the Air Force. The effect of being a father on me is beyond profound. There is nothing like the love a man has for his children and his children have for him. It will endure even beyond this earthly life. Being a father drives me to be better and do things better that will be remembered well beyond any failures.

Yes, the Air Force made ALL the difference . . . and to think I almost destroyed all my opportunities in the Air Force with one little incident. It was a lesson I'll never forget. Let me first give a little background.

I was raised with the Great Depression, WWII mentality, mainly from my father. This generation learned hardscrabble ways—scrimping, saving, scavenging. They never threw out an empty cottage cheese container as "We can use it for something." Yes, Mom was a child of those eras, too, and gave us the example of hard work, love, kindness, manners, and principles. But under Dad's roof, it meant that if a thing wasn't nailed down, it was fair pickings. I remember loading up used railroad ties lying next to the rails. We needed them for the farm, as they were very good for roads, building things, and borders; and they were "free." So many things needed to be "repurposed" back then. But let's be clear; taking them was a felony! We were just following Dad. This life example meant it was okay to cut corners, even ethical corners. It took me a long time to undo that lesson. As a traditionalist, I believe honesty is the best policy: You never have to remember what you said or hide what you did.

A half truth is a whole lie. – Yiddish Proverb

The railroad tie example set us kids up for troubles, transgressions, and tragedies. How did we know? It was how we were raised. Much later in life, I saw that one little indiscretion can destroy a reputation that took a lifetime to establish. I came within a whisper of ruining my career in the Air Force.

In Officer Training School, OTS, we were tested for character and worthiness for commissioning. We had timed tests. At the exact time the test ended and time was up, we were to put down our pencils. Well, I had the answer to one more question, and it was easy to mark the bubble. The timer sounded, I scratched a little lead in the bubble, and it was done—an honor violation. A fellow officer saw it and reported me to the student honor board for adjudication. That one act was justification enough to get me expelled from officer training. Imagine the consequences!! No commission, no remarkable life accomplishments, probably no doctorate, no trip to Iran, no Cindy and Nicole. The likely path was to work in a nondescript company somewhere in northern Ohio, nearly anonymous, just getting by, as is the pattern in northern Ohio.

Luckily, I went to school with an OTS student honor board chair who remembered my work as an undergrad and determined my act was out of character. What a lesson. Even the remembrance brings an actual shudder. Still, it took many more years for the lessons of traditionalism to work their way through and into my life and conduct. Let me repeat: Growth as a humane human being is a process to the very last day, and that is the blessing of it. Begin the journey as soon as you can. Learn to:

Live with virtue, strive with character, thrive for a lifetime. – JK

It takes wisdom and courage to notice the many, many opportunities that are cast at our feet: One, to notice them and their potential and two, to have the ready guts to pick them up with the dogged determination to see them through to their logical end. That end makes so many more opportunities possible.

For example, my Air Force experiences made it possible for me to get a job with the North Carolina Governor's Crime Commission as the Federal Policy Analyst. While the political environment was, well, disappointing, I continued to have an impact.

This prompts me to say: If you are alert, persistent, and diligent, it will serve you well, and:

Opportunities everywhere are useless till tightly grasped
by an enlightened, prepared person.

How Was Your Air Force Experience with Combat?

The next generation of warriors. Nicole at Edwards AFB, weekend duty

There have been 268 days of peace in the past 3,421 years.
– Will Durant (1960)

It was the Vietnam Tet Offensive of '68.

I was on temporary duty to Bien Hua for the usual 60-day rotation. Little, so little, did I know, nor expect. I was on the other side of the world seeing and doing things my high school chums could not even imagine. No one could have imagined what lay ahead in the next 60 days.

I am fond of saying that in 1968 I was off doing what legions of hippies were protesting back home. I knew naut of these things, as I didn't have a radio and no news. Only a 50-cent weekly movie at the Bamboo Theater at Clark AFB, the Philippines. The "theater" was an outdoor covered grandstand with boards for seats, overlooking a grass parade ground. It became a theater when a flatbed trailer mounted with a huge screen was towed to the viewing area.

I was 19. Everything was new and focused. We worked about six days a week, extended shifts.

I can write about combat only in a casual way. I knew nothing about the insanity and horrors of two world wars that our grandparents and parents knew from the factory floors, supply lines, and especially front lines of those wars. My uncles on the Klopovic side, Ed and John, Dad, and Aunt Amelia all served. So did Uncle Russel on the Tucker side. I've related what happened eventually to Uncle Ed. He had been left for dead on the killing fields of the Battle of the Bulge, next to his smoking machine gun. A corpsman saw a whisp of breath and rescued him. "Cracked up," he wrote in a telegram from a European hospital. See my photo journals for that telegram to Dad. As I related earlier, Uncle Ed attempted suicide 16 years after VE day, when I was 16.

Uncle Ed, dear saintly Uncle Ed. He was in a senseless coma for a year, fed with a tube. He withered away to a skeleton then simply slipped into the next realm. He was a carpenter, a farmer, and a lover of poetry. What tortures he endured for over 20 years until he couldn't take it any longer and took a courageous way out. We kids knew not how bad things were.

Thankfully, I wasn't hurt, nor did I know anyone who was badly hurt. Still, I served in a theater of war.

I know not with what weapons WWIII will be fought, but WWIV will be fought with sticks and stones. - Albert Einstein

We crewed (fixed, maintained, launched, and recovered) F102 Convair Delta Daggers, we knew as the lead sled. We named so many things. Realize that our birds were based on WWII technology. The mission was to intercept Vietnamese flown Chinese fighters and shoot them down. Reality: During the 18 months I was there, only one rocket was fired from one of our Duces—a miss. None of our birds were shot down nor even shot at, that we knew.

We also ran detachments in Thailand—Udorn and Bangkok—and Vietnam—Danang and Bien Hoa. I did stints of a couple of months at Udorn and Bien Hoa. Bien Hoa will be my focus to keep things brief (much briefer than justified). Already the memories flood through me, even the smells, sights, feelings, tastes in that great kabuki of war. We suffered no personal losses. Thousands of flights, no big accidents. Hundreds of us in and out of Southeast Asia.

Only one fella suffered from combat—an Italian, Mancouso, I seem to remember. Plump, round of face, liked to drink Jim Beam, eat, and play a little cards. He caught a piece of intentionally ragged mortar shrapnel in his aft section while running to the makeshift cement-block "bomb shelter" in Bien Hoa. The incident resulted in a Purple Heart and the habit of grabbing a bottle of Beam at the blast of the klaxon warning of attack before skittering to the shelter. . . .

Shelter? Our Air Force brought the best design wizards, combat vets all, no doubt, to our mortal preservation from flying death from above. Shelter for life and limb consisted of two parallel rows of hollow cement blocks about seven feet high, girded by a stack of sandbags. I guess "they" determined we had a force field to protect us if a mortar or rocket grazed us. For the record, a hand-launched 122mm rocket hit a barracks a couple of hundred yards behind us and killed seven army troops in their beds—so we were told. I did see the wrecked corner of their barracks. We were not permitted to trash our flashlight batteries as the VC could use them to hand launch those 122mm rockets, aimed (again, as we were told) by leaning the rocket against two crossed twigs to "eyeball" the target. It's astounding the determination and ingenuity of guerillas fighting for home and family, even if it's for Communism.

> *The true soldier fights not because he hates what is in front of him,*
> *but because he loves what is behind him.*
> – G. K. Chesterton

So, it was my time to rotate to Bien Hoa. One maintenance crew came in, the other left with barely a nod. We had two complete complements of enough mechanics to do the groundwork and launch birds, so we could work 24 hours on and 24 off month in, month out. Each crew stayed in one of two mobile homes near the end of the runway, just a few running strides from five birds in steel revetments on alert for launch. Those revetments were about six feet thick, stuffed with sand, taller than a fighter, and open on one side to taxi to the takeoff pad a few minutes away. The thought was that if a plane were hit, the fireball wouldn't damage the adjacent birds. That theory was thankfully never tested. Each spot had "coffins" to store the six rockets that made the Duce aircraft lethal. The revetment ensemble was completed with a cockpit ladder, a huge air compressor used to crank the engine, and chocks for the main gear. Yes, only one engine, hence "lead sled." No engine—no fly.

We would scramble full tilt as soon as the klaxon went off. It was the most startling, screaming beast mounted inside the door of the trailer about ear high—naturally. It would blast in one ear, careen about the noggin for about 15 minutes, cross the eyes, and rest in the remaining vacuum. We would race out the door and be at our alert bird in seconds. The object was to be in position on the cockpit rail ahead of the pilot to help him strap into the staged parachute with his left hand first through the shoulder harness so he could grab the throttle stick and start the compressed air cranking the engine turbine within seconds of the still-whining siren's blast. Within a few more seconds, we would have him strapped into his parachute and seat, then release the canopy strut, pull the canopy to within his grasp, then hurl down the ladder. Then we'd wait a few more seconds till the engine ignited, dangerously knock the air feed off port (not a safety-approved maneuver), remove the chocks, and position ourselves at the head of the bird, thumbs outward to signal chocks were removed and all was ready to marshal the pilot out. In a few minutes from the klaxon, the pilot would be taxiing to the active runway and launching, the *priority* being to meet the imminent threat from the air.

I came to the Philippines, commonly called the "PI," at 5 feet 11 inches+ and 135 pounds. I left after 18 months at 129 pounds and could eat three meals a day with double servings of Friday fried shrimp at the chow hall. Evenings were fueled by a couple of huge cups of coffee, free after the first 10 cents, and a very large Butterfinger candy bar. I had my head in my cubby with my college books every evening.

Another memory is how the MDs got us ready for the tropical war. A gamma globulin shot supposedly afforded some sort of force field that would protect us from disease. ("They" invented a lot of those.) Naively, trustingly, we stepped up and exposed our tenderest parts. Pick your weakest cheek, yes, the one you sit on. We didn't know it would disable its victims to a hobbling mess for hours, if not a day or two. Then there was the anti-malaria pill. The result of that one, for me at least, was a violent stomachache and retching—proving the old saw that the cure is worse than the disease. We then returned to the detachment, the trailer, the revetments, and our jet fighters.

Imagine the wet tropical air, the fetid smell of the *clong* (swamp) competing with JP-4 kerosene fumes that assault more than a nose, hot exhaust swirling, sun blazing. And our laundry! We sent it to be washed and folded by locals. The pile came back smelling like vomit. Truly!

This was how war was "done"—entrusted to the all-too-young to know what was happening.

Thus, the days passed, 24 on–24 off–24 on–24 off. Routine helped them pass. Maintenance crews changed after a briefing on aircraft status in just minutes. We knew the deal. We might go to our bird to wipe it down (they were always leaking) and check things out. We might help a specialist fix a gig. I remember doing ab crunches from the rocket coffins (containers), toes under one, back over the other. Then it was return to the trailer to wait for the klaxon. We weren't disappointed.

That trailer and those birds were our lives, occasionally interrupted by a trip to the BX (Base Exchange) for toiletries and maybe a haircut by local barbers (35 cents) and a shoulder massage. I remember being in line with an army helicopter crew member who tossed out a casual comment about his pilot getting "shot in the ass" and killed with a small arm round that came right through the underside of the bird. What rotten luck. But that's war—and it's why most small observation aircraft, O2s, and helicopter pilots sat on their flak jackets rather than wear them.

The trip took us past the O2 (observation prop) birds parked in nice rows. Mortar holes pockmarked the flight line where shots were marched down the row, searching for a parked plane. How did they do that from that impenetrable jungle with crude WWII-era mortars? Surprisingly they missed all the O2s when I saw them.

> *War is always a great evil, but in some particularly extreme circumstances,*
> *it may be the lesser of two evils.*
> – Bertrand Russell

The days went by. An 18-month tour in the Philippines is one countdown to the next. Upon arrival it's 547.86 days to the "freedom bird" home. Or 45 days to return to Clark AFB from Southeast Asia. Or 30 days to the "freedom bird," then 29, 28 . . . . Then we had a litany of "short" (as in getting short on time remaining in the PI) observances to describe leaving. "I'm so short, I gotta step up on a chair to get my utrau on." Our fatigues were well faded, and our unit ball caps fit to a T with wear and grease. I felt a bit of sly giddiness at the thought of the "freedom bird" outa there.

So much unbelievable contrast from my world in Ohio, between the home in Euclid to the farm 29 miles away, then to the other side of the globe with its monsoons, typhoons, an earthquake, the South China Sea 100 feet down—and war.

Back to my bit of actual combat.

Ready are you? What know you of ready? – Yoda

Day 1: Act one—Morning—It begins.

Something was up, we knew not what. We were ordered into the officers' shack and unceremoniously lined up by a barred door to a closet. Each of us got a WWII helmet, webbed belt with canteen, two full bandoliers of .233mm M16 ammo and the M16 to go with it. Imagine 129 pounds of teenager, still trying to figure out how to shave whether I needed to or not, strapped with an X brace of ammo across my chest. We were told, "If they come through the *clong* (swamp before the jungle), we are it," or words to that effect. Heck, our commander, a very young major, wasn't that much older than we were—about 30 something. We epitomized the insanity of war necessarily trusted to youth. Age brings great pause, if only fear.

We retreated to our homemade bomb shelter. We mechanics built our own shelter behind the trailer from an abandoned water tower. We competed with our pilots for a spot, closer than cheek to jowl, every time the klaxon howled. The live shooting began, with helicopters, fighters, roaring machine guns, and the jungle in balls of napalm flame and smoke.

I was dangerously, naively curious. I crept out and, most of the time, sat by the corner of the officers' shack, peeked about, and watched the spectacle, or feast for the senses that it was. Oh, the stupidity of youth. I might as well have painted a target on my forehead. But it was like a front row seat to La Bohème or a Beatles concert.

Defense of the base was the work of aircraft. First F100s. Again, WWII technology. The J57 single-engine, 25-feet long, blew the F100 into the air armed with a 50mm belly machine gun capable of about 750 rounds per minute. I saw a film of the belly gun in action. The pilot strafed a line of old wooden boxcars on an abandoned section of railroad, shattering all to bits and pieces of kindling. The F100 would roar down the runway in flaming afterburner, rotate the nose, and accelerate nearly straight up, loop over, then take a run at the jungle at the end of the *clong*. Yes, quite near. You could feel the bird when the pilot hit afterburner, meaning when more JP4 kerosene is atomized and injected at the rear of the engine, virtually exploding into more thrust. The jolt is dramatic and necessary to get the tons of steel, fuel, napalm, and ammo off the ground. A fighter doing its job is an amazing thing to see. And most vital. No modern war is won without air superiority.

From our distance, the gun sounded like a mythic tiger roaring. Next, the bird would loop again and loose two wing-mounted canisters of napalm about 12 feet long into the same piece of jungle which was just strafed, which would erupt into an orange fireball then into the smoke of napalm, incinerating trees, vegetable matter, and earth. What could survive? Not much did.

We were told the VC came with families, as they planned a complete takeover of many bases. Key was Bien Hoa, mainly because it projected superior airpower and was one of the most active airfields in the world. . . . No chance.

I can't expect loyalty from the army if I do not give it. – George C. Marshall

Airpower also meant helicopters, in many ways more deadly than the F100s as the helicopters were relatively precise and horrifically deadly. Imagine two mini guns, one on each rail, both going at about 600 rounds per minute. Flight crews mentioned that a 'copter would back up with the recoil.

A couple of bursts began as the birds flew over my head, I'd guess less than 100 feet above me. Guns screeched, blasting away at the *clong*—nothing but grass and swamp to be seen. The sound of jingle bells is what I remember as the casings danced on the tarmac close to me. The dual mini-guns on the helicopters sounded like an angry, full-throated buzz. And the fighters flew on. Flight after flight the ground shook as the 100s took off in flaming afterburner to destroy jungle and leave a fireball rising into black smoke, marking an inferno. Seemed so small against the expanse of the jungle. What in the world are they shooting at?

Then the ground shook, yes shook. Somehow one of the largest bomb dumps in the world had been hit by something. Bomb dump bunkers are positioned as far as possible from anything and anybody for a reason. I never saw the aftermath. That did not dispel the fact that I felt those distant blasts through my feet, through my belly. Every sense I had was involved in some way to some degree. That war was mainly a deadly feast for the eyes—blue eyes that "see" it even now.

Day 1: Act II—Nighttime—Beyond Spectacular for the Senses

Oh, the night. This time the night sky was always alight with white hot phosphorus flairs in the air, launched from wishing-well looking structures surrounded by sandbags, which housed two AF security policemen. The flairs were fired in an unending succession, a chain which kept the night daylight bright. Those flares soared into the air, floating so beatifically to the end of the burn on a little white parachute. Then another traced its embers, utterly stunning at night, leaving a trail then clouds of heavenly white burnt chemicals and phosphorus to the ground. Swoosh, pop, and another swung its descent to the *clong*.

The 100s at night continued exciting the senses. We could hear them taxiing to the takeoff position. Fat with huge wing tanks of fuel and napalm, with the 50mm machine gun pod bolted to its belly nearly scraping the pavement it seemed, as the bird was positioned at the active runway. Then wah, *wah, wah,* the turbine quickly whined to a fiery max thrust before the afterburner exploded. The ground shook. Nighttime was the show. The remarkable contrail from the tail began as yellowish white then morphed into oranges then reds. It took a racoon-tail-striped shape of hellish circles that had to be 30+ feet long. Imagine a cutting torch flame with those circles, the extreme tapering to a tip that was bent and deflected at an upward angle by the runway cement as the afterburner hit. The F100 rolled, accelerated, then leapt into the air and accelerated upward nearly vertically, hurtling with tons of fire.

It made a ballet-like loop to line up with the jungle behind the runway. Within seconds, a patch of jungle was mowed down. The bird made another loop, and wing tanks of napalm fell away from the plane in a manic tumble to the ground. Fire erupted, smoke billowed.

So beautiful, so alarming, so exciting to the senses when so disconnected from it, this thing called war.

The soldier's heart, the soldier's spirit, the soldier's soul, are everything.
– George C. Marshall

Back to my perch at the corner of the Ops building. The flairs lit the way for the helicopters, buzzing, whining away at 1200 rounds per minute. Carefully staged, directed, and enacted. They came in twos, with the lead bird's belly floodlight scanning this way and that. When it detected something, the following copter, blacked out, erupted with spraying streams of lead. The deadly beauty of it all was that every tenth round was a red tracer, screaming a path to the ground in a ribbon of crimson. I can see it now. Smoke hung in the clear night sky, stars twinkling as they should. Flairs were relentless, 'copters too, all night long. And there I sat, at the corner of the officers' shack, cross-legged, my M16 in my lap, with my helmet, canteen, and a few hundred rounds of ammo.

I think about it much more now than when I was there. I am lucky to be here, I am sure. So many things happened and didn't happen. It has made me a lover of peace but with the necessity of a strong force and the willingness to use it. How can anyone know unless they experience it.

Day 2: Act III—Daytime—War Buddies

I maintained my perch, cross-legged, head stretched 'round the corner of the officers' quarters, staring at the show for hours. Reflecting years later: How young, how stupid to be peeping around a corner at the enemy. We all had a price on our heads, so we were told. I was more valuable as an aircraft mechanic than a foot soldier. I helped put the fire and brimstone in the air.

More of the same all day long into the second full 24 hours. I maintained my position, only taking breaks to eat and such. I remember visiting one of the guard stations to chat. Upon my return, a dog, a terrified mongrel, came to me and sat in my lap, shaking in fear if not terror, and there he remained for the longest time. War buddies.

Day 2: Act IV – Nighttime Again—Routine

The next act of the same play came that night, all night—the 100s in afterburner, scorching the jungle. Brilliant flairs floating to earth. Helicopters in twos, red streaks and all. I can't remember sleeping, but I must have, as a teenager might.

Atypical was the M16, two bandoliers of ammo, a helmet, and a canteen. Not what a child should have, nor have to remember.

The more you sweat in peace, the less you bleed in war. – Norman Schwarzkopf

Day 3: Act V—Daytime—Result of It All

It happened in seconds. I was maintaining my position, cross-legged, semi-auto lying inert in my lap, neck craning my perfectly targeted head around the corner of the crew shack. I peered past the wishing-wells of security police, over a small ridge where a few more men lay prone, watching the *clong* and jungle. All of a sudden, the few guns on the small groundswell erupted. What were they shooting at?

The shooting stopped, the birds stopped flying, we walked around freely. My first impulse was to investigate what the shooting off the ridge was about. The police said a commie had made it to a small shack at the end of the runway then chanced a mad break for our Duces. He was peppered by M16s, gone, sprawled on the tarmac. Afterwards I saw the evidence painted—splattered really—on the cement.

Sobering then, sobering now.

I don't remember hearing an announcement that the engagement was over. We all just milled about the detachment area. I wandered a bit in the confusion—men, trucks, planes overhead—this and that going that-away and this-away. My gaze fell over it all—over the *clong,* scanning the jungle. I picked up a stray shell casing souvenir from the tarmac. In my periphery, I spied a small stake-bed ton-and-a-half GMC truck. It passed me, and I instinctively glanced at the load . . . a few bags of charcoal, piled up willy-nilly. Odd. Bags of charcoal. Then it hit me. Not charcoal but bodies of the enemy in their black "pajama" uniforms gathered from the *clong.* Who knows how close they got. We were told they were armed with satchel charges to storm our fighters and blow them up—and were supposedly "coked up" for the suicide mission. Our airpower must have simultaneously terrified and steeled them.

Remember our barber I briefly mentioned—wielding his straight razor about our throats and all? He was supposedly shot dead at the main gate. I didn't see it, but I have no reason to disbelieve it.

A question rolls around in my head to this day: Would I have pulled the trigger on a man heading for the planes? Perhaps. That's why war is given to the young. They wouldn't think at that moment, just do. My next thought is I would have never gotten past that day and into my seventh decade with the promise of more. Dead most probably. And if I did pull the trigger and hit my mark—as I am trained and capable of—my constant thought is, I might have killed a good man, perhaps better than I. A patriot, just fighting for his homeland. Then my thoughts move to thankfulness that it came out the way it did. I turned in my helmet, my webbed belt and canteen, those two bandoliers of ammo, and my cold M16.

Sobering then, more sobering as the years pass.

Know thyself, know thy enemy. A thousand battles, a thousand victories. – Sun Tzu

So many lessons, observations, realizations. Humans seem destined to fight wars. Even today a devastating war rages in Europe, Putin claiming Ukraine for "Mother Russia" and the Ukrainians killing and dying to keep their homes. Meanwhile, China fumes to claim Taiwan, the South China Sea, the world's resources, endless space, and domination of all. Didn't we hear this in the prelude to and during WWII?

So, what have I learned?

Love your country. It's the greatest experiment in government yet and worth protecting. Peace is assured as much as possible by the strength of a truly representative government and the willingness to use that strength for freedom. We will always need a strong, strong military and brave people to make it an instrument of peace.

Truly, it is good to be alive, in this country, at this moment in history!

To be prepared for war is one of the most effective means of preserving peace.
   – George Washington

How Does Veteran's Day Affect You?

Vietnam Helicopter Pilots Association, January 2023
It was an honor to stand with these true heroes.

I think of a hero as someone who understands the degree of responsibility that comes with his freedom. – Bob Dylan

As a preamble to my answer, I must mention I had a marvelous few hours with the Vietnam Helicopter Pilots Association at the Vietnam memorial in downtown Raleigh. Members meet annually in February to remember and give thanks to their comrades and to give thanks for their country. They remember MIA North Carolinians monthly. It's a remarkable honor to be invited to stand with these guys in their flight suits, all in their 70s. What's left of their hair is grey, and for the most part, they hike up and down stairs with stiff joints.

Conversations ranged far, wide, and distant. Talk usually began with the physical pains of the day, from bunions to knee problems, hip replacements, backs gone (one in a brace awaiting operation), shoulder replacements, neck injections, and cataracts in various stages of going, going, gone. Plus, internal torments a plenty. It's called aging. Not to mention the noticeably thinning ranks. Many wished out loud they had minded their health from youth on! Still, I noted smiles, humor, plans for doing good things, and palpable, abundant gratitude for the day. All were glad to be alive and fairly able.

I return to my feelings about Veterans Day.

Why must we have war?! How did we come to this!

We have a saying: "No one hates war like a warrior." I have studied and practiced war for just over 20 years; but I will never stop thinking about it. It was a job. I was distracted with getting an education and the trials of marriage. The meaning of serving escaped me till much later. My foremost memories were of being in the Tet Offensive of '68 in Bien Hoa, Vietnam, which I've described. At 18, it was a show for me. In my 70s, it is surrealistic and tragic, giving me much pause. War truly saddens me. It seems we will always breed despots. What an unspeakable waste of the gallant and the treasure of nations. I hope the horrors of modern warfare alter history to one of preparedness, overwhelming military capability by freedom-loving peoples, combined with a "coalition of the willing" who will stand up against any despot who tries to weaken or even destroy liberty. But history belies my hope.

The society that separates scholars from its warriors will have its thinking done by cowards and its fighting done by fools. – Thucydides

Thucydides describes our current war with Russia and Ukraine. History is right; we have not been able to escape war for now nearly 3,500 years.

My overwhelming thought through the years is I consider myself most fortunate that I did not shoot or kill anyone. Or, more likely, be the recipient of a bullet. Serving is a privilege, yes, and certainly formative. As Dad would say, the military experience makes a good man better and a bad man worse. He bucked a bit at his experience in WWII—never talked about it. Nor did Uncles John and Ed. We children never knew our dear uncle suffered extreme post-traumatic stress until he attempted suicide and was in a coma for a year, fed by tubes, withering away to skin and bones, detached from reality, staring vacantly. He had been a strapping and most capable man. I would come down to the barn and find him cooking an oatmeal breakfast on a small burner and singing to an old 45 record: "Ahm gonna sit right down and write mahself a lettah." And he would belt out the "lettah" like the artist. Smiling. His eventual fate still saddens me today. I think he would have burst with pride to see his nephew and grandniece in uniform.

Veteran's Day is a constant reminder that we must be prepared, individually and as a country, for the next war and the next. It will never end, only be delayed by opposing decisive capability and a strong arm. The older I get, the prouder I am of having served. I used to shy away a bit when someone thanked me for my service. Now I quite sincerely say, "You're welcome. It was an honor."

What does being a veteran on Veteran's Day mean? My buddy Bain Black invited me to the ceremony to honor his Vietnam Helicopter crews' MIAs at their annual meeting. Quite solemn to be among those heroes. Their company had a 100 percent replacement rate due to deaths and casualties during Bain's tour. Think about it. Those who eventually survived gathered for their annual group photo—and just before the shutter clicked, Bain invited me to stand with that group of real heroes. Imagine that! I was both proud and humbled to think they knew I belonged there. It still brings a tear to my eye. Then I was given a gratitude quilt crafted by women who just wanted to give us something tangible in thanks. It's on the couch now, signed by me no less. Keep it sacred if you will.

I know Mom and Dad were proud of me, especially as I progressed in the military. Children of the Depression and WWII had great respect for the military. While it waned in the '60s, I note a growing respect for those serving, thank goodness. Dad thought my becoming a sergeant was a really big deal. When I became a lieutenant, Mom and Dad burst with pride; I know it. Dad squired me around introducing me as "Lieutenant." I wonder what they would have said if they could have seen me in my insignia as *Major* Klopovic. And more, seen their granddaughter as a captain in the Air Force Reserves, Medical Corps. *Wooha!* as I am fond of saying.

What a proud moment for an ex-Airforce mechanic—that my daughter Nicole is now a commissioned officer, and I administered the oath of office. Yes, I'm proud to busting! How a difficult life for us both pales in comparison to its blessings, wonderments, and testaments to hard work and perseverance.

Nicole, you and I began our rapprochement in Arlington, Virginia, where we saw the Arlington National Cemetery. I write of this later in the Travel section under "Where's a favorite place you've traveled and why?"

Knowing I will be buried there is remarkable. Imagine me with all those revered and honored heroes. I do hope you will visit occasionally—and that it will be difficult to forget where I am waiting. Then all can have a good meal with fine wine, perhaps a good Napa Cabernet Sauvignon afterwards, on me, . . . and remember.

Veteran's Day offers necessary moments to give us pause about the tragedy of war and its inevitability. A fact of the human condition is we will always breed those who would rather "take it than make it," no matter the unfathomable costs.

The farm made me; the military made me over; life tested me and I bested it. I am so proud to be a veteran.

Americanism means the virtues of courage, honor, justice, truth, sincerity, and hardihood—what made America.
– Theodore Roosevelt

TRAVEL

What Was Your First Big Trip, and How Did It Affect You?

My study and antique walnut executive desk at which I sat for years

True wisdom comes to each of us when we realize how little we understand about life, ourselves, and the world around us. – Socrates

I was five years old when Mom decided to make her first trip back to Australia with two of her sons, me and John. Little did we know it would result in a disaster for our family.

John was an infant in arms. For some reason, David remained home. Maybe he was too much of a handful—or the three of us together might have been. I'm sure Mom was the proudest in all of Momdom in Sydney those few days. She always wanted children and devoted all she had to us.

It hadn't been but a few short years since air travel had become commercial. No doubt it was very, very expensive for Mom and Dad's Old World, Depression era, WWII rationing mentality. Thus, we traveled by ship. The only memory of the trip I have was when we crossed the equator and "Neptune" (a crew member dressed in the part, trident and all) appeared to conduct the crossing ceremony. I can still see him on his throne. The rest of the voyage I remember not, but it would turn out to have monumental consequences that crowd out other thoughts even today (see below). I am lucky to be fit and alive.

I have two overarching memories of Australia—the outhouse with the iguana lizard living beneath it and Bondi beach. I suppose those are typical memories for a five-year-old.

On the first day of our return, Aunt Amelia noted that John seemed a bit listless (my word here). One of the biggest disasters had befallen our family: John had contracted polio, probably on the ship. The Salk vaccine had just been introduced. The entire family was altered. Mom soldiered on as before, even though her work tripled. John needed intensive mothering, dressing, feeding, bathing, chauffeuring, caring. Dad, again true to character, remained distant. He did nothing to ease the constant attention John needed, let alone the demands of four more offspring who clamored like little wild chicks in a nest.

John was stricken hard—with withered legs, curvature of the spine, and much internal damage. Operations attempting to lengthen his legs and straighten his spine were complete failures, as medicine was quite crude then. As a teen, he put a halt to the surgeries proposed by too-eager surgeons. He spent untold hours in hospitals in one contraption or another. They mounted a halo on his head to support threaded rods to his legs to increase the downward pressure in the effort to lengthen his withered legs. No doubt that contraption was patterned after the rack of the Inquisition jailer. All failed. Our neighbor had a polio-stricken daughter who died, striking home that dark and dire possibility.

Still, today as he passed his 70th year, John is alive and surprisingly well—despite the hereditary arteriosclerosis (Dad), Alzheimer's (Mom), diabetes (Grandma the elder), alcoholism (Grandpa the elder), and cancer (Aunt Carolyn) in the family. He's retired from a career in accounting and has been successfully married for thirty-five-plus years. Man, he lucked out with Diane. He's as active as his affliction allows and has learned to love reading and the daily news. In fact, John is quite capable, if a self-imposed recluse. He drives with his hand-operated "gizmo." He refuses a wheelchair, even though both shoulders are blown and beyond repair from using his arms as legs with custom crutches many decades old. Still has that wicked humor to match his curmudgeon lifestyle. Unfortunately, he has nothing to do with his siblings and offers no explanation. What I've gleaned about him I learned from my reconnection with him after my divorce. Since then I've tried to connect with visits, projects, and calls. Nothing. Regrettable but final and okay. We move on.

That trip to Australia was by far the most significant trip for me because of what didn't happen! We three—Mom, John, and I—stayed in the same accommodations, ate at the same table, slept in the same room, and visited the same people, both family and strangers. John was afflicted, I was not. Ahh . . . fate and luck.

> *Fate rules the affairs of mankind with no recognizable order.*
> – Seneca

What Later Trips Did You Take with Your Family?

Here I am with a king salmon, caught while staying at Tikchik Narrows Lodge, Alaska, July 2018.

A road trip is a way for the whole family to spend time together and annoy each other in interesting new places. – Tom Lichtenheld

Dad loved fishing but rarely went. Still, he did arrange several fishing trips to North Bay, Ontario— Lake Nipissing, I think it was. He made a connection with an old German who built log cabins on the lake for fishermen and tourists. Man, that was waaay kool. Fishing every day. Mom fixed three meals a day for seven and kept the cabin shipshape and the home fires burning as usual. To our amazement, she spent a day fishing with Dad and loved it.

On the first trip, when I was probably six or seven, I caught a small-mouth bass on a dropline, which I dragged about for as long as I could then had it cooked for supper. I was hooked, shall we say, and my interest in fishing grew at the pond on the farm. I've mentioned I sold seeds one year to "win" a spinning rod. I got a yellow jitterbug top-water lure for the bass, which I caught after a rain. Put a few in the fry pan, too.

Back to Canada.

We trolled for lake trout on the main lake, which was surrounded by smaller lakes, each labeled for the predominate species in it—e.g., Bass Lake and Perch Lake. We'd tie off at Bass Lake, I'd catch leopard frogs in the grass with David, then we'd portage our canoe and three-horse motor through the woods a mile or more. There's nothing like a huge big-mouth bass nailing a surface frog. The ponds were rarely fished—paradise! And the next day we'd load up at Perch Lake.

Canada was fun, as it was a real diversion from strict home and farm work. David and I managed to get firecrackers, which we lit in the woods next to a German farmer's place. His wife was worried someone was shooting, scaring the hens. Believe it or not, Dad offered to help Ulrich Von Doeler, the farmer, put up hay, which he did with two Belgian draft horses, one named—wait for it—Dave.

The monumental achievement came when I was a teenager and the whole family pulled off a swing through the U.S.A.

Dad fixed up an ol' Corvair minivan and got an inexpensive (i.e., cheap) cartop carrier. A canvas bag hung from the front grill for cool drinking water, and a torpedo-looking "air conditioner" was shoved in a window. Just one for the seven of us.

We sashayed down ol' Route 66, the southern route to San Francisco, to visit the Klopsons (which is another story). We stopped at as many attractions as we could, including the Carlsbad Caverns, the Mormon Tabernacle (yes, we heard the choir) and the Petrified Forest. I can remember crossing the deserts, especially Needles, California, with the 120°F temperatures, windows up tight to get a whiff of air from that window "air conditioner." While with the Klopsons, we went to Muir Woods and hiked the "canyon" near their house in Richmond. We returned the northern route through Yellowstone, the Tetons, and Mt. Rushmore, stopping frequently to sightsee. It was all quite dramatic to a teenager; everything was so big.

Between every two pines lies a doorway to a new world. – John Muir

Every night we set up camp for seven. Perish the thought that we would stay in a motel. Each of us had an assigned duty. We got good at it, so soon it went fast. Mom had a hot meal ready for supper, a hot breakfast, and provisions for lunch along the way. Nary a restaurant was bothered. Dad's self- appointed sole duty was to connect a string of lights from the car battery to the picnic table then reverse the process in the morning in time to be on the road rather early.

I remember two "life-threatening" moments.

The first was when Dad, ensconced in his self-appointed head of household role, took offense at something his "ungrateful" children said or did and informed us we didn't "deserve" such a trip. To this I uncharacteristically and reflexively blurted out, "We didn't ask to come." I know my siblings, and especially Mom, thought it was all over, at least for me. I heard a collective gasp for the soon-to-be dispatched brother. . . . Dad must have been stunned. He just turned, sat at the picnic table, contemplated the truth of the moment and his explosive rejoinder to retake command and said . . . nothing!

The second came during our endless hours of driving, Dad at the wheel. I sat shotgun, where I read several books, one in a single day about Custer at Little Big Horn. The reading was exciting.

I would occasionally cast my eye from the page. Dad was forever saying, "Look ada view, look ada view," whereupon he'd cast his gaze at "the view," away from the road ahead, ignoring the potential for a head-on or a glorious catapult into an abyss. On one such occasion, while I was riding shotgun and reading, I looked up to see we were headed for the immovable barrier to an exit, a micro-second away. I shouted, "Dad, where ya goin'?!"

His response was "oooooh," as he swerved a hair's breadth to the left and the barrier posts ratcheted past like a frenzied picket fence. I'm trying to paint a picture here. Silence for a mile or so. Then he merely said, "Someone has to ride up front the rest of the trip." Not, "Hey son, thanks; I screwed up, and you saved this trip and our family." Oh well. I'm content to think it was a sentiment on the tip of his tongue.

We must have looked a sight, the seven of us sardined into that minivan, tooling across the country and back. Again, I refer you to Mom's (Grandma's) many albums to see the quaint Kodak chronicles. This is the family from whence you came.

In retrospect, it was a good trip. Well, monumental actually. Dad had his moments. It took months to put it together with road maps, having no Google. Every day had to be planned as we needed to find camping in time to set up, cook, eat, clean up, and stow seven people. I think we were gone about two months, including a lengthy stay with Uncle John, Auntie Wanda, and the five cousins. It took years for these moments to sink in, along with more travel and living in the Far and Middle East and a right many states in this U.S. of A. Age and accumulated awareness taught me to appreciate the length, width, and breadth of this great, great country and especially the brave people who settled it and kept it going. We are fortunate. Realize that and do your bit to build on it.

"... for there is nothing either good or bad but thinking makes it so." Hamlet
– William Shakespeare

What Is the Strangest International Experience You've Had?

Grayson Highlands Park, Virginia, on the Appalachian Trail with "wild" ponies, August 2017

They nibble—no bite—your pockets, as they know where the carrots are. Ol' Sea Biscuit here is already an accomplished panhandler.

All we have to decide is what to do with the time that is given us.
– J. R. R. Tolkien

Strangest international experience? My mind is trying to sort out the bizarre from the significant from the eventful, all of which can be strange.

Was it the trip to Russia, strange because it was so stage managed by U.S.S.R. officials to demonstrate the "glories" of Communism? The lecture by a Communist party apparatchik at the Kremlin was surreal.

Was it hunting for wild Russian boar in Iran? We were running one down along a river. It crossed the river, so I rushed headlong over the riverbank—and stepped on one sleeping in the brush. I offered a *yippie ki-yay*, as did the boar. I still don't know which one of us was more startled. Oh yes, the gun jammed. Luckily, the gun functioned as the beast bore down on me, so I put the river escapee in the chili pot and on the chow hall serving line nonetheless. We dressed out about 250 pounds, we guess. These aren't Hollywood boars. While they're wild, they don't know what a gun is, as those are illegal for the locals, so the huge beasts are free to get as fat and big as they wish. (See my first photo journal.)

Perhaps my strangest experience was the Tet Offensive of '68, which I've recalled in these pages under Military: How Was Your Air Force Experience with Combat?

Or was it the bazaar in Incirlik, Turkey, or in Shiraz, Iran, which seemed to be pulled right out of an Indiana Jones movie—surreal?

Could it be the Coast-to-Coast (C2C) hike across northern England, freezing in a whiteout at 3,500 feet then sunburned traversing the moors? All along the trek I was in awe of the beauty, the people, the history—even the food and ale. From the Viking artifacts on display in York to the well-preserved Viking dung, an archeologist's pot of gold, the experience was out of the ordinary.

Wait, wait, there's more! Let me tell you about watching Iranian fighter jocks live fire Maverick missiles in the moonscape desert near Bushehr, Iran. Sphincter tightening stuff.

Rick, a buddy from my years at George AFB, was an F4 fighter IP (instructor pilot) and thus coming to Bushehr on the Persian Gulf to observe Iranian pilots display their chops where the rubber—or metal, wires, and high explosives—met the road. He called: "Hey Jim, wanna watch the Iranians blow stuff up?" No need to ask.

Rick caught a ride from Tehran on our turboprop Cessna 12-seater air taxi, rested up a bit, and we were off. We pointed our Toyota Land Rover on the only road north across the desert, tumble weeds and all. With more than a bit of by-guess and by-golly, we found the range, which was more than a challenge as the range was third-world homemade, secured by a ramshackle sheep-and-hog fence. No signage. Somehow, we located a gate to the sheep-wire fence and encountered the rotund gunnery sergeant standing by with a gleaming smile ear to ear. He was proud to have visitors—any visitors. He couldn't have been more like one would imagine, with a tan work uniform that matched the sand, untucked to accommodate his girth, and a bare, bald cue-ball head. He sported that universal grin of pride at the prospect of hosting two American officers.

The sergeant could not have been warmer and more welcoming. So far so good. Too good.

He ushered us through a few sand dunes and shrubs to what looked like a stubby fire observation tower, which couldn't have been more than six feet off the ground and was in need of repair—no, replacement. So up we went on the rickety steps, sat on a plank bench, and peeped through a rectangular window overlooking the range spotted with derelict car hulks—the "enemy." Looking sharp and full of anticipation, we should have been thinking about a last will and testament. But I'm getting ahead of the reality of "live fire" Iranian style.

Rick had a hand radio ("brick" we called 'em, as they were as heavy as a brick), so we were in contact with each pilot as they made their run. Nary a car hulk was safe. In fact, most anything within a five-mile range was not safe.

The first pilot kept us informed of his "attack." It went something like: Vector this way and that way, lock on, missile away—*KA-WHAM*. A hulk twisted into the air and gasped a last breath. Big fun. Then the next pilot lined up. Same story as the first pilot, and another hulk was sent to Allah. We were thoroughly entertained. Then the next pilot lined up. Let's call him Mahmood.

Mahmood went through the approach protocol, then "Missile away." We were both glued to our binoculars and the hulks, anticipating more of the same. Then *KA-WHAM A LAMA LAMA*. The missile went off what seemed like a few hundred feet to our right, which is inches in missile speak. "Oh, sorry sir, sorry sir, sorry sir," bleats Mahmood. "Misfire, misfire!"

Misfire, misfire, my a___! You nearly killed us! He locked on to a hulk very near our observation tower and blew it back to essential elements on the periodic table. This to prove that if things can go wrong, they will—and reaffirming that life is good, if you're blessed with a bit of luck.

The poor gunnery sergeant was mortified to his bones. He could not apologize enough. Luckily, we had no result other than this story. Yet one more failed approach by the Grim Reaper. Over the years, I've way surpassed my allotment of nine lives. I lost count at about 16 encounters with Mr. Grim Reaper, and who knows how many more went unnoticed. The day did end on a memorable but much safer and quite tasty note, though.

The sergeant took us to lunch just across the street to an establishment of cement blocks made of the same sand we walked over. Imagine a brown block building with a tin roof, a few mismatched windows, and a squeaky screen door needing another hinge, with a few chickens in the yard. They were there for a reason. The sergeant ordered for us after we sat down to a rickety card table for four in mismatched plastic chairs to complete the decor. . . . Just where did those chickens go?

Soon enough, the proprietor came out with a huge steel platter, hammered with Middle Eastern scenes, filled with perfectly braised, succulent chicken halves, smothered in delectably sauteed onions with the local Barbari Persian flatbread and dreamy butter, plus the obligatory Coka (Cola). To die for! No pun meant. I've had some splendid meals, but they were equaled that day by that superbly braised chicken, seasoned no doubt with an ample dusting of "Man, it's good to be alive" herbs and spices. What a day. Nearly nuked and dining on the finest braised chicken meant for a Persian princeling potentate. Life is strange and good.

Life can only be understood backwards; but it must be lived forwards.
– Soren Kierkegaard

Where's a Favorite Place You've Traveled and Why?

River rafting the Middle Fork of the Salmon River, summer 2020

Demand not that things happen as you wish, but wish them to happen as they do, and you will go on well. – Epictetus, *The Discourses*

This is an easy question to contemplate. A favorite place of travel? Its *anywhere* with you, Nic. I love being your *dad*. It's just wonderful to have an adult relationship with my adult daughter. And yes, I still hold out a thread of hope that I can have the same with Cindy, in the same way, with the same result. But back to the question.

Ah, the memories—more than just one favorite place. Was it to the Atlantic Ocean, the North Carolina mountains, or the Pacific? Was it a nice meal at Heron's at the Umstead here in Cary? Trips to California? Perhaps a tour de force to the farm. Aunt Carolyn thinks you're a genius, Nic. I don't doubt it; and you're a *kind* genius. On our last trip to the farm, for your oath of office ceremony June 2022, we went straight to splitting firewood. As you lifted the hugest logs as if they were BBQ bricks, Aunt Carolyn turned to me and said, "Is there anything she can't do?" This is just one of many reasons my travel these days is to have experiences and make memories with you.

Maybe a favorite trip was biking with you in Holland. Or, maybe it was river rafting the Middle Fork of the Salmon River, Idaho, for a week. You won over each of the 30-plus guests and crew, boogie boarding and navigating your one-person dinghy, whitewater and all, the *whole* of the way for about six days. Plus, you delivered expert medical care to one very ill traveler. I can see the whole experience now, the two of us sharing a patch of ground under the stars for a night's sleep wrapped in nature.

> *What is the good of your stars and trees, your sunrise and the wind,*
> *if they do not enter into our daily lives?* – E. M. Forster

Oh, I remember your visit here and my visit there in the summer of 2020 to close on your first of two houses in about a month! Your house in Sacramento and a rental here in North Carolina. Who does that!? And just before Apple announced its East Coast HQ a few miles from your rental here. You are doing so well, with the promise of progress in so many ways.

How d'ya like this rooster fish I caught off the Mexican peninsula?

A trip bonus is always fishing. I really love to fish! And I am also smart enough not to get a boat so I take these trips or accept invitations to do a little fishin'. It usually involves good people and good times. I note there's a difference between fishin' and catchin'. Naturally, the latter is the goal. How about fishing for tarpon of a lifetime off N. Miami Beach? That was a winner! Or catchin' rooster fish off the Mexican peninsula, Pacific side, at Ixtapa Zihuatanejo.

Nic, do you remember having a remarkable Michelin meal at Fiola Mare, DC, where you had the sommelier teach you about your first glass of wine? Or that weekend in Yountville, California, Napa wine country, staying at the Maison Fleurie BnB, complete with welcome chocolates and a bit of wine?

One of my favorites was the perfect dining experience at the French Laundry. Chef Keller took a knee to thank you for your service on your pending swearing in to the Air Force Reserves Medical Corps—conducted by your father (ahem, yours truly), a retired major no less. Ahh . . . and that indescribable ceremony on the farm by the pond.

How could I leave out Africa in 2022? We went on "safari" in Nairobi, April 23–May 2, 2022. Twin elephants had just been born. Please refer to the photo journals. The pictures are worth those thousand words, no, two-thousand words, even if they don't do justice to such an experience. We were hosted by a Masai village. What talented gentlemen and women were the native black Africans who served us. We climbed the Sacred Mountain. Enough; see the journals. Go, travel, experience, be in awe and wonder.

More travel favorites were fishing N. Miami for tarpon. Then in 2023, the year of this entry, we visited the Culinary Institute of America in California to learn plant-based cuisine. Right on the heels of that, we flew to Bali, each from our respective coasts.

Will my favorites be vacations anticipated? Snorkeling the barrier reef in Australia, vacationing in a Croatian villa on the Dalmatian Coast, an epicurean cruise anywhere on a luxury liner, visiting Israel, a luxury barge trip down a famous European river? . . . Or just cooking in your kitchen? Gotta stay in contact with the farm, too, for sure.

Who knows what's next?! My skeet friend Dustan Taylor has a shot (oooh, pun) at the Paris Olympics in 2024. Gotta get that passport ready!

Nic, you make a trip, any trip, endless wonderful memories.

My favorite must be your first trip to DC, when you were exploring medical schools, now years ago. It was the first time I heard you call me Dad in more than a decade. I took you to Fiola Mare, where wine was poured by the sommelier. Then you tried an oyster shooter at the famous Old Ebbitt Grill. I warned you that the drink was "challenging." I still remember your face. That drink is a ghastly thing. Didn't I say you would try most anything?

I also remember the following trip to DC, when you were designated by UC Davis to be the student representative to advocate for Physician Associates in Congress.

That first DC visit, however, had ramifications that will echo down the years, long after I am gone. We had some time to explore, so we drove this way and that—got lost, really. We ended up, very much unplanned, crossing the Potomac River over the bridge to Arlington National Cemetery (ANC). We were there, so I suggested we go in and perhaps catch the changing of the guard . . . and we talked like we hadn't talked for years.

If you'll allow me a digression, I adore your every phone call, which might be about the concerns of the moment, such as how to fix a squeaky door, my opinion on buying something, or how the days are going at the clinics. It's wonderful to have my own personal medical specialist "on call." On the other end of the conversational spectrum, our call might be about coordinating buying two houses . . . just as the housing boom began. What timing. What luck. And I got to "be there" with you.

I can listen to you for hours even when you tell me, "Dad, you're not funny." Or, "Dad, I know; you already said that . . . several times." Ahh, back to ANC.

You, as intuitive, kind, and penetrating as usual, asked about my final wishes while we strolled Arlington. We began the kind of father-daughter conversations and connections a father wishes for and dreams of in a fraught world. I decided to voice my thoughts on being buried at Arlington and have made the decision to do so. So much came of that discussion. Because of that walk, I now plan for legacy.

I work on leaving a respectable name. I leave my love of books, books written and many books in a small library marking my journey through life. I pass along knowledge especially about financial security. I'll leave a journal, this memoir, some money with which to do good, and photo journals, which tell my experiences and travels pictorially. I will leave heirloom gifts—and perhaps a small book that we write together yet to come. You make so much possible. Who knows what is next. You make me a very lucky man.

I always wished to have worthy children, and you are one of the worthiest. Our discussion gave me the impetus to revisit my estate documents, which are rather extensive for a small "estate." These documents have now gone through at least four iterations and include an "ethical will," a brief bio, and instructions to succession executors. With that, my finances—our finances—took on new meaning and urgency. Later, I decided to write this memoir and flesh out a few details of our history (which now exists because it is written). It's my fond hope that you and, perhaps later, Cindy and your progeny will appreciate knowing the history from whence you came.

> *I had an inheritance from my father,*
> *It was the moon and the sun.*
> *And though I roam all over the world,*
> *The spending of it's never done."*
> – Ernest Hemingway

Legacy is of growing importance. Most people leave the scene and are forgotten. No one knows where they are buried, let alone visits the cemetery, and certainly doesn't remember from whence they came.

So, I kept saving and conservatively investing so you have an example and know how to conserve and grow money as a tool to do good works. I just paid off my house and will spend two years upgrading it inside and out. It will make a great residence or rental for you. I persist in writing books and this memoir, so you remember what's important to me and then to you.

A vital result of that chat at Arlington is that it led me to begin The Nicole and James Klopovic Charitable Foundation, which I know you will grow and do good works. (For more details on the Foundation, see the section If You Could Have as Much Money As You Wanted, How Would You Spend It?) My next publishing project after this is to finish producing the four-volume set on Capacity Building, which will serve as standard operating procedure for our foundation, which is to *Build permanent solutions to permanent problems.*

Also, I make the effort to live a good philosophy of life to leave you a role model. I strive to constantly strengthen being good and doing good for the common good. Imperfect, yes. But trying matters. Having worthy goals matters.

You get it. I simply glow when I see and realize the countless ways you affect lives in being the best physician associate you can be and the best Air Force officer you can be. You have no idea the footprint you leave!

My hope is that my legacy will continue to guide you and yours for generations to come.

Oh, and there will be more travel, as Hemingway and Twain would wish.

Broad, wholesome, charitable views of men and things cannot be acquired by vegetating in one little corner of the earth all of one's lifetime.
– Mark Twain

Chef Jim learning about plant-based cuisine at the Culinary Institute of America with Nicole, April 2023

How Has Travel Enriched You?

Nic at Katz Deli, NYC, September 2017, at the very table where "Harry Met Sally"³

The world is a book, and those who do not travel read only one page.
— Saint Augustine

We have many ways to discover life's truths and possibilities. We have formal professional and technical, butt-in-the-seat *education,* including the odd class of interest. We also learn by doing—say, cooking, beekeeping, and how to load your own shotgun shells. Then there's the purely *experiential* school-of-hard-knocks type of education: Nothing like farm work, with its attendant sun-bleached hair, toasted arms, and palms like shark skin, to teach and mold a young'un. *Reading* (combined with writing and speaking to learn and do rhetoric) far and wide trains us to think, persuade, and do. No one avenue should be slighted, as together they prove again that the whole is greater than the sum of its parts. With all of that, we learn—and if worthy, we're granted the wisdom and grace to pass the lessons of life and living to the next generation with the message to keep paying it forward. All forms of learning work together to shape the child, mold the man, and inspire the sage in us all.

We continue the topic of travel—from considering strange and favorite travel experiences to how travel enriches. This question, it seems, is best served by recounting my travels . . . so far. Each encounter with people, places, and things brought me something memorable, if not extraordinary, and certainly edifying and enriching. Golly, I have traveled (and read and sat in classrooms and worked many, many jobs in many, many places) much, much more than most, with the promise of even more. I have tried to learn and put those lifelong learning lessons into practice. Now I hope to pass all this on to those who follow me.

Give me a little more time to see this remarkable world with you, daughter of mine. Somehow, with luck and focus, I would like to camp *inside* a glacier. Pick grapes in France. Bake a pie with a grandchild. Cruise famous oceans and rivers and . . . . Travels and life have expanded and informed my view of civilization and the stark fact that I continue to push the Grim Reaper aside. I imagine when he does come, we will have a laugh at all my clever evasions. I have a reason to be here, now that I have reconnected with you, Nicole, with the potential to make a difference.

Forgive any redundant recounting here. It's an overview. I begin with one of my most meaningful trips, to a land that provided me half of my DNA—"Oz."

Australia – 1953. Mom took John and me back to her homeland when I was five and he was about two. We took a ship, as I suspect it was less expensive than flying, which was newly invented. On that trip, John got polio; I did not. As I have mentioned before, this was the most monumental of my trips for what did not happen. Had we both gotten polio, this memoir and so much more would simply not exist.

Canada – The family went fishing several times in Ontario, Canada when we were children. Dad's choice; he loved to fish but had little time to do so. Imagine seven of us in a Pontiac Bonneville with a cartop carrier. No surprise, Mom did the bulk of the work—especially magically materializing those three meals a day. Dad was in his element; we all had a big time. The memories come back.

On the rowboat trip to the remote log cabin, John got hung between the dock and the boat as it slipped away from the dock. Imagine him, slung there, hooked by his toes over the gunwale, braces and all, his fingernails clawing the dock and screaming like an incoming buzz bomb. He had to have been paralyzed with the fear of going under headfirst, feet "nailed" to the boat. I instinctively jumped in to prop him up, secure in my arms, screaming in terror a fraction away from my ear, which still echoes with his cry. Afterwards Dad asked, "How did you know how deep it was?" Ah me. Not a variation of, "Good going, son; proud of ya." The question says much. P.S.: I wasn't thinking; what knew I of ready? (Yoda again.)

Many a trip continues long after movement in time and space have ceased.
– John Steinbeck

Next, in about 2003, a group of Ohio guys and Carolyn's husband Tom took me to the Gouin Reservoir, Quebec, for walleye. It took *two*, two-hour trips there and back to haul our tight party of six and all our gear to the cabins. Remote is an understatement. But the hand-built log cabins were complete with running hot and cold water, gas refrigerators, and heat. (The trip back took only one boat ride, the only difference being the beer had been consumed.) I caught the biggest fish—a 35-inch northern pike—and won the pot. I had a great time reading by the evening fire; then the guys came to the fire for hours of stories. We called ourselves the Order of the Black Arrow. Michele, a six-foot-two lumberjack of a guy was the life, humor, and soul of our party. In a quiet moment, he confessed his beloved young and only son had drowned, stuck under a small wooden pier. Yet he was able to find fishing, humor, and comradery. So many lessons in life right in front of us.

Philippines – Air Force, 1968-1969. Made about 30 dives in the South China Sea. On one dive, I dropped overboard into a school of countless sharks, churning the water with fins and teeth. I scrambled back into the handmade *bangka* boat (outrigger canoe), known as the tsar of the seas, much faster than I'd left it moments before. My fellow divers roasted a sea turtle on the beach where we pitched camp. Turned out that was just below the tide level, so we were soon chased inland, soggy gear and all. We knew little about camping on shore. . . .

Traveled the length of the main island of Luzon and spent a weekend at a mountain golf resort built in WWII for the officers. Enjoyed the Baggio farmers market, unique in the world. How about pineapple nearly as big as a watermelon? Spent another weekend at Pagsanjan Falls, with a luau suckling pig roasted in the ground and traditional dancing. Sucked fresh coconut water hacked out of the treetops by boys with machetes as big as they were. While stationed in the Philippines, we had temporary duty (TDY) in Southeast Asia. Our squadron— the 509th FIS (Fighter Interceptor Squadron) maintained and flew F102 Delta Dagger fighter interceptors armed with six missiles.

Thailand, Udorn – My first TDY of 45 days was to Udorn, Thailand. We were housed in the maintenance shack at the end of the runway. These tin-roofed barracks held nothing but two rows of WWII bunk beds and a huge fan at one end to stir up the thick air, with only screen mesh between us and the elements. Ever adventurous, I'd go into town to see what there was to see and have a meal. One time I purchased a bowl of Khao Phat, fried rice, and a coke for 35 cents. As I began eating, I noticed one of the rice grains crawling this way and that—quite the study. What was one to do? I continued to eat around him (or her) and, with a few grains left, ordered a replacement bowl. Heck, that 35 cents was big money. On another occasion, I traded places with my unmotorized *tuk tuk* tricycle "taxi" driver just to see what it was like. Like!? I couldn't control it and into a wet ditch we went, I mortified and the driver squelching a belly laugh, hoping for a bigger tip.

Oh yes, another memory . . . taking a shower. There was enough pressure to get the occasional pencil width of cold water to issue forth. One time I was standing there all shiny with nothing on but a few soap bubbles and one of the housemaids walked by. Demur as can be, cute as can be, looking straight ahead, hand over mouth and giggling uncontrollably. My sense of manliness has suffered ever since.

Vietnam, Bien Hoa – We had 45-day rotations to fly MiG cap for the base. (MiG stands for Mikoyan and Gurevich, the post WWII Russian fighter aircraft designers and their company. MiG cap was to fly above, hence cap, our protected airspace to keep the allied skies as safe as possible.) Two maintenance crews of about 12 mechanics each stayed in one of two 60-foot mobile homes, which facilitated continuous readiness, 24 hours on and 24 hours off. During that time, we had several mortar attacks, a couple of missile attacks, and the famous Tet offensive of '68. Every time the warning Klaxon went off, we beat it to a rather exposed two-walled cement-block shelter the AF called our "bomb shelter." It did not engender the appropriate confidence. Probably designed by horticulture grads stationed in Slab City, California. So, we, the maintenance crews, built our own. When the warning klaxon blasted, we all ran, scrambled, crawled, and muscled in with the pilots, cheek to jowl like kissin' cousins. All hoping not to take a direct hit, not daring to speak of it.

War, actual battle, is an extravaganza for the senses. Even after experiencing it, it's difficult to describe. (Nevertheless, see my effort to do so in the section on Military: How Was Your Air Force Experience with Combat?) One must be there. Again, I reflect often on the fact that I didn't have to shoot or kill or be killed. I still wonder if I would have pulled the trigger.

Mexico #1 – 1970. Just over the border to Tijuana. Mouth permanently singed by the pickled carrots. Never again.

England #1 – 1978. In traveling for a year's assignment in the Persian Gulf city of Bushehr, Iran, I laid over in London and did the tourist thing. I love the history, tradition, pomp, and ceremony. Stayed just off Trafalgar Square, which is guarded by one of my heroes, Lord Nelson. Took a Cook's tour this way and that, even to where the first English steeplechase was located. The *original* steeplechase was between the steeples of County Cork, Ireland. Why the steeples? They were among the tallest structures in the county. The English Grand National is one of the toughest in the world, with 30 fence jumps. Saw the crown jewels and climbed the Tower of London to view a chopping block complete with ax blade slash.

Iran – 1978. I was stationed on the Persian Gulf, at Bandar Bushehr, strategically placed north of the straits of Hormuz, through which most of the Gulf oil must pass. Toured the nuclear facility being built by the Germans c/o the Shah with our petrodollars. The Germans "let" the Iraqis build the cement plant . . . only! Shopped the bazaar in Shiraz, still much in the seventh century. Went wild Russian boar hunting. Got seven of them, which were turned into chili for Friday dart night and "roast beef" by the detachment cook. Toured Persepolis, the ancient kingdom of Xerxes the Great. Watched men sitting in front of a handloom, weaving intricate wool and silk carpets from pictures—some, hundreds of stitches per square inch.

Russia – 1979. Mid-tour in Iran, everyone was nearly ordered to go on vacation to "get away." (Iran was/is a strange place for a Westerner.) Sat in the Kremlin, nearly brainwashed by a party apparatchik. Traveled the overnight train to St. Petersburg (or Stalingrad or Petrograd—might it be Putingrad next?). Toured Catherine the Great's summer palace, reduced to rubble by the Nazis and rebuilt to unspeakable splendor by Russian masters. The entire building and grounds are works of art. We were given thick cloth booties to wear while walking on the floors, which were inlaid with two dozen exotic woods. Stood entranced before about 20 Rembrandts confiscated from the Nazis.

The world is a book, and those who do not travel read only a page. – St. Augustine

Italy and Spain – 1979. Newly wed. Returning to Tampa, Florida, MacDill AFB, we laid over in Rome and Madrid. Had chestnuts on the Vatican plaza. Stood in awe in front of St. Peter's Basilica and marveled at the Colosseum, wondering, *How can men build such things?* While in Spain, we drove to Toledo past ever so docile bulls. Drank sangria on the Plaza Mayor in Madrid, ate paella as only a Spaniard could prepare it. Put down $100—all we could scrape together from pocket bottoms and wallet corners—to buy a classical Ramirez (luthier to Segovia) guitar.

Europe – 1984-1987. Finishing up 20 years with the Air Force at Pope AFB, North Carolina. Our mission was to fly C130 Hercules cargo birds all over Europe. We staged at Mildenhall, England. Before rotation to Mildenhall, I was sent on a tour of all our sites to prepare to manage maintenance for an upcoming rotation. Was the *only* passenger in a C5 Galaxy, a flying football field, it seemed to me. So, I did the gadfly, catching hops to:

Germany – In and out of Germany. I had a fabulous dinner of medallions of pork. Perfect. But allow me to explain more fully by referencing my story under the question about the Worst or Most Bizarre Food I have tried.

Greece – Tried ouzo—once. Marveled at the Parthenon. Pondered the greatness of the ancients. Perhaps laid the seeds for my continuing study of ancient philosophy.

Turkey – Incirlik, another bazaar. Bought a Meerschaum clay pipe souvenir. Have since lost it.

England #2 – When I returned to Europe, sometime around 1980, I was the Officer In Charge (OIC) of 118 maintenance troops for 90 days. Staged out of Mildenhall, England, we provided supply support for Europe and kept the birds fit in case of exigencies and emergencies. Spent a day each touring Oxford and Cambridge, inspired by the luminaries and geniuses past and present. Had "chips" in a pub, a big bowl of limp shards of potato doused with malt vinegar.

Best was returning to Pope AFB, Fayetteville, NC, as you were all there behind the security ribbon, quarantined for a drug sniffing dog, all looking like China dolls. Nic, you—looking especially doll-like—burst under the ribbon to hug me before the guards knew what had happened. Can't buy that with money.

> *No one realizes how beautiful it is to travel until he comes home and rests his head on his old, familiar pillow.* – Lin Yutang

Goose Bay Labrador – Flew back from England and laid over at an air base in Goose Bay Labrador to ferry the C130s back to Pope. No cars, just snowmobiles parked between two telephone poles atop about eight feet of accumulated snow. The poles allowed the 110v chargers to rise as the snow accumulated. The roads were mini canyons between plowed and piled snow. I thought I knew snow.

England #3 – 2003. Hiked the Coast-to-Coast trail from the Irish to the North Seas. Too many memories. Do this while you're young and quite fit. It nearly killed our young companion, Wes Riffle, who got bleeding stomach ulcers from ibuprofen overdoses to stem the pain from a sore knee. He nearly bled to death in the hotel room bathtub. "Near death," according to the doc. Got him to the hospital in the nick of time and into surgery. His blood pressure and pulse had collapsed. More about this hike under Travel: What Is the Strangest International Experience You've Had?

Belize – About 2010. Fishing for bonefish, tarpon, and profit. I said fishing, not catching. Toured Mayan ruins in the Lamanai Archaeological Reserve, once a major city of the Mayan civilization. Remarkable; only 10 percent of the geo-located ancient civilization is excavated and preserved. Monkeys on an island (can they swim?) ate bananas from my hand. Snorkeled the reef and hand fed sardines to a loggerhead turtle as per the guide. Some things are just not smart in retrospect. Think about it. What else cruises the briny deep and probably loves a sardine with your arm.

Jim "Tarpon" in Belize, Central America, November 2015

Mexico #2: Ixtapa Zihuateanejo – Fishing all day with a predawn breakfast Mexican Cantina style served from a four by eight-foot sheet of plywood. Then off to get bait, travel to the breakers to breathtaking sunrises, casting into the surf all day. The trip home passed schools of bonito, boiling the water frenzied for tiny shrimp. Just cast into the boil for supper ceviche. Ate next to the pet parrot who pecked at the tourists. Got an eight-foot sailfish, fastest fish in the ocean (60 mph)! Returned it to the deep.

Holland – Began foreign vacations/tours with you, Nicole. Biked Holland. Simply marvelous to be with you, talk with you, see who you are and what you are becoming. You "posed" for the Dutch masters, capturing the light in a replicated master's studio. We toured the Delft porcelain factory, eight employees keeping the historic art alive. We were lost all the time in the wonder of the moment.

Wandering a central market in Holland, May 2018

Everything neat as can be and clean. We witnessed a city parade for children's groups. Last in the procession was a street sweeper and men with brooms and blowers. Not a fragment of a gum wrapper remained. No wonder the Dutch ruled the world for a time. Seemed to be a cathedral on every block. And the canals! We toured, snacked, drank a bit, with you, Nic, at the wheel.

Alaska – Nic, you and I went fishing at Tikchik Narrows Lodge, July 2018. You got a 35-pound king salmon in the first half hour. We chose a remote experience, deep in the bush. The chef made hors d'oeuvres, cedar plank salmon, and blueberry cheesecake. Remarkable, have-to-see-it-to-believe-it experience. The "tent" even had a flushing toilet. . . . You took the place by storm—especially the young men and the occasional patient. We fished sockeye on the spawning run. Salmon were so thick, we could "walk across the river on their backs as the ancient indigenous Innuits did." The fish seemed to move in clouds. Caught 'em faster than the guide could fillet them. Fished near a moose grazing on underwater river grass, in three feet of water—only up to his knees; I measured it. Nicole, you flew the float plane to the lodge.

The real voyage of discovery consists not in seeing new landscapes, but in having new eyes. – Marcel Proust

Nicole fileting a king salmon – July 2018

CULINARY UPS
AND DOWNS

What Was Your Favorite Thing to Eat as a Child and Young Adult and the First Thing You Cooked on Your Own?

I enjoy feeding you, Nic, because you appreciate it so much—all five courses.

Food is symbolic of love when words are inadequate.
– Alan D. Wolfelt, The Olympian restaurant

I see where you came up with this question. Food is sustenance; more so, it is love. I tried to do all this when you were growing up; perhaps the gesture stuck. We both like food, appreciate food, and are most willing to learn and experiment. I look forward to creating nice meals with you—those that last hours and feed the conversation and the soul. So, to the questions.

The first thing I cooked? . . . Hmm. . . . It was probably toast, as would befit any hungry child. Other than that, it would have been Cream o' Wheat. Simple to do, so I must have done that. We children left the cooking to Mom and Grandma, as was the separation of powers in the '50s and '60s. However, as you were growing up, I had to do the bulk of the cooking—especially holiday meals. I'm better at it now. Memories, memories.

I remember once I tried to barbecue a suckling pig. I couldn't get the fire right. Tried the oven and the pig wouldn't fit, so I made it fit. But then it was not fit to eat. I have progressed.

I have often said I could live out my days with Cream o' Wheat in the morning, Kentucky fried chicken (just a little grease on my chin), and a bowl of Chinese noodle soup for supper. I have come a long way from that, too. Though my daily routine is quick, it's hopefully nutritious. So, these days, I must have breakfast of granola, hemp seeds, protein powder, wheat germ, Greek yogurt, and fruit. Don't forget the Nespresso coffee and honey with a dash of half and half. This is the best coffee I have ever had in the oceans of it that have passed my lips. Even better because the Nespresso machine just showed up at my door, an unexpected and absolutely wonderful gift from you, Nic.

Lunch is a protein, veggie(s), and some carbs. Sometimes it's a half sandwich of honey roasted peanut butter and fruit. More than likely, it will be a lean sandwich, some lettuce, a bit of fruit, and maybe cherry tomatoes and a few olives, too.

Supper is a protein (chicken or fish), microwaved vegetable medley, and 90-second whole rice. I may snack on a keto blend of nuts or have some fruit with that peanut butter. Yes, I indulge in an adult beverage every early evening, but I try to hold it to one. I watch my weight by regular vigorous exercise, monitoring how my belt fits. When it gets snug, I just cut back on a few calories for a few days. Another of my rules to live by: "It's much easier to nip something in the bud than it is after the thorns have grown."

While I was single in the military, I lived in barracks then in mobile homes while at Oklahoma State then in Adelanto, California, while at George AFB for four years. Then it was off to Iran. While I had a kitchen, I really didn't have "chops" in the kitchen. What did I cook as a young adult then? I can't recall specifics. I do remember that Mom and Carolyn sent me a regular "care package" while I was at Clark AFB in the Philippines, 1967-1969. They also sent me a box of Cream o' Wheat—but where to cook it? There was no way in the barracks, but opportunity knocked. During the movie at the maintenance shack at Udorn, Thailand, I would sneak to the back of the communal breakroom to a hotplate and make my beloved Cream o' Wheat. A treasure, a trip down memory lane. I make it now but put in a half can of condensed milk, a squirt of vanilla, a blast of cinnamon, and a scoop of hemp seeds. Oh yeah.

I do remember when you girls were young, I would cook major meals for, say, Christmas, New Years, Thanksgiving, and birthdays. They were good—no, better than good. I would sip champagne, get a lovely turkey with trimmings all set, and then we ate—all too quickly. After dinner, I attended to the cleanup. I know I was planting seeds of communication, togetherness, and family—which we, Nicole, now occasionally experience. Taking you to a nice restaurant is fun. In fact, we visited the Culinary Institute of America, Copia, Napa Valley for four days of their inaugural course on plant-based cooking and enjoyed a tasting at the Venge vineyard.

These trips are now in the family archives. You make things remarkable, Nic. First the CIA, April of this year, 2023. We had a class of about a dozen, food enthusiasts and professionals in the food industry. In five days, we made nearly 70 recipes in their Heston, best-of-the-best kitchens. We got a briefing at 0900 then off to stations, each with his/her own dish to do. The trick was it all had to be plant based. Tough to do when one has a meat-based rearing. Then we ate and discussed the dishes. The tables groaned under the fare.

We also toured the acre or two of herbs and had an evening meal by CIA chefs. Ya had to be there. I asked you, Nic, to find us a decent but frugal place to stay. So, with you at the wheel, we pulled up to a Fairmont!! I had no idea. Please see my photo journals. Naturally, you got an upgraded room with fireplace, balcony, and overlook to the 100-year-old manicured trees and gardens. The huge entrance border trees were lit up spectacularly with thousands of tiny lights. Look up *Fairmont* Sonoma Mission Inn and Spa. There's not enough room in this memoir to tell the tale. But I have to say, it is something to go to the bar with my baby and have *her* buy the drinks! Surreal.

Cooking started more seriously for me when I bought 208 Courthouse Drive and made it my own. I took a course or two for "cooking enthusiasts" at the local community college, then closed my eyes and leapt off the culinary cliff. I took a week for devising a menu, shopping, inviting guests, prepping, and printing the menu on parchment, complete with the meal title and toast, paired wine, at least five courses, and chosen guests. Then I'd don my bistro apron and side towel and just do it; first with appetizers, wines, and introduction of guests with a tidbit about each. At one such early meal of my "good ol' boy" friends and their wives, my eight guests stayed nearly six hours, deep into stories and a "little" wine (nine bottles). It was memorable, but oh so much work. What a wonderful surprise when no one would let me clean up.

And I have cooked for you, Nic. What fun! You with your endless sense of true wit and humor.

Why it is just plain fun to serve my daughter.
I can almost hear her saying, "Please, suh, may I have another?"

Here's one such menu of mine that describes the culinary aspect of an especially delightful meal we enjoyed together for Thanksgiving, 2016.

Nicole
Thanksgiving ~ A Homecoming
November 26, 2016

Irish Toast:
May those who love us, love us.
And for those who don't love us,
May God turn their hearts.
And if they cannot turn their hearts,
May he turn their ankles,
So we may know them by their limping.

Apéritif
Smoked Salmon Endive Boats
Blackberry Lemonade
Kir Royale Champagne

Le Potage
Fennel Soup
With Hazelnut Cream
Farmer's Sourdough Bread
With Hotel Butter

Plat Principal
Stuffed Roast Leg of Lamb
With Savory Cherry Sauce
Savory Polenta
Baby Mapled Carrots
With Hericot Vert
Penfolds Koonunga Hill -
Shiraz - Cabernet 2006

Fromage
Walnut Date Bar
with Vintage 1833 Barbe's Cheddar

Comme Dessert
Candied Fruit Ciabatta Bread Pudding
With Crème Auglaize
Espresso and Brandy

Let's cook together, eat together, laugh together . . . often. You have the cooking genes, which go back generations. As an aside, I dream of teaching grandchildren to cook. We'll start with Cream o' Wheat, then bake my Great Geauga County Fair, 2002, Grand Prize pie—*apple,* of course. Then, we'll take on the Fair itself and enter your *apple* pie with Aunt Carolyn to win your own Grand Prize silver bowl and big purple ribbon. We'll celebrate the event with toasted marshmallows at the pond, with you, the fourth generation to tread that sanctified ground; hoping for a fifth generation.

> *For what is the worth of human life if not woven into the life of your ancestors by the record of history?*
> – Cicero

What's the Worst or Most Bizarre Food You've Tried?

Breakfast with Nicole at the River Front Inn–Grassy Creek, North Carolina, February 17, 2020
No, *not* the worst or most bizarre food!

Food is a pretty good prism through which to view humanity.
– Jonathan Gold

Nicole, you asked another food question as well:

I am also curious to know if you enjoyed trying new foods and how you developed that, considering you grew up in a very homogeneous and somewhat isolated place.

What follows touches on both your questions and more. I'll cover food on the farm and food international—both the good and the bad. The difference between my experiences and those of my siblings is that, thanks to the Air Force, I have traveled much, much more than all my siblings combined and more than most people. I'll start with our common food experiences on the farm.

Farm food – Back in the mid-20th century, the best dietary minds suggested meat and potatoes. If it was white, it was a staple. If it was beef, pork, or chicken: Wooha! Fish were sticks, quite unidentifiable as to species of fish, if indeed it was fish. Sugar was quite okay—loads of it. Potatoes? Stuffed, mashed, fried, baked, in salads—pile 'em on. Veggies were cooked to mush. Dairy was quite okay, whole milk for sure, and Wonder Bread built "strong bodies 12 ways." How did they figure that? Especially when all the goodness, whole grain, and germ were processed out. Wonder Bread was just that, a wonder! It became white glue when squished in a sandwich for lunch.

Mom was a "right proppah" British subject, which included manners, an even, stoic temper, and a remarkable work ethic. So, to go along to get along, she cooked American, a bit of Croatian, and Australian/British. Thus, she brought to our table organ meats.

We had stewed kidneys and potatoes, liver and potatoes, beef tongue and potatoes, and once we had beef heart, as I remember. One has to skin it then really grind away at the tough meat. Imagine, buffalo tongue was a delicacy at one pioneer time. We had tripe (a cow's udder inner lining, a rubbery thing, no need to try it) with potatoes and creamed calf brains on toast (mmmmmm, *really* mmmmmm); no need for potatoes because Wonder Bread toast did the trick. All dinners were with some sort of veggie, usually from the farm when the huge gardens materialized, and frozen for eating all winter long, all boiled to mushy perfection. Of all the above, the tripe was most horrid. I even had it prepared as a Filipino dish later, and it was still horrid, still off-tasting and quivering on the plate. And I have a remarkable constitution for this and that. My favorite was the calf brains. Haven't had 'em for probably 60 years. Man, I can taste 'em now.

> *The only real stumbling block is fear of failure. In cooking, you've got to have a what-the-hell attitude.* – Julia Child

On the Croatian side, gadzooks. Dad had Mom go to Grandma's for a few "lessons." Mom learned a bit, but Grandma, my grandma, was a legendary cook. As an aside, Grandma Amelia Klopovic came from Croatia at 14 and took to house cleaning to support herself. Once she cooked for a client, that was it; the secret was out. She was a fabulous Croatian cook. Not only that, she had all her survival skills as a young teen! I mean not just the cooking from scratch but the making of mattresses and the birthing of children at home. She and her huge garden, a cow, pigs, and chickens were how the family made it through the Depression and flourished. Grandpa Ignatz Klopovic Nearly right off, she was engaged to cook for weddings, large events and parties. She could afford her own apartment when she was still a teen. Think about it.

Grandma Klopovic was "illiterate." She took ages to scrawl her signature—but only for dire emergencies. Therefore, she didn't use recipes. She had scores of intricate handmade dishes all in her head. She kept a bucket, yes, a small bucket, of lard under the kitchen sink. Flour came in sacks and sugar in large bags. When I came along, the chicken coop was still in use, but the cow and pigs were gone. The smokehouse still stood, and it smelled otherworldly wonderful.

Gardens flourished under her hand. I remember her planting by scooping a handful of fresh manure out of a bucket to throw *scherlop* in the hole ready for a plant. The house was full of one-of-a-kind doilies. She could doily the likeness of a flower. Everything she touched flourished. She had two splendid apple trees in her yard. Under those trees I would hunt nightcrawlers for fishing by the fist full—yes, at night with a flashlight. Even her worms were tubby, long, and sassy. They could grab their hidey hole till they snapped in half. We used to slice them into steaks for barbequing (wink, wink). As the first born, I was always urged to eat, especially by Grandma. Food was love. Where does one start . . . ?

Aunt Carolyn has a very small orchard, mostly of apple and peach trees.

The fruit trees were for more than shading nightcrawlers. We needed fresh fruit for applesauce, pies, and jam to die for. The trees flourished on the farm under the care of master gardeners. The apple trees were so laden with fruit that the branches had to be propped up or they would snap at the trunk.

Breakfast on the farm might have been sausage, potatoes, and eggs, cooked any way. The best was fried, as the edges were always crispy. Grandma put in a tablespoon of water and covered the pans so the tops would steam, and those edges would crisp. Otherwise, the yolk tops were doused with blazing bacon fat. There was always something on the stove. She would make her own noodles; store-bought wouldn't do. She always had some kind of soup going. Stews, meats, soups, salads, and dazzling pastries flowed. The potica, a Croatian nut roll, was at the top of the dessert tree. Aunt Carolyn, she of the inherited cooking gene, makes a great *potica*. You would be the fourth generation to master this one. So many good memories.

Loved the jellied pig's feet. (Never waste an animal part!) Boil the split foot in water with a bit of garlic and salt and pepper. Put one half foot into a shallow bowl, pour in the liquid, and set it on the porch to cool and jell. I would gnaw and suck the bones clean and white. I remember Italian (pronounced 'talian) bean and potato salad: potatoes boiled just right, broad beans from the garden, vinegar, spring onions, and S&P. Man! The skills Grandma (Klopovic) and Mom, your grandma from the Tucker side, had when they got here were stunning. Nothing fazed them.

Oh yes, in the Old-World way, the Carlovics hosted a couple of whole-lamb roasts for the neighborhood. Scores of people! We had lamb that roasted on a spit all day, with all the Croatian trimmings, including glasses filled with cold water, sprouting sprays of spring onions (Croatian table pieces), which we dipped in salt and ate raw. Man, Eastern Europeans know how to eat. Then they die young. So just sample, enjoy, and live to eat again.

Mom adapted to the cooking. Don't forget she fixed three full meals a day for six plus herself each day every day all year. (I recall we went out to eat *once* a year. Dad would splurge at China Gate.) Breakfast was usually hot. Lunch was in brown bags all lined up to go to school. Dad had a lunch bucket full to the brim. Supper for seven, desert included.

We ate American, as Mom was influenced by magazines, news, and a cookbook or two. Breakfast was some sort of eggs and bacon with white toast and perhaps jelly. The best jelly was the jelly she learned to make—grape from wild grapes and peach and plum from the orchard were the best in my opinion. Oh yes, and homemade applesauce to die for—or did I say that? We had cereal, dry and hot, with a little milk—and sugar, of course. I loved Cream o' Wheat then and adore it now, as I've mentioned—a little too much, so I ration it. Cooking and eating has evolved with the knowledge of what promotes health and longevity. Skinny rats live longer than fat rats!

Another treat was creamed chipped beef on toast, adoringly known throughout the military as SOS, s_ _t on a shingle. I suppose that's why I was so suited to the Air Force. I could get as much SOS as a fella could pack in. Man, I could eat. At home, the horrid part of breakfast happened when we started to have our own cow's milk, which ruined my beloved Cream o' Wheat. It had a kinda blue hue—no kidding. Mom pasteurized it as the cookbook said, and it remained undrinkable, as it belonged to one or two cows, with none of the blending that milk gets today. If a cow ate corn leaves, it did something awful to the milk. The blue-looking cream was siphoned off. I don't know where that went, and I don't want to know.

I'd rather be on my farm than be emperor of the world. - George Washington

I do have to mention that we butchered our own meat. Just a few chickens and a pig. It was way too much work to do it more than once. How did the pioneers do it? What I would do with the chicken selectees is hang them by the feet from a clothesline, take a dull, sorry, butcher knife—all I had available—to the stretched neck, saw, saw, saw, then jump back. They bounced and contorted on that line like, well, a chicken with its head cut off. Scalded 'em just enough to loosen the feathers, then plucked them endlessly, gutted the chickens, and readied them for roasting or the cookpot. That process of too many hours never got all the feathers off. And just think: Grandma would make chicken soup by culling the flock, taking the guilty one that wasn't laying up to snuff to the basement, hold it down with a foot, and, well, you get the picture. But if only you could have tasted the soup, thick with the best dumplings known anywhere.

Next came the pig. A shoate of about 180 pounds had to be held down by four men, because hogs are unimaginably strong beasts. The guy renting one of our trailers to help on the farm was skilled in butchering. He slit the hog's throat, and all the drama was over in minutes. Then the carcass had to be scalded in a 55-gallon drum of water boiled over a log fire and stripped of hair with a curry comb and wire brush. Any remaining hairs had to be burned off with a blowtorch. That whole process of pig killin' was a great bother, even for Croatian farm stock. The trimmings and scraps were handmade into sausage and the skin boiled into cracklings. It made for a very, very, very long day.

After that pioneer experiment, all meat went to a pro meat-packing house "just down the road a bit." The meat came back in a day or two, processed, packaged, and labeled according to meal-sized numerous cuts.

Besides the labor of Sisyphus, the smell of boiling pig fat for cracklings is, well, unique. I still love cracklings but haven't had 'em for years. Don't love the process. Such food killed Dad at 60. His arteries were "brown with atherosclerosis."

International foods – While in the Philippines, I looked at *balut*—a "fertilized developing egg embryo that is boiled or steamed and eaten from the shell" (courtesy of Google). Not for moi. A little more appealing were the fish I speared while diving. Preparation left something to be desired, though. The outrigger *bangka*-boatmen just threw them on a fire and turned 'em frequently in the embers, then we ate them by first scraping the scales off with a stick and then finger-picking the flesh. No seasoning.

The fruit was fabulous, in uncountable varieties that never make it out of the country. Huge pineapples, marvelous real strawberry jelly, and my favorite, Atise or sugar apple. It's an avocado-looking fruit with pebbly skin and packed with black seeds surrounded in white pulp. You scoop out a spoonful of seeds and pulp, pop it in your mouth, and separate the seeds from the good stuff by spitting the seeds out for the sublime reward. It tastes something akin to bubblegum, only better.

I've also had young green coconut, harvested from a treetop that looked to be 500 feet up by a boy with a machete longer than he was tall. He lopped off the top of the coconut with the blade, a fraction from his fingers. In went a straw, and *that* was coconut water the way it was meant to be. Not the store variety. The ground and pressed coconut meat makes coconut "milk." The meat was thin and rubbery—quite good. Love that mouth feel. Most of the time, the green coconut became a creamy pie.

I always make sure to explore wherever I am so I took the Rabbit (bus) from Clark Air Force Base to Manila. What a day, seeing the real Philippines from a largely wooden vehicle, the villages swarming with people trying to sell stuff at my window. For lunch, I popped into a neat looking restaurant on a main street, Rizal Avenue, as I recall. It had to be one of the best. Dish after dish came my way. Did I say I could match a bear preparing for hibernation back then? Ah, the meal is rising from my mind recesses of 50 years ago. Most memorable was the bird's nest soup served with a raw quail egg suspended on the top and still cooking in the lava hot broth as I watched, mesmerized. Every dish a treat for the eyes, nose, tongue, and wallet. The whole of it was a bit more than $10. Ah, the good ol' days. On to Europe.

I traveled Europe and Great Britain a bit. No food complaints there. Delish, in fact. For example, the Lamb Henry (many dishes are named for kings) braised over night in wine and herbs by a skilled chef was incomparable. In Shap, England, the inn prepared lamb taken from no farther away than a few miles and prepared immediately. Spirits, and especially the beer, were the best. Well, German and Dutch beer are close rivals. I like a hearty well-crafted beer, a good bourbon, and a fine red wine. I think fruit-flavored beer is an abomination. It took centuries to get beer right; don't tinker. Then came the English desserts: How about a spotted dick with clotted cream and coffee? Well, . . . look it up.

I had lamb in phyllo pastry in Athens, Greece. Roasted chicken from a street vendor in Toledo, Spain. The best yogurt ever in Iran. A buffet to die for courtesy of the base commander General Reahi in Bushehr. The thick Iranian Barbari flatbread topped with sesame or black caraway seeds and consumed with whole butter was yet another gustatory mini death, especially when served with baked chicken halves served on sautéed onions accompanied by a coka (cola). (As I mentioned before, the serving platter was hammered, decorated metal—and as big as a garbage can lid.)

Then I flew a round-robin to England, Germany, Greece, and Turkey with the Air Force in preparation for being the maintenance officer of a crew of 118 mechanics on C-130s. The rotation was 90 days in Mildenhall, England.

I settled into the Bachelor Officer Quarters at Wiesbaden and called a taxi with dinner on my mind. A gleaming yellow Benz showed up, of course, a hint of things to come. It was meant to be a memorable evening. I asked the driver to take me to a good restaurant—the Rosengarten in the top 10. I think it still exists. I had medallions of pork, sauced perfectly, with all the trimmings, plus chocolate dessert and cognac with half a cigar, all served by a rather stunning waitress in Bavarian dress, standing by, attentive to my every gustatory need. I ate one savored bite at a time and read *American Caesar* (Douglas MacArthur) by Manchester for three hours! It don't get no better! Do not forget the Benz return ride with one mellow-satisfied major on board.

So many places to go, so much to sample. I dream of taking an epicurean cruise and an "orient express" to have a rolling dinner, and staying at French or Italian wine estates to learn and cook local dishes. Onward . . .

Food is not rational. Food is culture, habit, craving and identity.
– Jonathan Safran Foer

We river rafted through that waterfall and magnificent jungle in Bali, April 2023.

Do You Have Any Tips on How to Host a Great Dinner Party?

In the kitchen at The French Laundry, Napa, California, with Chef Keller, July 2021

If when he eats, he can be just, cheerful, equable, temperate and orderly.
– Epictetus on eating acceptably

A great dinner party? Just do it. Try not to obsess. Choose good company, which means good conversation. This cements friendships and makes good memories; these matter. A good five-course meal with wine and fresh-baked ciabatta bread, pudding with dried fruit, and candied ginger drizzled with double-boiler-crafted crème Anglaise helps. Don't forget the wine for each course.

I knew my best way forward after the divorce would involve throwing myself into an array of pursuits outside of work. Of course I also had to buckle down and not let work lag, as that was also part of coping, then healing, then progressing. Oh yes, part of those pursuits included little things such as doctoral school and publishing books.

Learning to cook to host a dinner party was logical and potentially quite rewarding, even beyond the event. The most important thing for me was and is to make and keep friends. Feeding people is a way to the heart and continued acquaintanceship. Now how to make it memorable and fun?

> *My doctor told me I had to stop throwing intimate dinners for four unless there are three other people.* – Orson Welles

Luckily, North Carolina has one of the best networks of community colleges in the country, culinary arts being one curriculum. I accomplished a smattering of the hands-on experiences, more for the cooking enthusiast than the newbie. I learned some things, but my main revelation was that I could cook—and that people really appreciate a good meal where conversation and conviviality flow.

I had just begun extending networks—"good ol' boy" southerners who came my way and skeet acquaintances at Durham County Wildlife Club. I threw myself into all of it to rebuild myself and prosper. My first formal dinner was for my southern friends.

> *I cook with wine. Sometimes I even add it to the food.* – W. C. Fields

Background

Get yourself ready for a lifetime of cooking enjoyment and success. If you can, cook plant based. This is the most healthful cooking and is vital to focusing on lifespan. Then again, Julia Child lived well into her 90s fueled by butter. Sanity matters; *The body will not follow a discontented soul I say.* So cook classically—be reasonable with the butter, sugar, and salt. I highly recommend you take up Aunt Carolyn's—now my adopted—recipes for apple pie, cheesecake, and carrot cake. Share the results for the best experience. These basic recipes are meant to share with children as young as possible. This is legacy stuff. Make sure you get a copy of her cookbook, the result of decades in the kitchen.

> *Life is uncertain. Eat dessert first.* – Ernestine Ulmer

Cook! – You can read libraries of books, and while that's important, they don't really teach cooking. You need to *do* it. Begin with your favorite dishes. Try a soup and stew with carrot cake to see what it is like. Don't cook it if it can be done for you, the best. If you are blessed with a Cordon Bleu French Chef down the road, get his sourdough bread for the soup. You don't want to overshoot and discourage yourself. Then graduate to a five-course meal: menu printed on parchment, a witty toast, appetizers, soup, main dish, cheese/palate cleanser, dessert, and perhaps a special after-dinner aperitif and goodie. You need skills that come only from practicing. Have a no-fear attitude: Just cook. You will ruin stuff. And you will develop some stunning dishes. Guests are forgiving subjects for experiments and can hold a conversation. If you wish to have a friend, feed him.

> *A recipe has no soul. You, as the cook, must bring soul to the recipe.*
> – Thomas Keller, Chef, The French Laundry

Nic, recall we had the most soulful evening there (see the photo journals).

Take essential classes. – Look for courses at the local community college. Private schools are ghastly expensive and teach less. Take the "cooking enthusiast" classes. Don't get hooked on the celebrity chef of the moment and those shows meant only to hawk their swag. Concentrate on knife skills, the mark of a good cook/chef. Note: I very rarely use my food processor as I have developed adequate knife skills that obviate the processor. Again: Just cook. You must cook to learn to cook and maintain cooking skills.

> *You don't need a silver fork to eat good food.* – Paul Prodhomme

Research/learn with focus. – Get some good books, just a few. You'll be better served by books for professional chefs. You might look for a volume each for cooking in general, baking, and entertaining with a dinner. I recommend Mastering the Art of French Cooking by Julia Child, for example. Study matters. A good recipe matters. Get so you know when to add a pinch more of this and a dash of that.

> *I only drink champagne on two occasions, when I am in love and when I am not.*
> – Coco Chanel

Design your kitchen for efficiency. – Hopefully, you will have or design a good galley kitchen. Mine luckily allows me to pretty near pivot on one foot to reach the stove, sink and prep area, fridge, and most equipment. Get the best major appliances you can afford. Cook with gas. Get the best coffee machine you can afford. I now have a Nespresso Vertuo.

> *A balanced diet is a cookie in each hand.* – Barbara Johnson

Equip your kitchen properly. – You don't need much. This is why you get the pro cooking books (not books by entertainer cooks); the intro focuses on kitchen essentials. Start with basics and add only what you will *use*. Begin with the best set of knives you can afford. The Shun beginner set is quite good. Knives set the stage for everything else. Maybe add a slicer to the entry block of Shuns. No gimcracks or geegaws. Keep essential tools—spoons and spatulas, a good balloon whisk and such, for example—on the side of the stove for instant access in decorative pottery. The pro cookbooks will give you the basics. Only add extras if they will be used well and often.

To eat is a necessity, but to eat intelligently is an art. – Francois de la Rochefoucauld

A treat – If you can and if you wish to be inspired, visit Julia Child's kitchen in the Smithsonian. She changed how the American family functioned with a remarkably humble kitchen. And with the curator's inventiveness, you can step inside it and hear her cooking demo.

Always serve too much hot fudge sauce on hot fudge sundaes. It makes people overjoyed and puts them in your debt. – Judith Olney

Back to putting that dinner together. Once you have the essentials of the "how" (there's that word again) under your belt, you can determine the "who" of your most memorable meal.

Guests

Let's begin with the guest list. Ideally, guests would have the potential of at least getting along, if not having a common connection. For my first dinners, it was fairly easy to pick a group with commonalities. Let's begin with a dinner for nine. My guests grew up together in Dunn, North Carolina. I got to know E. B. Jackson because he was the deputy director of the Crime Commission. He got me involved with hunting and conservative connections. He would come with his wife Teresa, who had also been his secretary. He had her moved to another, nonconflicting job, so he could court her. EB connected me to Bobby Rupert and Sue. I would say a word about Bobby, but it's impossible to say "a word" about Bobby, if only to say he was the embodiment of a "force of nature." Ah, so many adventures. Then came Bruce Hudson and Margaret Ann. Bruce is one of the finest people I have ever met. Humble, humane, and humorous. Self-made into one of the key people in the cotton agribusiness in the entire country. The National Cotton Council comes to him when Congress needs to be informed. He sits atop one of the biggest regional cotton agribusinesses around as he commands the complete chain of cotton production—from planting, to ginning, to warehousing, to shipping, and more. What an assemblage.

All happiness depends on a leisurely breakfast. – John Gunther

What a bunch. Wickedly intelligent, great storytellers, good guys—and at *my* house. What an honor is a dinner guest list, especially this one. I must say, they didn't know what to expect but they came to dinner with just an invite, which is compliment enough. Then it was up to me to perform. These folks love to eat and share stories—wonderful, wonderful, full-of-humor stories.

They began to arrive at about 5 p.m., and the last guest was gone around midnight, leaving a testament of nine empty wine bottles and memories we all have today. Most importantly, Bobby is gone and the memories remain. They were in the moment; even more so, several hands pitched in to plate and serve, several more did the same with cleanup—the ultimate compliment. Ahhhh.

My weaknesses have always been food and men in that order. – Dolly Parton

Menu

Critical of course. Begin with the menu so you can copy each recipe. I suggest that the menu begin by selecting the protein then construct the main plant entrée and move backward and forward to complete the meal. From the recipes, you can create a shopping list, the prep sheet, the assembly schedule, the *mise en place* (a culinary process in which ingredients are prepared and organized—google the five principles of *mise en place*), the flow of cooking and serving. The serving order determines when to cook and serve, which becomes better focused after planned prep. Watch your guests closely, let them eat and converse slowly at a gracious pace then sneak to the kitchen, cook, plate, and serve, then join in.

Yes, I went a bit overboard, being new at this dinner hosting. I say again, start simple—a stew and bread and carrot cake. However, if you're adventurous and industrious, work up to five courses. Let me describe this better with a copy of my menu—in 12 pt Edwardian Script, which was printed on blue hued parchment, tri-folded:

Dinner with Friends
August 6, 2011

(Fold to open at toast)

Irish Toast
May those who love us, love us.
And for those who don't love us,
May God turn their hearts.
And if he cannot turn their hearts,
May he turn their ankles,
So we may know them by their limping.

(Fold to open at menu)

Appetizer
Mini Quiches
Wild Mushroom Crostini
Blackberry Lemonade

Soup
Corn Chowder
Wi
Black Walnut Sour Cream

French Farmer's Sourdough Bread
&
Hotel Butter

Main
Veal Scaloppini
W/
Mushroom Marsala Sauce
Alice Leather's Cornbread Pudding
Mapled Carrots Rondelle
W/
Pear and Cranberry Chutney

<u>Dessert</u>
Key Lime Crème Brûlée

Espresso & Cognac

The menu is an essential from the git-go, as it's the source document for the whole shebang: grocery shopping, sourcing (e.g., wine), the prep schedule (which can begin days ahead of the event), table arrangements, the sequence of prep (which may happen days ahead of the event), and then cooking with guests at the table. Each course must be served according to the flow of eating and storytelling, plating, serving, and the pace of the meal. Some of this will be intuitive, but you'll need to keep in mind what food will be "ready" when. Eagle eye here and finger at the ready to learn and test for perfect doneness and last-minute flavor adjustments. Keep plastic spoons in your bistro apron for the opportune taste.

Don't forget the cleanup. I've never had a dinner when the guests—always the women it seemed—didn't automatically pitch in with cleaning up. Though when the meal was on a roll and I asked for a "li'l he'p," there arose a minor stampede to help plate and serve smartly. On the he'p with cleanup: Good thing, as I'm quite whipped with the more than weeklong affair. Teaser here: It was well worth it!

We all eat, and it would be a sad waste of opportunity to eat badly. – Anna Thomas

Oh yes, a five-course affair with paired wine is quite expensive. Again, you may want to start with that simple meal of a ragout and French bread with a scoop of ice cream for dessert—and say "yes" when folks want to contribute a dish and wine.

Now for more details! After all, "the devil is in the details," just as the "proof is in the pudding." Why stop here: "Chefs don't make mistakes, just new dishes."

Appetizers

Have an appetizer with appropriate drinks ready—one nonalcoholic. I like blackberry lemonade. Kier Royals, which are champagne and a blast of Chambord are festive for the imbibers. If you have a hot appetizer, cook it when most guests are at the living room coffee table to serve hot from the stove. Wear your bistro apron, side towel perfectly draped, as it helps set the stage for more to come. When the hot dish is served, join the conversation, which should be underway if you chose the guests well. Discreetly leave to begin the last cooking of the main course. Seat them, plate the food, serve. Have fun, too. Most stories are memorable. Listen much more than you talk.

Process

All is prepped, tables are set, perhaps a few flowers grace the table(s), and mise en place is staged in the kitchen for the last cooking, plating, and service. Cook just the moment before serving hot food. (You'll serve from the guest's left, women first in order of rank, if they have one.)

As guests assemble, have something to say about each guest by way of introduction. Read them the menu with a little flair. Mention you would love volunteers "here and there." Have a menu ready at each place setting. They can keep their copy as a souvenir—or gadzook, have a pen with each so they can comment on the dishes or on the experience and leave it with the host. Some may wish to "grade" the dishes by way of complementing the chef.

The only time to eat diet food is while you're waiting for the steak to cook.
– Julia Child

Now, just a couple of suggestions to help yourself and the progress of your evening. I never try to bake bread—devilish to do it right—because I have La Farm French Bakery minutes away. Order ahead for the appropriate loaf. Serve it just warmed in the microwave in a decorative basket and wrap, with the best butter you can get. Be creative with the art of the dish; it will speak to you. When I go to a good restaurant, I take a good, long look at the plating; less is more—and more elegant. Food can, must appeal to all the senses.

Portion control: Don't serve too much. You can always ask to refresh a plate. Pace each course so the meal lasts and relationships meld. Little things matter and are a professional touch. I put a spoon of jelly on the middle of the soup plate and top it with mascarpone and minced pistachios. Study plating when you have a fine meal. Learn when a dish is done to perfection. Trust your taste to adjust seasonings, as recipes need refining to taste. I'm not a chef, per se, but I know enough to follow a recipe and do minor adjusting for flavor and seasoning.

Life is a combination of magic and pasta. – Federico Fellini

Soup

A light soup is simple to make and can be made early in the day to keep warm on the back burner. I do a fennel soup with mascarpone following a recipe I got from *Eat, Love, Pray* by Elizabeth Gilbert. Have the bread in two small baskets wrapped in cloth and sided by that good butter. You can cut pats then decorate them with the tip of a knife and add a few sprinkles of diced chive. Enjoy soup with your guests, then quietly drift back to the kitchen when the main course needs final cooking, plating, and service.

It's difficult to think anything but pleasant thoughts while eating a homegrown tomato. – Lewis Grizzard

The Toast

I've found that a prepared toast, glasses raised, delivered with a bit of theater is a hit. Have something ready as it's tough to do one spontaneously. Try some humor.

Laughter is brightest where food is best. – Irish Proverb

Main Course

While the usual meat and potatoes and peas can be done well, it's not as memorable as an unexpected menu prepared with a little skill and that touch of soul. People can taste soul. And folks are tired of the usual. A pork chop can become medallions of pork with cherry-rosemary sauce on polenta with sesame bok choy. The polenta can be wild mushroom polenta made the day before, chilled, then fried golden. Build the medallions jauntily on a cookie scoop of polenta, sauce with a flourish, and put the greens just to the side, just a few. Garnish, always garnish, with a small sliver or cross-three of orange rind. Make sure colors complement. You are painting. You get the idea. Again, join the table and the conversation. The pace of your eating—slowly—will help pace the table. Just as each course is served, you may want to say a few words on its preparation or history. See that the table always has a bottle or two of wine. Take care with your own tippling; you still need concentration and strength.

One cannot think well, love well, sleep well, if one has not dined well. – Virginia Woolf

The Palate Cleanser

Oh yes. Unexpected. Easy to do. A fruit bar and a speck of cheese tossed "carelessly" on a small plate does it. Fingers okay.

Everything you see, I owe to spaghetti. – Sophia Loren

Dessert

This can be the crown of the meal. Practice this one. Have a couple in your repertoire. I do a French silk mousse topped with fresh almond-flavored whipped cream and a coffee bean—just one. The most elegant offerings are the simplest. I put it in champagne flutes.

Add freshly made coffee to order. I have my Nespresso coffeemaker, but it only makes coffee one cup at a time. Worth it. Then there's always a good Australian Sauternes (a sweet white wine that originated in Sauternes in the Bordeaux region of France).

Ice cream is exquisite. What a pity it isn't illegal. – Voltaire

The Finishers

Offer cognac, or better yet: Pause a bit before guests take their leave to drive home. Tell them not to forget their menus. For those who drive, tactfully say that the coffee is superb and a treat on its own.

Do *not* refuse help with cleanup. I can't say this enough. You will be rightly pooped, and morning dishes aren't the way to cap off what will be a great experience for all. Many guests will say they've had the best of times, cleanup or not.

Age and glasses of wine should never be counted. – Unknown

A Reminiscence

Feeding people is an act of friendship, giving, and even love. It's returned in so many ways, mostly by making or cementing friendships. Bobby reminisced about playing elephant polo with a maharaja. Bruce told of cajoling lettuce out of the deserts of Saudi Arabia for the royal family. EB recounted his job in Washington DC while assisting a congresswoman. All told stories of growing up in the deep South. We laughed till we could barely laugh anymore. The last guests parted at the stroke of the new day with handshakes, hugs, and a blizzard of thanks. We can now cherish the greatest of memories together as an extended family.

The next morning, I had to count the empty wine bottles to be sure of our grand time. As Benjamin Franklin observed quite well:

. . . Wine is constant proof that God loves us and loves to see us happy.

Nic snaps a photo of dessert French Laundry Style

VALUES

Have You Ever Had to Make a Moral Decision? How Did It Turn Out?

Dad figured out how to manifest a chicken BBQ for hundreds.
Yes, those handmade spits all rotate in sequence.

The greatest way to live with honor in this world is to be what we pretend to be.
– Socrates

I wonder what Dad would say to this question about moral decisions. He had many sides to him. One thing for sure, he was quite intelligent. Before I give my own answer, let me comment on the photo above. Dad began learning how to barbeque chicken in front of our fireplace at home in Euclid. He liked it well done, crispy. Then came the Masonic Lodge annual picnic at Joe's farm, which he did several times. At least 250 guests would come as he split and spit 125 chickens. He handmade the electric spits. This BBQ tradition is very Croatian. This photo was taken at the town square in Huntsburg for the Youth Group's BBQ in May of 1976. Dad was in his element but would die within the year. So much left undone and unsaid. Despite his moral lapses, he did a lot of good.

As to moral decisions, "Question is good, this," as Yoda would say. It is best answered briefly as it could take volumes. Again, less is much more.

The first thought that comes to mind is that we must make moral decisions frequently during each day. That's the beauty of moral growth. We're never finished and are continuously gathering insights and practices. All day we can hone our whole-body growth until it becomes as automatic as possible, constantly improving. Thus, we learn justice, the difference between what is right and wrong, then practice doing what is right—even when no one is watching; as I often say, even in the middle of the night. Thinking right, doing right, for the general right must become second nature. One must be disciplined about doing it. This is probably the main aspect of living the Good Life, whereby we learn the practices to live a "life worth living" then *do* them.

Yes, there are moral dilemmas aplenty. The one that flashes to mind is divorce. When I said, "I do," I meant it heart and soul—which I needed for the years to come. Although divorce would not have been my moral choice, circumstances left me no choice. I am here, when and if you wish any retelling of the history of the separation, divorce, survival, and rebuilding from my perspective. One of my values is honesty, as best I can provide it.

The farm helped. I went there immediately, having to take a motel in Charleston then landing in Huntsburg, quite in pieces.

It was amazing the unexpected help I received, which displayed the character of the helper. In this case, it was my great and true friend Marty—Don Martin, my buddy from our early days in the Air Force. When he heard of my troubles, he was driving and had to pull off the road as the tears overwhelmed him. He knew of what I was experiencing; moreover, he *felt* it when and as I experienced it. Marty began calling me every Sunday for 15 years (!) until he died.

Shared joy is double joy; shared sorrow is half a sorrow. – Swedish proverb

I wanted to be married, and I loved being a dad! The pain was and is that I loved you then, love you now, and will love you both as only a father can. But you two needed the marriage—so one-sided—to end, as it had not been a marriage for a long, long time, if ever.

Make no mistake; if there were even a hint at a rapprochement satisfactory for you both, I would be there with all of me. However, there was never even the slightest attempt to find a mature way forward. You can't applaud with one hand.

The truth will out, it is said.

How did it turn out, the other half of this question asks? Much better. Much, much better.

Nic, you are thriving as a professional woman, beloved by all who see you, especially your patients, and certainly not the least, your father. *Oh, to hear you say "Dad"!*

Your intelligence, sincerity, and kindness draw people to you. You are growing in goodness and are strikingly beautiful inside and out. Golly—and you joined the U.S. Air Force Reserves Medical Corps in June, 2022! I was thrilled to administer your oath of office in my old dress blues. I gave you your first set of captain's bars and have my old set of major's leaves when you're ready for them—and yet another milestone ceremony. What an unspeakable, humbling, and rare honor. You made that happen, Nic.

> *Every father should remember one day his [daughters] will follow his example, not his advice.* – Charles Kettering

Allow me to call you my greatest accomplishment; a father's dream come true. You have done monumental things to be the person you are now and will continue to become. I am as proud as a father can be. How fortunate I am in a world full of parents. I stop here, as it would take more volumes to trace your trajectory through life even thus far. But that's why I kept a journal of your years growing up. It's why I keep a photo journal, so you know how I conducted myself since the divorce. It's why I write books and have started the Nicole and James Klopovic Charitable Foundation, our Donor Advised Fund (DAF) for you and yours to continue. I do try to earn the respect of respectable people. And more. I am concerned that I leave you a good legacy. You are my purpose in this life. How fortunate I am.

Me? Well, even with the scars, both physical and in the soul, most of my painful memories have now truly faded. I know I did my best under that great weight, which is confirmed by the many who know me. For example, when tracing the evidence, my domestic attorney commented that never in 20 years of practice and dozens of cases had she witnessed a case like ours. And my counselor, with 45 years of clinical psychology and having known me for upwards of 25 years, confirms that from what she knew of the facts, it was one of the most wicked cases she'd ever taken on. All the more remarkable, she says, because I am "one of the sanest people," she knows. She's one of more than a few folks who know me who say that I truly did my best, beyond what most would not, could not, endure.

As I write these truths, I say with conviction that I would do it again to have you two—and especially you, Nicole, whom I have come to know as an adult. What an unspeakable blessing you are! I am reminded that:

Without mud there is no lotus. – Chinese proverb

How is it turning out, you ask? I thrive by many measures. I am reaching just about all my life goals. A few more are well within reach, for example, publishing my Capacity Building four-part series of book, the SOP (standard operating procedure) for the Foundation. I am respected by respectable people. I have reasonable health and can exercise vigorously five times a week, age appropriately. I have even completed mini sprint triathlons. I am vital and vigorous for a man of 74 (weighing just a couple of pounds more than I did in my 26th year). I am retired and will never have to work for money again if I am careful with my savings and investments (a state of giddy release). Working and progressing and doing some enduring good for 45 years in two careers is more than enough. Recall that I began as an airman at about $87/month and retired as a major at age 38, enabling another career.

Then, at the Governor's Crime Commission, I began as an entry-level statistical analyst (numbers baffling me, but I made them work). I retired in 25 years as a senior-level federal policy analyst. All GCC grants are still selected with the ranking matrix I wrote in the early 1990s, and it was automated per my suggestion. I also did the study for making schools safer with School Resource Officers. This resulted in a $10 million general assembly bill to hire hundreds of officers following my model and the establishment of the Center for The Prevention of School Violence, which still exists today.

In truth, my working life began when I took over most of the work on the farm at 16, and I really haven't stopped working. The "plan" is in place, and so far so good. It has always been to have a career in retirement, perhaps my longest at 30 years, doing what I wish to do while trying to do a bit of good.

Now I practice living a meaningful, worthwhile life, although I'm still getting used to relaxing evenings with streaming. It's wonderful to have the time, and my doctors assure me of more than two more decades. More time to travel, make and keep friends, relax, and collect and read the greatest books ever written, leatherbound to be sure. Hopefully you will keep and add to them, Nic. I also plan to cook a bit, learn more about good wine, get better at skeet shooting, visit the farm to split firewood, mind my health, and revel in the wonders of being the dad of a dynamic, beautiful daughter.

> *The greatest legacy one can pass on to one's children and grandchildren is not money or other material things accumulated in one's life, but rather a legacy of character....*
> – Billy Graham

And that life is good and worth the work of it! – JK

We enjoy good food, hard meaningful work, and the honest sweat of well-being.

If You Could Have as Much Money as You Wanted, How Would You Spend It?

In the Senate building. With dozens of trips to DC, I got legislation passed.

For the wise man does not consider himself unworthy of any gifts from Fortune's hands: he does not love wealth, but he would rather have it; . . . and what wealth is his he does not reject but keeps, wishing it to supply greater scope for him to practice his virtue.
– Seneca

Who doesn't think about this question!? I suppose it began for me as a very young preteen. I schemed to make a lot of money doing something like . . . shoveling snow. This consisted of trudging through sometimes 12 inches of powder-dry snow to shovel someone's driveway, the walk to the front door, and the sidewalk passing in front of the house. I triumphantly strode to the lord or mistress of the manor to claim my due: 25 cents! Big money. Now, I've heard of youngsters turning up their noses to shoveling a couple of *inches* of snow on the drive for $25! Because it is work. Believe it or not, that hard labor of shoveling snow, digging ditches, and hoeing seemingly miles of crops taught me this: There *will* be that last shovel full, that last row.

I guess I started out to be "rich." Since shoveling snow, I have kept at setting money aside and "retiring early and often," as I was counseled by a senior AF officer. I am doing well enough now, in my 74th year. That is, I'm not rich, but I am *wealthy*. I know the difference, and I'm quite happy in that calculus. I own my own little "Hobbit Hole" and pay as I go. I haven't had an imposed credit card balance for nearly 25 years now. What freedom.

When I married in 1979, I had about $93,000 from investments and savings, including a little borrowed. In two years, we were foreclosing on properties and living debt ridden, paycheck to paycheck. This financial precariousness continued for 25 years.

The day I detached from that financial doomsday, I paid off that credit card and never looked back. I rarely went out, packed my own lunch, and wore the same clothes I'd had for years. Still stylish, too. How many outfits can one wear at one time anyway?

Luckily, I continued to save, even if marginally. I paid off my Hobbit House in about 15 years and retired from working for money at age 66, when Social Security kicked in. That "savings" I now plow back into the house in fixing, maintaining, and improving it—and enjoying things and life. I love to make memories with you, Nicole. Plus, I would like to try the guitar (simple stuff of a few chords for a base voice), and as always, I *read*. . . . *If* things are paid for in cash. No more debt. I look forward to at least 20 more years; do I dare ask for 26 more to hit that unheard of 100? . . . So much for a little background.

> *I think everybody should get rich and famous and do everything they ever dreamed of so they can see that is not the answer.* – Jim Carrey

I dreamed, and still do so, of coming into a lot of money. Yes, I do buy the occasional lottery ticket when the payout is over half a billion dollars. I say it affords me a few hours of entertainment to imagine spending it. If I *do* win: Number one: I would tell no one. Number two: I'd consult friends with money regarding how to act with it, how *not* to squander it, how to *grow* it, how to *conserve* it, and how to do *good* with it. Number three: I would engage in philanthropy full time with you, Nic. Naturally, I would take care of me and mine with a few worthy gifts to worthy daughters. Doing federal grants for 25 years with the Crime Commission helped me learn how *not* to do granting/philanthropy. Anyway, how does one contemplate a truck full of lottery money when shoveling knee-deep snow for a quarter was a fistful of gold?

What would I do with such a galactic amount? . . . What I'm doing now—just more of it.

My priorities have matured. Again, I am not "rich," but I am "wealthy." Being rich is self-defeating as it's largely about acquiring stuff—and there's always another trophy. Then it's about power. That is unending and burdensome.

Being wealthy means I can live as I choose, so I do. Thus, I study how to die well. Answer: Live well.

> *It's simple arithmetic: Your income can grow only to the extent you do.*
> – T. Harv Eker

I'm fond of saying I can go where I want when I want to, do what I want when I want to, and eat and drink what I want as well. I'm warm when it's cold, cool when it's hot, dry when it rains. I sincerely don't want that much. I realize I live *very* well indeed, as I have seen the Third World. I have a builder-grade house worthy of fixing up and a great car, a 2010 Honda Insight with more than 240,000 miles on it, which I put on myself. It gets 40 mpg in the city, and the lavish insurance is essentially "free" with USAA. I pay my bills and have a balance left over, even after tithing to the Foundation. It is life affirming to have nice things (but I always get a deal), do fun things, be healthy, have a growing number of acquaintances, enjoy companionship, and sit and relax in my backyard Shangri-la. . . . Against stiff odds, here I am.

I have a full wardrobe—for me, anyway: a Canali suit (a gift), a Hamilton Jazz Master Swiss watch (a gift), Australian Uggs slippers (already sewn up), two sets of pajamas, which I wear most of the time, and my 'round town uniform—usually jeans and Simms hoodies. I wear Tommy John unmentionables till the bottoms go out. The point is that, relative to my means, I don't want that much. Especially if I must get it on credit, even if it's only a month extension on my (one) credit card. When graciously asked by Visa if I would like to increase my credit limit to $25K, the answer was easy. "NO. In fact you can reduce it by half." I know they were disappointed.

I remind myself that I live much better than a pasha of just a few generations ago. However, I can dream of an automobile that will take me where I want just by telling it to do so. Give me three more years; gotta pay cash for that new wondermobile. They are designing it as we speak. Of course, "they" consult with me nearly daily on all the goodies I require (ahem).

So, what am I going to do with "all that" money? As much as I want. Essentially, maintain my present lifestyle and habits. Luckily, I have continued a study of philosophy, Stoicism mainly. Thus, I try to live a life that considers virtue, character, well-being, and legacy—and have some fun. Yet we must work on being healthy, living frugally, and earning the respect of respectable people. I admit, people occasionally take advantage of me. Still, it's better to believe in, even expect, kindness from our fellow humans.

Fortune sides with him who dares. – Virgil

I do work on being a good father. You be the judge of that, Nicole. I look forward to the day Cindy and I can spend just one lovely day together, the beginning of many more, with mutual love and respect, as it should be. Both of us have much to gain from a good relationship.

I write and publish books, which hopefully will be read before and after I'm gone. They're part of my journey. I also keep a photo journal of my life since I began life on my own again (nine brimming three-ring binders covering the past 20+ years). What luck that I read and discovered anyone can be a philanthropist.[4] Anyone can budget and do it. This legacy of "wealth" is about leaving a good reputation, some accomplishments, and memories of being a good friend and citizen. These matter.

If I won the lottery, I would do the same. Do a little for friends and family. Make memories. Work on being good, doing good, for the common good. My common good, intergenerationally, is via the Foundation. With a lot of money, I could do a lot of good way beyond my mortal years. I work on longevity to be able to complete the footing to my legacy when I'm gone—footing being a good reputation, some money, and the DAF (Foundation).

> *You have not lived today until you have done something for someone who can never repay you.* – John Bunyan

The Foundation's guiding principle is to *Fund permanent answers to permanent problems* (at the local level of government) with capacity building. I have drafted four volumes on capacity building for reentry of people coming back to the community after involvement in the criminal justice system. It's a proven take on helping people who help themselves. My 25 years with the Governor's Crime Commission led me to realize that is one of the best ways to direct very limited public dollars where they will do measurable good then have immeasurable effect. There must be a return on investment in the community. This set of books was drafted as my doctoral dissertation; the topic is pertinent and perennial, and it becomes more so with time. The one on *Decriminalizing Mental Illness* is already on the bookshelf. Together, these books will form an operational manual for how to do DAF granting that makes a difference for the long haul. Further, they will inform others how to do granting with impact that shows a real return on investment. I list them here to give you an idea of their scope. If I won the lottery, I'd have more than enough money to get them all published—and who knows? Maybe I'd write more.

Capacity Building Series

Volume I. *Building Capacity from the Bottom Up: The Key to Sustaining Local Services* (in the pipeline as of this writing)

Volume II. *Decriminalizing Mental Illness: A Practical Model for Building Sustainable Crisis Intervention Teams* (in print)

Volume III. *Accelerating Juvenile Reentry: A Practical Capacity Building Model for Sustaining Aftercare* (in the pipeline as of this writing)

Volume IV. *Accelerating Adult Reentry: A Practical Capacity Building Model for Sustaining Post-Release Transitional Services* (in the pipeline as of this writing)

Nicole, you are most capable. You are doing better than so many, as you are maturing well in what matters, working hard, giving service to country, understanding what is right over wrong, developing mettle to face the day and overcome, being frugal, and becoming wiser and wiser. Your life and that of the Foundation are in good hands—lottery winnings or not.

If you think you can or you can't, you are right.
– Henry Ford

What Qualities Do You Most Value in Your Friends?

Billy Don "Marty" Martin[5] – my Cicero's "one true friend of a lifetime"

The only way to have a friend is to be one.
– Ralph Waldo Emerson

What a great question. Allow me to refer to Cicero's *On Living and Dying Well*. He has a section toward the back of the book titled *Friendship*.

Cicero observes that we are fortunate to have *one* real, true friend in a *lifetime*. Yes, we will have plenty of people who refer to us as "friend." They are really good acquaintances, the people one needs in the day especially as we age. In passing, calling or being called "friend" is meant to be, well, friendly, but it's not what a friend can and must be. I have been blessed immeasurably, uncountably with Don "Marty" Martin as a true friend. I helped him produce his memoir—*Little Stories: A Legacy of Learning, Laughing, and Loving*—after prodding him for years. At least I prodded him each time he'd tell a story, dozens of them, new every time he told them. Finally, I convinced him he could record the stories just as he would tell them. Success. He threw himself into the task, sometimes dictating several stories and editing them. He had never typed so much in his life. Then he could see the value of editing the crude dictation. I did a hunk of the editing and mustered the many talents of my production team to make it worthy of my friend.

He loved selling it, enough to make his money back. He would sell in the grocery store checkout line: "Hey, did ya know I'm an author?" Then he told a story, and they were hooked. Magically, he had a copy with him to sign and sell. He worked with urgency, spurred by the knowledge he was dying of prostate cancer. He humbled me by letting me know the book project kept him *alive*. We laughed page by page, nearly word by word, even through the tough stories with tears close to the surface. There can be only one Marty.

Marty and I attended basic training together in 1968 at Lackland Air Force Base, San Antonio, Texas. He was an "old" man of about 23 and, by golly, *married*. Gadzooks—he even had to shave. From early on, he was the kind of guy we all gravitated to. Somehow the Air Force kept us together for nearly four years.

What sweetness is left in life, if you take away friendship? Robbing life of friendship is like robbing the world of the sun. – Marcus Tullius Cicero

After Basic, we went to Airplane General tech school at Sheppard AFB, Wichita Falls, Texas. In about three months, we knew everything about gassing up and changing the tires on a fighter aircraft. Then off to the Philippines. We stayed in limited contact but aware of each other to make some stories happen (see the Little Stories book). Marty wangled jobs away from the flightline, as did I. Man! The flightline was work! It centered on the acres of cement where the airplanes were parked. We had to launch them, recover them after a sortie, and ready them for the next flight. They had to be cared for like infant children: cleaned because they leaked all the time, inspected daily up to massive inspections in the hangars. The flightline is where the birds were fixed after a flight. Pilots and any of the ground crew, including me, could write up discrepancies, every time a bird flew. Oh what power.

We could be fussing with them most of the day and into the night. In the tropics. With trench foot. Greasy. Sweaty. For 18 months. Marty and I had other things to do.

He worked in inspections and at the Alert Shack, where our F102s were scrambled (mobilized) for anything worrisome in the air. I wangled that job putting LOX (Liquid Oxygen) on the flyers twice a day so I could study during the workday and go to school evenings. No temporary duty to Thailand or Vietnam except for the odd weekend, so I could collect that hostile-fire pay: about $100 for a long weekend—big, big money.

I remember Marty spent off-hours building and flying model airplanes and entertaining the troops with the antics he could do with them. Flying fascinated him, but he never got licensed as he had a real fear of an accident. So, he made model airplanes, built from scratch, and had an audience as he flew them outside the barracks' front door. Ones and twos would gather. Then he invented stunts and curiosities. He jerry-rigged a quick-release launch. Then he invented detachable landing gear, which floated to the ground on a hankie. And more. His audience loved it when his creations crashed. He could fix or build anything. Again, see *Little Stories*.

Next, we were shipped to Carswell, AFB, Fort Worth, Texas. We were staff sergeants by then (whoa—*Sergeant* Klopovic), so we knew this and that about fighters. And we knew how to work the system. Marty got a job filing Technical Orders—simply done, indoors, no sweat. I got a job in another squadron as the Maintenance Training NCO. Working the flightline is just not a joyful thing. He kept up with me. I remember being invited to Marty's home for "Mescan," southern for Mexican. We were connecting, though I didn't know nor appreciate it at the time. Well, he got out to be a family man and I got wangled into becoming an officer. We lost track of each other for about 25 years.

But Marty and I knew we were thinking about each other. I had no way of knowing how much Marty would become to me. He knew it though, innately. He had been through a hardscrabble time on a "dirt farm" as he called it and a pretty tough marriage.

> *A true friend accepts who you are but also helps you become who you should be.*
> – Unknown

Then the divorce happened, and Marty knew, felt in his bones and heart, that I was in trouble—big, big trouble. What kind of person hears a friend is suffering mightily and is so overwhelmed at the news that he must pull off the road to weep in sympathy and gather himself? I'll tell you. A friend of a lifetime. As I've said, Marty called me every Sunday for about 15 years without fail just to check on what I was doing and, more important, *how* I was doing. Only the friend of a lifetime does that.

I can hear him now: . . . "Klop, wacha up to?" We would talk endlessly. He could make a story out of a bolt and a nut and be informative, certainly novel, and inevitably funny. He loved to laugh, and we did. So we kept up.

I visited him in Rosenburg, Texas, several times, and we finally got in a deer hunt. This was a one-week process. It included: prepping the blind; mowing the shooting lanes; priming the feeders; shooting in the gun (adjusting the sights to be "dead on" a bullseye);[6] packing in all the gear before daybreak on two four-wheelers; putting trails of deer corn on the shooting lanes; taking a deer (they were kind enough to walk toward us eating corn nibbles); skinning, quartering, and deboning it; packaging prime cuts; making sausage and smoking deer sausage and deer jerky to die for (all day); and then eating it—not quite all in a day! Man, Marty had to have a pile of jalapenos with it. Another trip to the hunting camp was necessary just for the rickety handmade BBQ pit. It completed the process and made it an event that's now an indelible memory. That's the way it was done. Let the stories flow.

Nothing—no nothing—like fresh-smoked-over-a-pit deer sausage with barbequed onions and baked beans. Oh yes—and grill-toasted bread, too. All with a once-in-a-lifetime *friend*. We had become quite close over the years and the faithful Sunday calls. I'm being all too brief here, as Marty is a book in himself. Cicero would approve, and would have loved to have indulged in barbequed smoked sausage with us.

> *A (true friend) is the best and most beautiful equipment for life.*
> – Cicero

Marty making deer sausage like no other, November 1, 2018

Allow me one more picture of so many, many words. Study it. Allow me to put a note to it.

Marty, only Marty, when confronted with having to hand grind hundreds of pounds of meat just had to do it smarter, better—and nearly for free. He cannibalized an old washing machine motor and geared it down to an old timey hand meat grinder. Then sausage making became enjoyable, even nearing the end of a weeklong Homeric odyssey preparing to hunt, "harvesting" a deer, fitting the animal up to eat, smoking the meat, and freezing it. Then having a celebratory meal of sausage, onions, pork-n-beans and jalapenos at the ramshackle hunt camp to cap the ritual. Holy smokes, he had six refrigerators and freezers packed to the proverbial gills. Food defined him. Food eventually did him in.

He would hand mix a mountain of meat on his kitchen counter. The ground sausage meat would sail into the casings while that ol' motor hummed a pulsing tune, *harrum, harrum, harrum*. Marty, only Marty, not surprisingly had a spreadsheet that computed and recorded the exact amounts of all the carefully selected spices and pork butt for any weight of deer meat. Just weigh the meat, follow the formula, perfect every time. That's after a day-long fruitwood fire at the smokehouse, a little shed that leaned a bit too far to the left. Then again, at this age, we too listed a little to this side or that.

It took Marty years to perfect that recipe. He epitomized so many things: determination, attention to detail, giving freely with no expectation of any return. Never an unkind word of or to anyone—though he'd occasionally hint at a bit of guarded displeasure at this and that, this one or that one. His sausage was the result of going 'round and 'round to the most noted smokehouses and meat packers in the Houston area. He cajoled and pried recipes out of the butchers then formulated his own concoction. You guessed it. His was the best sausage in Houston and surrounds.

Marty lived to serve others. It was in his DNA, if there is such a thing. And he worked ever so hard. I remember on one of my visits after he started to decline, he wanted to make me some special scrambled eggs. He had a lot of trouble standing at that point, so he scooted around the kitchen in his five-wheeled chair to get it done—which he did.

He was and is loved by so many because he embodied what he was with no pretenses. Virtuous of character, giving. Laughing, always laughing, and thus others did with him. We'd laugh at the same joke over and over. So much, so much, so much. He could go on and on about pec*ah*ns as he said in his Texas twang by way of Arkansas. I would correct him by telling him it was pecans, with a northern nasal "a" . . . because one goes to the grocery for a can of beans, not a c*ah*n of beans.

As an "ol' timey shop teacher," which he called himself, Marty took the most troubled children by the hundreds over 30 years. His students loved him—and parents would plead to have their children in his class because he taught them more than "shop." Much more than what they got in their other classes. They learned manners, respect, work, and humility—at least. No doubt his students teach his lessons to thousands, and those to tens of thousands. What a legacy.

And he is my friend. I can hear him now, love him still.

What is friendship? How do you keep friendship? How do you become a good friend? My answer is *Marty*.

Let Cicero explain:

> *Among the many great benefits of friendship, one stands out above all others: Friendship shines the light of hope into the future and keeps the spirit from becoming weak or stumbling. Looking at a true friend is like seeing an image of yourself. Even when absent, friends are near; although poor, they bring riches, although weak they are strong, and what is especially hard to express, although dead they live—for respect, memory and longing pursue them. In this way the dead are blessed and the living worthy of praise.* – Cicero, *On Living and Dying Well* [7]

Small Things Matter; Which Matter to You Most and Why?

Learn to cook . . . make new friends. See my recipe for this carrot cake to die for—plus a Grand Prize apple pie and a cheesecake like no other!

Great things are done by a series of small things brought together.
– Vincent Van Gogh

Yes, small things add up. It's important to get in the practice of recognizing small things that are profound, especially when done regularly. This is why I meditate daily. One of my themes is gratitude, the recognition of which takes extended practice, as our many blessings can be crowded out by daily, even minute-to-minute, struggles.

An example: It's a wonderful feeling to finish a vigorous workout, to still swim a mile in about 40 minutes, then reward myself with a sit in the sauna. Simple yet profound. Look at what that represents, what it means. It represents years of realistic conditioning for all the right reasons: health, well-being, contentedness, and capability. It also recognizes that longevity responsibly spent is important. I will experience the unimaginable. Again, I say, all this work and trying to improve is worth it, as the next day, which could be tomorrow, may be the best day of my life.

Attention to detail is not obsessing; know the difference. – JK

Here are more "small" things in no particular order that I do and for which I'm grateful—because they mount up to a life worth living:

Delivering a homemade carrot cake. – I take great pride in delivering a carrot cake or apple pie to a get-together or just a casual visit, because I know people genuinely swoon over it and offer heartfelt praise. It's just a cake—or is it? It has become much more as it's a small thing that allows important things to happen, such as connection to good people.

Working on the farm. – I truly enjoy hard work with people who know how to work. Countless people still chop their winter firewood, but still more don't know the reward of hard physical work. It's most gratifying to watch that cord of split wood mount and take shape. To work with people who know how to work together, wordlessly, efficiently, and enjoy the result of honest sweat, yes even on a frosty day, is a joy diminishing these days when we have more and more conveniences or a harmful sense of entitlement. If grandchildren come, they will spend time on the farm, mainly to work because work is fun. I do hope they get to experience being so tired from honest toil that they go to bed too tired to eat.

Having a picnic on the farm. – To have a picnic at the pond on the farm presents a moment to reflect on the generations who now have trod those 56 acres. To see the pond Dad had built when I was five. To roast sausage on an open flame. To perfectly toast a marshmallow without losing it to a gooey blob in the fire—there's an art to it. To chat as family should chat—to reminisce, to joke, to tell stories, to smell the sweet, newly split wood being placed on the fire. To make memories galore. It's a moment that reminds me there is tradition, that family means something, that life is good.

Relishing unexpected moments. – Then there are the unexpected moments—especially those that arise from trying to accomplish worthy things. Lofty stuff but worth the effort, the Stoics would say. It's remarkable and gratifying to hear someone say out of the blue that they got worth from one of my books. It's remarkable to hear by chance, over the breeze if you will, someone thank me for making a difference in their lives. Let me give an example. I got our skeet club, the Durham County Wildlife Club, to sponsor Dustan Taylor in his skeet game. This allowed him to continue practicing and going to competitions. The Army "found" him and enlisted him to shoot. He's now an Olympic contender. But that's not the whole story. . . .

I was at a shoot at Ft. Bragg when a beaming woman of the South, full of life, took a seat next to me. She announced, "You know, you are a hero in our household." I was truly taken aback. It had to be a mistake. Then she introduced herself. "I am Dustan's mom." Life is made of little moments.

As I write, this story progresses. Dustan called to say he was in town and he asked if I would come to the club, as he was fishing—one of the things we do at the club on our 12-acre pond—and he wanted to see me. We spent the afternoon chatting about this and that. Yes, he is very much a contender for the 2024 Summer Olympics. Imagine! And we are going fishing with the *Tarpinator* this January. Dustan wants to be a fishing guide after the Olympics and the Army!!

> *Never forget that you are one of a kind. Never forget that if there weren't any need for you in all your uniqueness to be on this earth, you wouldn't be here in the first place. And never forget, no matter how overwhelming life's challenges and problems seem to be, that one person can make a difference in the world. In fact, it is always because of one person that all the changes that matter in the world come about. So be that one person.*
> – R. Buckminster Fuller

Receiving a Father's Day card from you, Nic! – There was a time when that never happened. I didn't know I missed them till one showed up after some years of being estranged from my daughters and disillusioned about my dreams. Then there it was. Even the envelope was beautiful and meaningful. DAD was written in a scrolling, artful hand above the address. Within was a message of thanks for "all that [I] am because of you." And an expression of love as only a daughter can deliver. A moment to live for.

"You know you want to." – Add those moments when you, Nic, coyly ask for something with the justification of "Well, I'm worth it." Or, "You really want to do this." Or, "I'm only doing this because I know it does you good." I am defenseless. My heart smiles (and my wallet falls open of its own volition).

Reflect on moments, these "small" things. They are the stuff of life. Continue your path and they will happen regularly. Learn to recognize them, and then . . . relish them.

Gratitude turns what we have into enough. – Anon

How Would You Describe Your Politics?

At a Washington Conference, February 2020, with my then-new book, *Decriminalizing Mental Illness*

You want a friend in Washington? Get a dog. – Harry S. Truman

Be good, do good, for the common good. It seems this overarching theme pops up frequently, no matter the question. This, I think is the action statement, motto for a traditionalist and an Independent, which I consider myself to be. Traditionalist means to me that I believe in our founding principles. I am an unabashed patriot. I feel privileged to be an American. I try to tell the truth, work hard, respect others, pay my bills, and be responsible—which I expect from others. I have little sympathy for those who expect an unearned handout. Or those who besmirch our truly great country, one of the greatest, no greatest in history.

Being an Independent as well as simply independent, I try to do my own thinking about what is right and wrong and act accordingly.

Being a traditionalist compels me to study philosophy to determine how to live well. I've been aware of philosophy most of my life but have only begun to study and apply it in the last two decades. This is not to say I wandered aimlessly through life. I was always disciplined, determined, and driven. I just did not have the focus on life's essential principles that I now have. What I've divined from this study weaves its way through this memoir and my other books, so I can be brief here.

Being a traditionalist is to live with virtue, character, and well-being. Know that our purpose is to improve the general good, mainly by example. The sooner one learns these things and applies the lessons of living well to die well, the better. I am living proof that it's a worthy, if not the only, way to go through life. Still, as Aristotle asserts, we are not ready for philosophy's lessons until we're about 48 years old. Start this study as early as you can, then work on becoming a philosopher.

If you become a philosopher and practice it, live the Good Life, and are conservative, in many ways you "best" those who become politicians for the wrong reasons. I say they "play" politics for personal reasons rather than "do" politics to improve things. Even if they begin with the greatest of intentions, people are flawed, and thus they do harm. The power has to be intoxicating to the point of self-delusion. Politicians must/should compromise for the common good. So many are unwilling to compromise and certainly too selfish to serve the common good. They have not studied. They have not read. They have not traveled. They don't understand the human condition and how politics can work from strength to strength.

Democracy has been tried for centuries even millennia: It rises for the common good, is overtaken by the wicked, then is subject to revolution and dictatorship and goes through the slow grind back to democracy. Still, I emphatically say that the American experiment in freedom is the best idea mankind has ever had. It's been tested and tested again and survives, even thrives, even though the genius of the Founders is at present being sorely tested by extreme, harmful liberalism. Too much is, well, too much.

Let me quickly say that I am optimistic, even sanguine, that we will work beyond this moment in history and rebuild the republic of Washington, Jefferson, Adams, Franklin, Madison, and Hamilton. I see hope in the undercurrent of the next generations who are working hard, keeping a family, raising good children, and making a mark. It has always been this way. I hope I live to see the turning of the tide to the greater good.

As a traditionalist, I understand "there's no such thing as a free lunch," and that everything has a cost. To be worth anything, a thing, a pursuit, a goal must cost a combination of blood, sweat, toil, tears, and money—commitment displayed in many ways. These investments help us appreciate the worth of a thing and steel us to put up with the grind and occasional disappointments of working on that which is worthy. Remember that we're lucky enough to be in a country where, if we work hard, we can do well no matter who we are!

It is an object of vast magnitude that systems of education should be adopted and pursued which may not only diffuse a knowledge of the sciences but may implant in the minds of the American youth the principles of virtue and of liberty and inspire them with just and liberal ideas of government and with an inviolable attachment to their own country.
– Noah Webster

INFLUENCES

What Are Your Favorite Books, and Why and How Have They Affected You?

My book *The Honest Backpacker* at a book signing and presentation, Rocky River, Ohio 2017

A room without books is like a body without a soul. – Cicero

Oh, my goodness! Please look at my bookshelves! Take and read any that you wish! And perhaps remember me, as I've read them all—a few with a skim for the gist, some several times cover-to-cover, some a slow page at a time over weeks and weeks.

For brevity, I will answer as the whim of titles and authors strikes me. To be clear, I have *so many favorite* books.

Socrates – Defining the virtuous man. Exemplifying it. And dying to make the point immortal.

Aristotle – Much of civilization's progress traces back to this guy.

Seneca – A most sensible philosopher who explains the Good Life for us wee people.

Cicero – Defining friendship and so much more. He says things in the brightest, motivational, inspirational way.

Franklin – Demonstrating what an American can achieve. A polymath extraordinaire.

Washington – How to lead for the ages in war and peace. He made the Emancipation Proclamation possible because, as the most famous person alive in his times, he freed all *his* slaves in his will after his death.

Napoleon – The one-in-a-century who demonstrated what a human can do. His reforms continue to guide countries and thus civilization today, with centralized government, a higher education system, centralized banking, law, roads, and sewer systems. Oh, and there were the many battles won . . . and lost.

Lincoln – That farmer who walked miles to return a penny and righted civilization's course. How? By preserving America's union and, in many ways, giving rebirth to a country that would dominate the world with a compassionate, strong right arm.

Churchill – Oh, Churchill! "War is to teach Americans geography." Numerous achievements on a grand scale and 50 great books!!

Roosevelt – The "Teedy" one was instrumental in preserving our natural wonders.

MacArthur – "Duty—Honor—Country. Those three hallowed words reverently dictate what you ought to be, what you can be, what you will be."

Buffett – How to build wealth: buy and hold, thus freeing us from having to work for money.

Mark Twain – For rip-roaring stories. Most influential figure of the 1800s. He was one of the first, certainly the most prominent, to write for earned equality over expected equity.

J. R. R. Tolkien – Introduced a humble hobbit who enjoys a good meal and a good smoke, and saves civilization.

Spock – Dr. Benjamin, that is. Mom, his book nearby, raised us all by it. I have her very volume still.

> *A reader lives a thousand lives before he dies. . . . The man who never reads lives only one.* - George R. R. Martin

Somehow, I *love* reading. Thank goodness. Mom lit the flame. What a marvel it is for a child to snuggle next to their mum and hear her voice—better yet with a good story. I am rarely without a book. (I need to figure out how to read when I'm swimming.) You can see by my list and my stuffed bookshelves, which are hardly all the books I've read. Combine that with reading a daily paper.

A Meet the Author event about *The Honest Backpacker*.
The room was filled, and I signed a double handful of books.

My daily diet of reading begins with the morning *Wall Street Journal,* the best for me. Expert, detailed, data driven, relevant, informative, succinct, with expert opinions. Being informed is a must. It affects the entire day.

Reading is available to all. It takes you places. You "see" wonders and worlds and horizons. You have amazing adventures. You unlock secrets. You have coffee with the fabulous, the famous, and the infamous. I stop there. Create your own adventures with reading!

I was born with a reading list I will never finish. – Maude Casey

How, you may ask, does one "use" a book? Early on, I decided to learn at least one practical and pertinent thing from each book I read and put it to use. Just about any good book offers doable advice relevant to the day, even a life. Begin with practicalities. One of the biggest problems of life and in a marriage is money.

Read about money management. Please study how to build wealth and begin early. Dollar down, dollar a day, set it and forget it will support you in retirement from having to work for a paycheck. Learn the glittery stuff is hollow.

> *... I find television very educating. Every time somebody turns on the set, I go into the other room and read a book.* – Groucho Marx

Study great philosophy so you may be a moral person worthy of the wealth you accumulate, one who knows that just enough is a banquet.

Choose a book deliberately. Just make sure it's a worthy book—that it's edifying or enlightening, perhaps entertaining, and especially practical. Let the moment guide you: Shall I read a Nobel in literature (Pearl Buck, *The Good Earth*), or shall I read a rip-roaring western (Wister, *The Virginian*)? Shall I better myself with the ancient philosophers (Seneca, Cicero, Masashi) or a good travelog (Bryson, *A Walk in the Woods,* and don't forget Steinbeck, *Travels with Charlie*). All have improved me, informed me, entertained me.

> *The more that you read, the more things you will know.*
> *The more that you learn, the more places you'll go.*
> – Dr. Seuss

Get a bookshelf and add a few labels:

- Philosophy
- Building Wealth
- Health and Well-being
- Biographies
- Histories
- Nonfiction
- Fiction
- Travel
- Greatest Books Written
- (Your choice goes here.)

Do take the best, most interesting from my shelves. I truly hope you find my leatherbound editions worthy of keeping, cherishing, sharing. Read them, and we will discuss them no matter where I may be. What do you do with all this? Well, become your best, a work in progress. Most likely, you will become an interesting person who attracts like people. Reading is self-fulfilling—and much better than media-stoked agendas about what has happened, is happening, and will continue to happen.

I am slack-jawed at the myriad ways we can communicate, and at the same time, I am saddened (and angered) at how this ability is abused. Oh so many children graduate primary school and can't read! Gadzooks! It takes three hours to run about 13 minutes of Super Bowl football! The halftime shows are . . . help me with a word . . . debasing. Breaks from the game slam through sometimes as many as 10 commercials telling me what shirts I should wear and what cigarettes to smoke, said the Rolling Stones from the '60s. But I do get distracted. On with reading.

I am here, there, everywhere with the written word. Doing so has compelled me to do a little writing, too. Reading makes one more intelligent, worldly, capable, companionable than one has the intelligence to be otherwise. It is the "secret" to rhetoric, virtue (especially wisdom), and legacy. Discover why the pen is mightier than the sword in the right hands. Uncover that reading is legacy in the hands that write their own. Just be humble with your increasing powers. Read on!

> *Keep a book by your side . . . now. Die well read, content, made happy with a book in your hand to read in the afterlife.* – JK

What Book Really Made a Difference for You as an Adult, and How?

A picture worth a thousand words!

To learn to read is to light a fire; every syllable that is spelled is a spark.
– Victor Hugo

This topic requires another book to explain my literary journey, as I have a true love affair with books and reading. I simply love the heft and feel, even smell, of any book—especially the leatherbound ones. And I love where any book takes me. Good words well chosen, well ordered, well themed allow my senses to engage. Yes, I can see what I can't see otherwise. I can *smell* forests and dungeons. I can *hear* the painful beat and weeping of a heart; the lament of a dying warrior, his last breath for duty, honor, country. Oh, and the *tastes* of countless dainties. Feel? I can *feel* a sword in my hand. I can know the dread of battle and the evil of a lie without committing either; thus I learn. Each sense born of words informs and especially inspires the whole. Life is better, so much better, with a book.

As I've previously alluded to, this affair stems from Mom making time to read to us in the evening—such innocent little bits as *Little Black Sambo* and *Peter Rabbit*.

Somehow it's appropriate that I quote a poem from my present and second romp through Middle Earth: *The Lord of The Rings,* by Tolkien of course, a genius for the ages. This is from the 50th anniversary edition, page 179; look for it in my collection of leatherbound books. Read it and marvel. Every word has meaning for life.

> *All that is gold does not glitter,*
> *Not all those who wander are lost; The old that is strong does not wither,*
> *Deep roots are not reached by the frost.*
> *From the ashes a fire shall be woken, A light from the shadows shall spring;*
> *Renewed shall be blade that was broken,*
> *The crownless again shall be king.*

Read Tolkien to your children so they may do the same for theirs.

The only problem with a book is that it causes the *need* to read two or more. I note also that the magic of books is a recent phenomenon. Books used to be the birthright of the rich and powerful only. Then came a man called Gutenberg, who took the written word to the masses and me. Go to the Library of Congress to see one of his original bibles. Think about it. Experience awe. I did.

The question here is tough for me to consider, let alone answer. But answer I will, because that is the task. With my feet to glowing iron, I say a most personally important book must be—*Cicero*.

- Begin with *Selected Works.* Turn to the back and read Cato the Elder: On Old Age.
- Then *On Living and Dying Well.* Start with Friendship.

Not part of the question, but branching out from there, one of the best thought out and laid out explanations of ancient philosophy, specifically Stoicism, is— Farnsworth's:

- *The Practicing Stoic: A Philosophical User's Manual*

The genius of this book is that it explains and organizes profound wisdom and arguments for how to live. It's codified through the ages by the major ancient philosophers around the themes of living well with meaning, purpose, and result. Understand what virtue and character are. Learn the essence of what is meaningful and possible to do. Learn the limits of what to expect. Know what success is and how to achieve it. Know that life is good and must be lived properly.

Legacy and happiness are at stake.

Branching further in the hopes you'll forgive my digressions: Probably the book that started it all for me, even from my 20s, is by Miyamoto Musashi, Japan's most famous samurai. Famous first by his killing 30 men or more in hand-to-hand combat. Then renouncing all duels, as he was unbeatable and had nothing more to prove there, he went on to develop and practice a strategy for living as hard as he had trained in the martial arts. That masterpiece is:

- *A Book of Five Rings*

The book was written in martial terms, and thus it's abstract and seemingly disconnected from practical use. The beauty of this deception is you must read it many times as it reveals itself slowly but surely to you. Each time you read it, you peel back another layer of meaning. The advice can be summed up in his Way of Strategy, found on page 49 in my edition. Note that, not insignificantly, he begins with *Do not think dishonestly.* That alone demands a lifetime of practice.

Let these few books be your segue to a lifetime of reading and learning from the greats. Cicero was my beginning and continuing study of great, usually ancient Greek and Latin, philosophers. Not to discount very important modern and especially Asian (Japanese) observances of how to live.

They pose the essential question that can lead to a life well lived: *"How do you die well?"* Then they answer it: *"Live Well."* This brings us to the essential How, which is the first step to action. After all, we must do a thing to figure out a thing. For me, these books began a lifelong, I hope to the very end, continuous study to understand how to achieve a life well lived. This is legacy. I hope to be a role model for those who are around me and come after me.

A part of my legacy is some well stocked bookshelves of what I have read, each volume usually in its entirety. This is only a partial telling of my journey through life, as many volumes are "missing in action." It's my continued process as a developing human and humane person of, hopefully, some consequence. Please read them and see that they are kept well. Add to the collection and pass along copies of the best of them.

Books tell one's life story. They are much more than the mark of education, discovery, life passages, and evidence of digging for life's secrets. They're essential to what compelled then propelled my life's path. I would not have retired as an Air Force officer without books. I would not have been successful at the Crime Commission without books. Certainly, I would not be an author without them. Each title is a chapter of my life. They represent my growth. They represent my personality. They represent, frankly, a love affair with holding a volume, especially if it is leatherbound. They are me. They are yours.

Although I began with mentioning philosophy, that does not imply even slightly that philosophy is the be-all and end-all of my literary pursuits. I suggest you wake up reading and go to sleep reading. Always have a book within easy reach. Get in the habit of having a book with you *always*. Even if you're just going to the grocery store! As if to drive this point home; I had an appointment yesterday, left an hour too soon. I had 60 golden moments to continue Durant on Spinoza. Quite beautiful. You never know when you'll have a stolen moment, no better spent than in a great tale of wizards and goblins and powerful rings and the wisdom of the ages.

I used to plow laboriously through books especially because I was consumed with succeeding at school. I had to figure it all out as the first Klopovic to get a degree, and still the only one to go further, much further. The classroom and my little cubby in the barracks room I shared with two others began my learning how to write and think and persuade—a never-ending pursuit. However, now I shy far away from formal classes. I want to read what interests me, improves me, entertains me. Many times, I just look for a book's main points, a summary, or a tidbit on which to act. Try never to read a book without illuminating a helpful, practical hint toward achieving something. Again, look at my bookshelf: It is yours.

So, open a page of Cicero, perhaps on growing old, get a Riedel Cab glass from the cabinet, join him in a good Cabernet Sauvignon, and hear him speaking and laughing about growing old. The Stoics were fun-loving and funny, quite funny.

> *I am not at all afraid of losing my memory. . . . I never heard of an old man forgetting where he had buried his money.*
> – Cicero, *Selected Works*. Part II-5: Cato the Elder on Old Age

What Historical Figure Influenced You Most and How So?

Key Largo vacation with Mom and Dad and a 35# king mackerel, February '67. Drat. I wasn't in the big fish pool.[8]

Fishing is much more than fish. It is the great occasion when we may return to the fine simplicity of our forefathers.
— Herbert Hoover

This is a tough one to answer, considering all the books by historical luminaries I've listed as personally influential. So, I'll go with my first impulse. At the top of a list of my firsts is Sir Winston Leonard Spencer Churchill. "Winnie" is first for many reasons, not the least of which being he's a legendary wit.

He struggled as a child, even though a child of remarkable lineage, status, and privilege. Some would say he was a runt. Never excelled. Stuttered horribly and was reticent. He leaned on his "mummy" and her connections as a widowed, stunning, wealthy British socialite with American roots. (Oh yes, it helped a bit that she "visited" the Prince of Wales in his private, very private quarters.) Winnie taught us, me, so much. I have more books on and by him in my library than any other author.

Dogs look up to you, cats look down on you. Give me a pig. He just looks you in the eye and treats you as an equal. – Churchill

This witticism makes me laugh every time.

Churchill was so many things, and he gives us motivation, no, inspiration, for how to live! He didn't just talk about war, he was in the Boer Wars. He made one of the most daring escapes from behind bars, risking being shot or imprisoned, clandestinely sneaking away on a rickety old train. And of course, he wrote about it.

He wanted greatness and worked ferociously for it. He knew the power of rhetoric, this hopeless stutterer. He became an orator for the ages, wearing away the thick carpeting by a full-length mirror to the warp and woof. He knew about the power of the pen and, with the word, slew many, many dragons.

Our inheritance of well-founded, slowly conceived codes of honor, morals and manners, the passionate conviction which so many hundreds of millions share together of the principle of freedom and justice, are far more precious to us than anything which scientific discoveries could bestow.
– Churchill

As world war loomed, he was not favored to be prime minister. Many thought him too brash, a failure, not the man for the job. The hapless and vacuous hacked away at him. It is not funny that those who hurled these faults had them all. But he had readied himself for decades, and he compelled them to choose him.

Winnie is an exciting read! He came to us just as media became mass. We could see, hear, and fairly sense his presence. What a leader. The case can be made that he won the war by not losing hope but rather *giving* his countrymen hope. He also inspired, if not compelled, the rest of the world to do real battle as if civilization depended on it—because it did. Now we have truly great documentaries, movies, recordings, and written records about Churchill to burnish his immortal sheen. That's the way history should be written.

Talk about a polymath. Those who worked for him could not match his frantic pace of two full workdays each day—one with the sun, the next after a nap into the black of night. Likewise, they noted he could speak for hours, illuminating, enthralling, and dazzling his audience with his flashes of genius. It's been said that Winnie wrote, "History will agree with me because I intend to write it." This he stated as he "retired." Retired?

> *A fanatic is one who can't change his mind and won't change the subject.*
> – Churchill

Winnie painted 500 paintings of respectable note. He put 50 books on his bookshelf, all in tiny, tiny print, sans many pictures. His speeches are studied still.

He also accomplished much manual labor on his beloved Chartwell estate. His brick walls still stand and will stand. He was the only "lord" who had to earn a living to pay to participate in politics, and he did it by writing articles and books. Imagine footing the bill for a mansion, a staff, a stock of Pol Roger champagne, and a Rolls! His cigar humidors brimmed with cigars named for him—all gifts; he never bought a one.

He predicted war when "sheep" prevailed. He prepared for war personally and nationally because he saw it coming when others did not. He was the politician with a sense of purpose and was a key part of history. He held the country, the common good, above his own good. He fought war as a true warrior who put himself in real harm's way for the right reasons—from the Boer Wars to the trenches of WWI and during the WWII air raids—waves of 400 nightly Nazi bombers and rockets. Churchill often repeated his famous saying, "You can always take one with you." At the family table, his daughter-in-law asked, "But Papa, what can *I* do if they come?" He grinned and was more than a bit serious when he shot back, "You, my dear, may use a carving knife."

Churchill proved to hold more than a bit of destiny. On the Boer War front line, hot, hot lead whined like bees past his ear, and he was pulled to the ground by his sergeant as a fusillade of fire peppered the shadow he left on the hillock. Then, on the Western Front of WWI, the former First Lord of the Admiralty, busted to a lieutenant colonel when blamed for Gallipoli, followed an impulse to move a few steps down his greasy trench. Minutes later, a mortar landed in his boot prints.

He stood when and where few would. Ready, confident, compelling, inspirational. We owe him so much.

We did not come this far because we are made of sugar candy.
– Winston Churchill

AGING

Describe One of Your Most Memorable Birthdays

December 3, 2016. Nic's birthday—and we are together!

You were born with greatness. You have wings. Learn to use them, and fly.
– Rumi

I know, I know. This question is to direct me to one of *my* birthdays. Still, most memorable are those that happen on December 3 of any year—*and* that you may now spend with me.

The most memorable? Well, it had to be December 3, 1983! And what a birthday. There you were, pink, squirmy, and croaking a bit. You (and Cindy) were happy babies, a magical joy to hold. You loved curling up in my arms for a bottle or just to be held. I loved coming home from my job at Arizona State University to be mobbed by you two grabbing a leg, sitting on my foot, and having me Frankenstein walk you around the house. Any celebration was a big deal. I tried to make your birthday complete with homemade cake and a gift or two.

This birthday with you holding that cake got us "primed" for a very nice Asian fusion dinner. And I'm sure I did a bunch of cooking for you on your all-too-few visits. You were here because you wanted a place where you could study for your

PA board exams. Five surreal weeks here under the same roof. It must have worked, as you passed famously, as I recall. I was quite proud of you—and bewildered about and around the material you had to master. Forget the questions! I couldn't even wrap my tongue around the words.

Someday you will be old enough to start reading fairy tales again. – C. S. Lewis

I am now looking at your weekly study schedule where you mapped times for Zumba, Abs, Abs and squats, BP (?), BC (?), CF, and BJ. And you studied at your solid cherry executive desk, which was readied for the task. I resurrected it for the third time, its second resurrection being from the old Bost house, the first from the state salvage. I hand rubbed it with a deep, deep gloss finish of 24+ coats of Tru-Oil, because I knew you would sit at it again. As you will. My hope is that your desk goes with you and serves your children.

As you grew, you would ask for birthday presents, some quite pricey, with the most charming requests ever recorded. With pouty lips, a downturned face, and upturned eyes with lashes that fluttered a bit, you'd say after the request, "Because I'm worth it." More fluttering of the eye lashes. Indeed. Indeed. How could I refuse?

Over the years, it's been fun to get you things—trips, Michelin meals, stuff big and stuff small, all meaningful and memorable because you sincerely appreciate *anything*. My joy is returned many times over in your smile and chatter about it. (I'm reminded again that, at your swearing in, I gave you your first set of captain's bars, which you held for the remainder of the day and posed for anyone with a camera for pictures.)

I love your birthdays, and we'll have many more together!

Count your age by friends, not years, your life by smiles, not tears. – John Lennon

A birthday present can be gifted any time of the year, unless it's for the very young still under the familial roof. So many options.

Take 2022. You visited me here in the wintertime to go to Asheville to visit Jayne Henderson at home in her luthier shop to see about a fine handmade guitar. It went into production late that year. I met Jayne and her daughter Matilda at her father's workshop in Mouth of Wilson, Virginia, to take possession in June,

2023. All three generations of Hendersons were there. Matilda, at two, helped build your guitar by placing the ribbons on the sound board ribs. Wayne played an old-time country tune, which had him all over the strings and fret board to include harmonics. At the end of the tune, he simply said, "It's good." High, high praise from our modern-day Stradivari of guitars. Wayne, now nearly 75, has made just over a thousand guitars and other stringed instruments. He can make about 20 per year. He aims to make 1,101 guitars, as Antonio Stradivari by one count made 1,100 violins and cellos. But Mr. Stradivari had two sons and a helper at his side.

Jayne referred to the guitar as "she" and "her." This project was very personal. She actually put love into this guitar. The result is not only of the highest technical execution, it is beautiful. Jayne has her father's skills as a master guitar builder. As important, she is an artist. The detailing, the inlays, the fit and finish are stunning. Even my untrained ear can hear the roundness of the base strings and the sparkle of the high strings as Jayne noted. It can be called a masterpiece, one of a kind, because it is. Frankly, when I opened the case, I was speechless; words caught in my throat, my eyes blurred with true tears of joy. Our gift to you, Nic. Play it well. Play it long. It's another family heirloom for generations.

We also shopped for patio furniture, as I was putting the hardscaping patio project together, and who knows what else. You bring about a whirlwind of activities on any trip. We have already been to the farm for the commissioning.

In mid-November, we went to New Orleans. Dinner and show at the Ritz. Unfortunately, we both got food poisoning, so the planned air boat ride and tour of a plantation were summarily cancelled. Upon recovery, we took a Cajun cooking class. Well, it was a moment. Towers of cognac flames from multiple pans. In contrast, the paddle wheeler down the Mississip' was incredibly boring, skinning the tourists once again. We did spend time in the WWII museum. Stunning. Alone worth the trip.

In April, we went on safari in Kenya. Remarkable. Too much to relate. Please, again, see my photo journals. All came under the broad brush of birthday presents, although we shared expenses here and there.

We have also done the CIA and Indonesia, Bali, and Singapore. They are in the photo journal. So many memories. I will never forget you at the Raffles Hotel, of Singapore Sling fame, in a simple ankle-length dress, the most beautiful woman to be seen anywhere.

Who knows what else for trips and visits will (not might) pop up. It's about connecting and making memories. Yes, now birthdays are truly special—anytime they happen.

With mirth and laughter let old wrinkles come. – William Shakespeare

I do remember one birthday of mine, though. It was my 70th. I found myself on the farm around the holidays, which gave Carolyn a chance to do it up. Kind of a surprise. About eight family and friends sat 'round the table for some of the best possible home cooking—and a homemade cake, of course. Then came the gifts. I got an age-appropriate goodie basket. All items were well thought out: Geritol, Depends, Beano, and the like. Your Aunt Carolyn is quite endearing. Then we hit the never-ending to-do list. Truly more fun; I like the work, as it's gratifying to achieve things from one's sweat and effort.

Two people of the eight who celebrated my 70th are now gone, one too young. Do things like this while you can.

With some luck, I hope to hit 100 and still be vital and vigorous, age appropriately. Would that more birthdays be with youngsters. When all this and more washes over me, I say, "Life is good," and you make it so.

Nothing is more honorable than a grateful heart. – Seneca

How Do You Grow Old Gracefully?

Lamanai (submerged crocodile) Mayan temple, Belize, November 2015

*There is nothing noble in being superior to your fellow man;
true nobility is being superior to your former self.*
– Ernest Hemingway

To grow old gracefully, first ask as the Greats did: How do I die well? Answer: by living well. Then ask: How do I live well? And go about living the answer. "The stoic regards human lives as interdependent, and finds in this a source of duty, affection, and solace." This is a definition of living well.[3]

Work so you don't have to work for money later. – Then enjoy your money frugally and devote it to the greater good.

Understand the five uses of your time. – Time is the most valuable thing you have and the most misunderstood. The five uses begin with *maintenance,* i.e., sleeping, eating, and going about the chores of the day. Next is *work for pay,* versus working when a salary doesn't matter. Third is *relaxing,* when we do nothing, which recharges us. Fourth is *recreation,* when we partake in a hobby or activity we enjoy, which may be quite vigorous, but even if it's challenging, it's rewarding. Fifth is *leisure.* During this time, we can choose to become our best and invest ourselves in the greater good. Yes, you guessed it. Leisure is the goal of the natural man. Note how the driven, creative, moral person accomplishes so much. Don't just watch these people, emulate them.

Know that you are capable. – Take challenges, prudently, then make them work. Accept "bad luck" and know you can work through that, too. Don't give up on good pursuits. I have noticed that if I work hard, overcoming problems while conducting myself in a respectable manner, unexpected good things happen. Some of the best, really. A great reward to me is when, on a few occasions, someone looked me in the eye and said, "You changed my life."

Know that life is good, very good, if one just tries to live with virtue, character, and love. – Never stop learning, evolving, and being in wonder of it all.

> *How old would you be if you didn't know how old you are?* – Satchel Paige

This whole memoir is about my thoughts on life, how to live it well and live it long. It struck me recently that we need a goal to grow old gracefully. That truly is where we can make a significant mark—and have fun doing it. But we must be there. Where is "there?" A place and mindset and longevity to have the time to leave our legacy. And have fun. You even have to know how to do *that*, too, by experimenting with whatever gives you a bit of zest. It was wonderful to get a video of you, Nic, snowboarding, rooster tails and all, for a couple of miles like you have done it all your life. Could it have started when I took you to the roller skating rink and ran beside you holding your hand?

We now have done CIA in Napa and then Indonesia, Bali, and Singapore. With luck, I will be tarpon fishing in the Gulf of Mexico this fall with my friend Dustan Taylor, the one who has a shot at the summer Olympics shooting skeet. If he goes, and he's now on the team, we will do our best to be there.

We may take an epicurean cruise. We contemplate driving the Pacific Coast Highway, "The One." And may I say, I sit here contemplating with more than a bit of nervousness the two of us climbing Mt. Kilimanjaro in Tanzania. I shake my head at such good fortune, hard fought and won.

> *I wish for you that you grow old well and capably while being age appropriately vital and vigorous. – JK*

Again, time is your most valuable asset. Life conspires to rob you of it, and once spent, it is gone, then you are gone. How in the world do we live long enough to leave the nest, get a good education, read enough good books and discover their secrets, make a marriage work, make a career or careers work, raise respectable children of virtue and character, take care of our health, and live in the community of man with respect and courage?! And *then* have time, brains, and brawn enough to put the cap of graceful aging on it all?

Let's dissect the above goal for a good life capstone in no particular hierarchy. When you define your day in categories of time (see above), we have little time to reach our potential.

Only an hour or two, if not a few minutes, remain in the day to construct your legacy. Really feel the urgency of making your mark, especially by raising a moral child—yours or others'. The most successful people in our midst began early on with a sense of noblesse oblige. They are time management monsters. They are driven to productive yet moral accomplishments. They plumb natural talents, especially creativity and intelligence. Everyday people accomplish the exceptional every day.

Ask as early in life as you can ask, "How do I die well?" – You know the answer is "Live well." You will learn by bits and pieces. The question never dies, though it may fade. But certainly, put yourself on track to living well by the time you approach your 50s. Know that our lives are measured in hours.

> *In the end, it's not the years in your life that count. It's the life in your years.*
> *– Abraham Lincoln*

Grow old capably. – Work to be vital and vigorous, age appropriately, to your last day. This means that you have what it takes to live independently and well, physically and financially, if possible, till the last day. Expect to live to 100+ and you will. Imagine yourself then. See yourself still standing erect, distinguished in military pose. Be able to step out lively, not slumped over, shuffling from side to side with infirmity or too many pounds. Your head is erect, neither tilted up in arrogance, nor down in submission. Let your visage and capability speak of wisdom and kindness and strength of character born of many battles lost fairly or won honorably. Respect given and earned matters.

Develop good wit. – Good wit is the best of humor. Develop true Churchillian wit. It's not insulting. That clever turn of phrase is classy. Read any Mark Twain book to see how a master humorist spins a tale. A wry smile helps, too. So, what's a good witty example? Let me tell you; it's quite close to home.

I was commiserating with you, Nic, about the expense of our trips: "Golly," I said, "I had to sell my other kidney to afford this trip." Your answer was instantaneous and perfect: "Dad! You know your liver regenerates." Who thinks of that? This comment gets uproarious laughter every time I repeat it. But nothing like the first time "from the hip."

> *You don't stop laughing when you grow old. You grow old when you stop laughing.*
> – George Bernard Shaw

Work to be vital and vigorous, age appropriately, in body, mind, and spirit. – Expect to exercise vigorously, five days a week, generating an honest gentlemanly or gentlewomanly sweat. Always stimulate the mind, morning, noon, and night. Keep the written and spoken word, stimulated with reading, writing, and conversation. Ah, conversation: That's a mark of living well. Hone the art of rhetoric. Keep a happy soul, secure in how you have been and are living. Learn to meditate, at least once a day. The skill follows you morning, noon, and night. Determine to make it a life habit to unlock its secrets and potential.

> *No man has the right to be an amateur in the matter of physical training. It is a shame for a man to grow old without seeing the beauty and strength of which his body is capable.* – Socrates

Earn the one friend of a lifetime. – Learn early on how to make and keep a close stable of good, like-minded acquaintances. Keep searching for that one true friend. Be a good companion to earn a good companion. Friends are the elixir of life, more important than diet and exercise for longevity—and a whole lot more fun than dieting and exercising.

Realize what you can control and moreover what you can't. – Some of my motivation, again, comes from the Ancients, who observe that we have no control over our health, wealth, or especially our reputation. They mean this factually, so we know what to do about these realities. We could be stricken by any number of diseases and be gone instantly. But that does not mean we should give up living in a healthy manner so we have a better chance of living long and well.

The most legendary stories of wealth tell of generations of money that have been lost on a bet. So don't bet. Save and invest to be free of working for money, which is another passage through the doors of Narnia.

Mind your health. – We can be struck down by disease, accident, or folly at any moment. It does not mean we then abandon life and hope. No. It means we mind our health carefully every day to prepare for a complete "career" in a lengthy and meaningful retirement.

> *The body will not follow a discontented soul.* – JK

Gee whiz. Have a steak, not the whole steer. Have a good shot of bourbon or cabernet, not the whole bottle. Gasp! A couple of cigars a year is not bad. In fact, put them together: a well-aged cigar (short), a shot (just one) of Woodford Reserve double-oaked bourbon to preface a perfectly done T-bone (not a side of beef) is, well, life assuring—especially if enjoyed by and with that true friend. (P.S. Finish with French silk mousse and hand-whipped vanilla cream in a champagne flute.) Just *never* neglect the daily workout, usual and habitual frugal eating and drinking, and daily meditations. I've taken up the habit of a morning 10-minute guided meditation. That practice is now habitual and follows me throughout the day. Goodness, when I lose the confusion in my mind when shooting, I shoot better. When I stand on the station I physically relax, the best state for a better shot, so much I can feel gravity pull on my face.

Mind your wealth. – Eschew riches. They can be gone in a flash; one bad investment and *poof.* Minding wealth means we should not be cavalier and buy glittery things.

It means we invest wisely so we have many, many years of not worrying about paying for things . . . and having a little good clean fun, too.

When the wind blows calm, tighten your helmet. – Japanese proverb

Use that money to have a few quality but not expensive things, make memories, have fun, and do good. Again, I say, know when enough is enough. How much is enough? Very little, especially in this great country. Have the accoutrements of living sensibly. I'm quite proud to say I stay in my pajamas, sometimes a few days at a time, as I read and write and stream a little in the evenings. My uniform of the day is jeans, a Simms casting shirt, reliable underwear, serviceable shoes (mine have had three trips to the shoemaker), and darn tough socks, which can "live" forever. Note: My 13-year-old Honda has 240,250 miles on it, and I put 'em all there myself. Insurance is nearly free. I get 40 mpg in town, had *one* small part go bad, and plan to keep it four more years at least. It's enough. I'm waiting to pay cash for a car that is safer and smarter that I am.

Be jealous of your reputation. – People will think what they'll think and, for the most part, it's not complimentary. That's a downside to human nature. Continue to be your best because you are better than that. Golly, don't spend a moment with a clod, and try not to be bothered by the small minded. This also means you need to get the measure of a man or woman quickly. Don't even start if they prove perfidious.

Become respectful to earn the respect of the respectful—which, by the way, is the path to winning the company of good people and finding that oh-so-rare good and true friend.

Be reasonable. Live the Golden Mean. I work on all this . . . a lot. There is no try (Yoda again), just do, and I am better for the effort.

Work hard to enjoy yourself well. – Good, hard, conscientious work makes the good times better. Know what the good times are and recognize them when they jump out of the bushes in your direction.

Quality is not an act; it is a habit. – Aristotle

How Do You Practice a Philosophy of Good Health?

Bananas Foster flambé New Orleans style, November 2023.
Nicole is caramelizing brandy by igniting spices.
P.S. The chef in the background is *not* on fire.

Three things cannot be hidden: the sun, the moon, and the truth.
— The Buddha

Well-being is the long game of living the Good Life. That's the philosophy. Now we can get to the how of things.

Habits matter. — Establish healthy good habits as early in life as possible. It's impossible, well, nearly impossible and certainly most difficult, for an aged body to recover health and vitality once they're squandered. Just look around.

I can see in my mind's eye Bobby Rupert on his death bed say to his son-in-law, "I'd give all I have, all I ever had, for one more day to tell you how much I love you." It was close to the last thing he said. He lived hard and died in his early 60s *just as life got good.*

Plan for healthy longevity. – A lengthy, *worthy* life is worth a lifelong pursuit. Read up on lifespan,[10] live in service to others, plan on reaching 100 or more.

Remember that science has shown that the greatest factor in living happily to the century mark is sharing your life with someone[11] and have reliable people with whom to associate. It takes real effort to make, and especially keep, friends. They are vital. Say yes to people—good people.

Keeping healthy isn't complicated. Remember, it's about the pursuit of well-*being*, not simply wellness. well-being assumes you are on the path to be a good person mentally, physically, and spiritually. Goodness and health must work hand-in-hand. To simplify well-being or holistic living, consider the human condition as a whole mind-body-spirit system. Wellness considers only health, centrally diet and exercise. If one has well-being, one is much less likely to need the medical profession. (Not that it isn't vital and much appreciated when needed!) One is also more likely to reach a ripe old age and avoid many symptoms of the "disease" of aging. But how can we achieve well-being? "That," as Shakespeare would say, "is the rub."

First, have a plan. – I'm a planner. If you don't know where you're going, you'll likely end up somewhere else. Coincidentally, I just got an email from the founder of Athletic Greens, to which I now subscribe. I take the eponymous supplement every morning. Threw out a double handful of pills. Recently one doc reviewed my handful of pills and said that most of these wildly hyped magical things just make expensive urine. His advice is clear and advisable, and I agree. I follow these edicts:

- **Sleep** *as if you're on holiday.* Difficult for this senior patriot. Morning meditation and a pre-sleep story help.

- **Eat** *as your ancestors did.* Make whole food the cornerstone of your nutrition and calories.

- **Move** *as much and as often as you can.* I say much about proper exercise. So simply put, begin an age-appropriate regimen in your 20s and modify it as you age. Aim to be 100 still doing ring pulls and swimming a mile (if that's appropriate for you). Then bust 100 just for the fun of it.

- **Get outdoors** *under the sky everyday as much as you can, especially in the morning.* Every minute counts. Gadzooks; read our book *The Honest Backpacker!* Sit on the patio under the cedar and watch the bluebirds on the nest with the remote camera.
- **Have fun** *and socialize with the humans you care about the most.* Cultivate friends as early and often as you can. Look past the grumps. The world is filled with remarkable people—maybe your neighbors. With this, be a discriminating joiner to a good gym, a church, perhaps a theme-focused club; pick up a hobby. . . . Whatever brings you joy.

Most people have no idea how good their body is designed to feel. – Kevin Trudeau

Picture big goals then the daily work that leads to them. – Decide what is worthy or necessary, then do those things with vigor. Remember, I built the Bost house in Chapel Hill. It started with the architectural renderings then went to working drawings so the subs could be lined up. Then I called the surveyors to stake out the margins of the house and garage. All else followed until the moving van drove away and we had a celebratory libation.

That is, reduce projects to their doable essentials. Begin at the beginning. Make sure what you do fits you as you age gracefully and make these good pursuits habitual. Have the small things help you develop the big things.

Take my situation today as I improve my Hobbit Haven. I will now move from hard- and landscaping to modifying, improving, and doing a bit of decorating inside. I try to be flexible, balanced, and mindful.

Are you becoming more moral every day? Are you respected? Do you study and apply the wisdom of the Greats? Do you know how to manage your time, especially when at leisure? For that matter, do you plan leisure into your day even now? Does your life matter to those around you?

Determine your priorities. – Make living the Good Life a priority. Meditate. Eat healthy. Exercise. It takes time to make health happen, so start early. At first, a life well lived seems crushingly overwhelming considering other life demands. Be assured that living well is a matter of intention, determination, habit, and time management. Start sensibly to finish well. Become your better self.

The six best doctors: sunshine, water, rest, air, exercise, and diet. – Wayne Fields

Get past your "reckless youth" while you're young. – Get over youthful foolishness and folly and recklessness as quickly as possible. So many don't survive youth who should have, could have. Pity. Still, curtailing youth is like trying to stop an avalanche midway down K2 (the second highest mountain on Earth after Mount Everest). So be conservative in your approach to things, which means minimize risk. Wear a seatbelt. Don't speed. Never drink and drive, not even a thimble full. An auto accident is youth's greatest risk of disability, dismemberment, and death—more so than disease. Your accident or, horrors, death, kills your family over and over and over. You *never* have to be anywhere that warrants reckless driving. Be sensible, be temperate.

Avoid! – Let's consider what not to do. If you don't drink, don't. No cigarette smoking and vaping (again, I like a few very mild, quite short cigars per *year*—a shot of good bourbon, too). Be very moderate with alcohol. If you can't keep it to about two drinks a day for a guy (less is better), then quit outright. That said, a fine dinner is greatly complemented by a good cabernet sauvignon. I remind you again that the body will not follow a discontented soul.

A good laugh and a long sleep are the best cures in the doctor's book. – Irish Proverb

Realize your priorities must change if you aim for longevity. – Beyond these pages, your brain, your joints, and your plumbing will inform you of how to live sensibly. Listen to them. Better yet, live so they don't "talk" too much to you. I do hope you will evolve into having good—no! best—and highly effective practices.

Prioritize. – Let's prioritize exercising the body first. A great risk, some say the *greatest* risk, to longevity is falling down! Yup. Break a hip, get a clot, yer gone. According to a quick google, three million seniors per year hit the emergency room for a fall. Thousands die. Think about the aging process, which by the way is a privilege and a joy if approached well. Nothing like taking the stairs two at a time when you're 75 just for the joy of it. As you age, what goes first? Flexibility, balance, and coordination. I maintain we need to keep balance, flexibility, coordination *then* endurance and strength in that order. Imagine yourself excelling in all five categories in your 90s and you will. You reap the benefit of this physiological focus especially if you begin in your 20s. This thing about never being too late for health: Not true.

Do group exercises that honor how we age. – For me, having a place to go to exercise with a group coached by a pro is the way to go. I have tried to exercise on my own at home, and it doesn't work—though I did Zoom my workouts for nearly two years of COVID caution. Better than nothing, but close to it.

> *The first wealth is health.* – Ralph Waldo Emerson

Men, and now especially women, tend to go for strength and endurance; it's what youth does. However, strength and endurance routines of youth are what a man or a women graced with some years modify, and rightly so. Focus on these two extremes of strength and endurance is too difficult to achieve in the first place and certainly tough to continue unless they're modified and reprioritized with the aging process. Thus, you grow into effective whole-body exercise to the day you finally hang it up.

Work out religiously. – Work out so regularly that you miss it when you can't. I have a rule for myself: even when I'm incapacitated, which is rare, I'll still go to the gym if I possibly can, even if it's just to sit in the sauna. Likewise, infirmities coincidentally and usually hit either the upper or lower body, so I exercise the half that's able.

Work out hard, with intention. – Yes, this means to calculated exhaustion. The human body was meant to function at a high pitch when needed. It's good to maintain this bit of physiology. You know you have reached a HIIT (High Intensity Interval Training) state of physicality when you can't hold a conversation or say a complete sentence without gulping some air. Now you're cookin'.

Sweat for a minimum of 150 minutes or more per week of moderate to intense routines. This means at least five 30-minute, no-kidding-intense workouts per week. With a rain-or-shine attitude. These 150 minutes do not include driving to the gym, changing, being draped over a machine shooting the breeze, or showering up and driving home. Oh yes, I've seen it all. The same guys who do this need long tweezers to pull on their socks, if they wear them at all, and knickers—quite unsightly. Forget about tying laces. It was a sad day and it tugged on my heart to go bird hunting with Bobby Rupert, who lived for the hunt, to see him head into the snow in loafers with no socks as he could not manage to get them on.

> *To ensure good health: eat lightly, breathe deeply, live moderately, cultivate cheerfulness, and maintain an interest in life.* – William Londen

Use appropriate technique. – It's all about technique. A good rep matters. A good stroke matters. A good pace matters. Breathing is quintessential: out on the explosive move, in on the relaxed move. It's a learned practice as it's the opposite of our inclination. Breathing properly gives you maximum oxygen transfer to your tissues. You must concentrate on doing a repetition with proper technique. Every good exercise is designed to hit a certain part of the body a certain way, but only if done properly. You must have good variety. Just pumping iron is, well, silly when one shoots for 100.

As if to make the point for me, when we readied for the trip to Indonesia, I met with some guys to plan the last prep for our trip of a lifetime to Bali. We're all of seasoned years, and it's common practice at this age to review our latest forays into "health maintenance." Matt relaxed on his recliner, his hip stapled over a new titanium model. Another fella, Rick, drooped a bit, kind of sloshing 'round in his skin. He rattled through his litany: two new shoulders, a knee, and a hip—all of that titanium stuff—and he's just waiting for the remaining joints to go bone-on-bone.

I had to ask, "Uh, Rick, any comments on what caused this downward spiral?"
Two words: "Lifted weights."
So many ways to do living well wrong. Even exercise can be so wrong it does harm.

Do beneficial exercise. – Aim for five days a week of beneficial exercising. You can do yoga two times a week. Swim perhaps two days a week. Throw in a weekly bike ride if you want. Do whole-body, age-appropriate CrossFit, supervised by a qualified, attentive coach at least three days a week. Develop an active hobby for weekends. Have goals. Do things to keep you motivated and in the gym. Maintain youthful weight. Allow me the "deadly sin" of pride. I just weighed in at about 168, which is what I weighed when I was about 28. May have a bit to do with the fact that I've also shrunk nearly two inches from 5'11" and a smidge due to normal disc compression.

Have fun taking the stairs two at a time. How about a triathlon mini sprint once a year? Be a finisher. Compete against yourself.

This seems ambitious, but it's a matter of intention, motivation, and scheduling. The grand thing is we can be quite capable in the decades we have after working for money.

My gift to you is one of a healthy senior citizen. – JK

I can hear you thinking as you read! "Howma gonna do all that?" Well, I happen to know a 74-year-old, gunning for 100, who does it and finds it quite satisfying (albeit with the occasional foot-dragging to the gym). Once there and after an honest workout, he rewards himself with a sit in the sauna and whirlpool.

It's about the Good Life. Get the process down first. Not that you must be well on the path to being a virtuous person of character before you exercise. This whole-body regimen and character building can, yea must, be done together. We are, after all, a marvelous system, so keep yours running well. Start with the intent of making whole-body health a major part of your life's work.

Don't forget diet. – Learn to cook or assemble plant-based meals. Know and serve the three food groups proportionately: protein as big as the palm of your hand, carbs as big as your fist, and veggies that fit in your open hand, about twice as much as the other two. Season with good fat, which stays liquid at room temp like extra-virgin olive oil. Eat frugally—breakfast like a king, lunch like a prince, dinner like a pauper. No sugary, salty, or fatty snacks or drinks. Keep them at bay and they lose their allure. Just don't have them in the house. Well, the occasional whole grain cracker is okay. Aim to keep the weight and waist size of your thirties, if not your twenties.

> *When diet is wrong, medicine is of no use; when diet is correct,*
> *medicine is of no need.* – Ayurvedic proverb

Mind your soul. – Laugh often. See the humor that's all around you. Be of clever wit. Be with happy, carefree people. Relish the work your accomplishments took, and be satisfied in your persistence. Gee whiz! Have fun!

> *A sad soul can be just as lethal as a germ.* – John Steinbeck

These pages are quite full of hints on how to pursue whole-body health. Approach aging as a disease, as the Lifespan[12] approach to health prescribes. Managing aging well helps you prevent or delay or recover from all the most difficult of bodily failures: stroke, cardiac events, cancer, diabetes, Alzheimer's . . . just to start.

Allow me the understatement that emphasizing building a healthy body, mind, and spirit greatly mitigates the bothers and possible disasters of the day, and certainly of one's lifespan.

> *Life well lived is long enough.* – Seneca

BIG QUESTIONS

How Can We Make Up for Lost Time, If Only a Bit?

Nicole and her tarpon of a lifetime, February 3, 2021

Be aware of the sand in your hand. It is beautiful, and it is running through your fingers.
– Nicole Klopovic

About 10 years ago, you, Nic, got in touch with me, and we've been connecting ever since, never to be distanced again if I can help it. I've been working on making up for lost time and distance between us by scheduling interesting things for us to do such as traveling, fishing, river rafting, and dining. I also like to find ways I can help you, such as cleaning your oven on a visit while you were at work. Time can never be recovered, but I'm trying my best to live, learn, laugh, love, and leave a legacy. As I write this, we are making last preparations for safari in Kenya, 2022. (Now, in 2023, I reflect on this memorable time of times. We climbed the sacred mountain and rode the safari truck just a few feet from elephants and wild lions.)

While I answer this question in terms of making memories, there is much more to making up for lost time. I spend a considerable amount of time helping you,

Nicole, understand money. You know how to make it. Hopefully, I am educating you on how to grow it to be free of worrying about money and how to use it to live well. It doesn't take much as you "get it." Right so you have a financial planner, an estate attorney, my final wishes documented and more. We have the foundation. You will get this house which will help with financial security. And I do try to give you gifts with meaning, gifts to last lifetimes.

Now back to traveling and experiencing the world. To that fish above, tarpon to be exact.

I make it a point to talk to, if not befriend, interesting people. While shooting skeet, I met and connected with a fella named Antony Dillon. Since he sold fishing gear *worldwide,* I asked him about good, no *great,* fishing spots and guides thereof. He shot right back that we must arrange a trip with the "Tarponator," Capt. Russ Kleppinger, hailing from Miami. I met Antony on a Saturday, and by Tuesday, I was shaking hands with Russ. Took a trip by myself, got 11 tarpon, peacock bass, and several other species in three days. Note that 11 tarpon on one trip is unheard of. Most people fish for decades and don't boat that many. Russ *is* one of the best guides in the world. People enter world-class fishing contests then see if Russ can guide for them—all expenses paid, of course.

It says much about Russ that he has a pet racoon he raised from a kit. Put a marshmallow in your lips and Oreo will kiss it away from you. Russ would throw-slide Oreo across the linoleum floor, and she would scurry back for more. Nic had to come, so we made it happen the first February in 2021—prime tarpon season.

Oreo kissing a marshmallow snack, oh so tenderly.

Russ is the rare individual who really, humbly, surpasses his hype, if not his renown, both of which are legendary in the fishing world. We caught tarpon that people fish for a lifetime and never boat. This "small" one (190 lbs) in the pic with Nicole, took a shrimp hardly bigger than a thumbnail while we were trolling nearly under the balconies of the multi-million-dollar condos off North Miami beach. Nicole was in the fighting chair—determined to "win." It took her one hour and 50 minutes to get this female to pose boatside. Read that one again. Her left hand was almost permanently cramped to the shape of the rod. She also got five more tarpon and various other species of this and that. What memories.

It's illegal to pull tarpon out of the water because it kills them—a magnificent creature sacrificed for a photo. The greater waste is that a female can release between 4 and 20 million eggs per year! Appreciate nature, its bounty and its fragility.

Next: bluefin tuna. With luck, sometime it will be blue marlin off the Great Barrier Reef when we meet the cousins in Oz. One trip inspires the possibility of at least two more. These bits of life multiply geometrically. Just say yes and watch what happens.

But I do get distracted from this rather probing and significant question. Short answer: Time that is lost is lost. One can only live well to make amends. Travel with a great fishing buddy is one way—and after so many years without trips, all the sweeter and dramatic.

Obstacles are not in *the way—they* are *the way.* – JK
(Reprise of the Stoic principle voiced by Marcus Aurelius:
"What stands in the way becomes the way.")

Hiking and Camping at Joshua Tree National Park, Big Bear,
then Venice Beach (Summer 2023) with Zoey (Greek for "life").
Is that a happy dog or what?

How Did You Get Through Your Greatest Challenge?

A micro-termite mound, built of termite saliva a micron at a time, concrete hard to last decades, Serengeti, April 2022

The greater the obstacle, the more glory in overcoming it. – Molière

My greatest challenge was the divorce. It was the end of dreams. It was the great challenge because I had dreamed of a good marriage and beautiful children, girls at that. What got me through it? Knowing I can meet and beat challenges, especially the biggest—and that a better day would come, even after dreams were blasted. But before then? I endured some dark, dark days.

It was fall of 2001 as I recall. A Thursday evening about 10 p.m. I remember, as I had just gone to bed after a favorite TV serial, *CSI* (Crime Scene Investigation). You girls were in your late teens at the time. A ruckus arose in the living room involving your mother. I intervened, and police were summoned. They suggested that "from their experience," it was advisable for one party to leave. It had to be me; I could see that emotions were very much unsettled.

I left with a suitcase in hand and little more, not knowing where to go nor what to do.

I lit out for the farm after stopping at a bank teller machine for my latest pay—and to put a freeze on insurance policy cash values. It was late at night, but I had to move, to leave, to cope even though the drive is nearly 600 miles. I made it to Charleston and had to find a motel then completed the trip in the morning. It was near Christmas, not the time to be alone. What can I say? I could barely drive. If ever one was shattered, it was me.

That began three years of doing the discovery for the lawyers to save money while mustering the real courage and mastery over mind and body just to get out of bed. It was inhumanly difficult to see worth in anything. My limbs were all but paralyzed—too heavy to get out of bed from sleepless nights. But I did.

I had no contact with you, Cindy and Nicole, for about 10 years, except for the last appearance in court. Thank goodness that you, Nicole, finally reached out about 10 years later. It kept me going, as I lived and live for you two.

I also knew enough to throw everything I could at this, one of the most challenging upheavals of a lifetime.

I got a small one-bedroom apartment furnished with Aunt Carolyn's old, discarded kitchen table and chairs, and a blowup air mattress, which went flat around midnight, every midnight. I can still see myself humped over that mattress, blowing for all I was worth. Within the first few days in the apartment, I went down the three flights of stairs, lunch and attaché in hand . . . and my car had been stolen. The sheriff related it was sold before it could be retrieved, so I had no way to get to work. Your Grandma Klopovic couldn't drive, so I caught a bus to the farm to get her well-used Subaru, which I kept for years. I saved for and bought my present house in 2005—modest compared to what the bank suggested for me; but I wanted an accelerated payoff, which I accomplished in about 15 years. Having a place of my own helped greatly. Still does. I was building for the day when you would resurface. This house, everything in it, and more would be yours—a thought I found most motivating.

I was well into my career at the Crime Commission, which I started in 1991. I had to force myself to go to work and to do the work; I was the first there every morning.

I got counseling, which continued for 25 years. It quickly turned into an advisory relationship with Dr. Deborah Heil, who just retired after a clinical practice of 45 years. She was quite a godsend.

I kept in contact with people. Aunt Carolyn and Marty called every Sunday to check up on me. Marty called me for years and years just to keep in touch. We would talk about everything and anything and he told the same stories repeatedly, but they were "new" every time. Who would have guessed I would help him turn those into Little Stories, his memoir?

I plowed on. I investigated hobbies and activities in which I could immerse myself. Golf didn't stick; skeet it was—and is. It had to be something I could do for the rest of my life. I took a few cooking classes and had marvelous dinners. I had my good ol' boys Bruce Hudson, E. B. Jackson, and Bobby Rupert and their wives over several times. Some of the best of memories.

My work led me to my Ph.D. Doug Yearwood, my office mate at the Crime Commission—brilliant—found Charles Sturt University in Wagga Wagga, Australia. It had a great online program in public policy sanctioned by the Haig, Netherlands, the international city of peace and justice. I threw myself into it. What a distraction. As a result, I published my first book, *Effective Program Practices for At-Risk Youth*. The publisher related that it did well for them and called it a "bestseller."

Oh yes, and exercise. Staying fit and well in body, mind, and spirit has always been motivating. As a recovery tool, it did what it should and does what it promises. Let me borrow a bit of wisdom from Steve Leder:[13]

- The sooner we confront our problems the better.
- Adversity teaches us the importance of reaching out. Don't let pain isolate you.
- Know we can endure painful challenges and ". . . live and love more fully because of them."

We are naturally endowed to endure, mend, and especially flourish. I remember some of the difficult days and I'm learning to count my many, many blessings. Having children is number one. Especially children with real potential to have a good life by being good, doing good, for the common good. Nic, you are immortality to a loving father.

I've learned that it's worth the trouble to live the Good Life of the Ancients and to live it well, even just one day longer, too. It's a fact that the next day, the next morning, can bring an event or circumstance that makes it the best day of your life.

I look forward to the not-too-distant future when I can tell my car to take me out for a banana split and pick me up afterwards. I look forward to seeing people on Mars. I look forward to gene editing curing many diseases. How about real Artificial Intelligence, which teaches itself? Don't have to wait; it's here now.

I look forward to being a grandfather and to seeing you girls do well. I look forward to the day when you, Cindy, visit and simply say, "Hi Dad; it's good to see you." I look forward to turning the Foundation over to you, Nicole, and to seeing what you do next. You are magical.

So, with persistence, or perhaps stubbornness and sheer force of will, I did get through the divorce trauma, though it took a few years. Oh yes, my mind replays some of the drama, but that's infrequent and quick. I'm debt free, have resources to sustain me, and I try to be involved in life and, especially, be productive. I have good—no, great—health, so my doctors say. Sometimes I forget what day it is, yet I'm sharp enough to tackle 'most anything. I make new acquaintances regularly. I have a significant other, finally. My love affair with books remains and sustains. With luck, I will have 10 modest volumes of my own published. Right there, I have at least three more years of productive work—interspersed, of course, with "once in a lifetime" trips. One book project finishes and others are on my doorstep. Will I find a productive place at a nonprofit for my Capacity Building series? Might it be TROSA?[14]

I have always believed that life is worth the living of it. My many obstacles have made me stronger, and better yet, I am increasingly equipped to do life. Overcoming my obstacles has given me confidence that I'm capable. Golly, people seek my company!

Study the Greats or some proven source of wisdom. Read like today is the last day to read. Contemplate the hidden meaning and unintended consequences of your actions. Especially these: It is said that when a Monarch butterfly flaps its wings in Monterey, Mexico, a gale blows hundreds of miles away. Let me recall again the day a young man visited, and the first thing he said was, "You know, you changed my life." The best part is I had no idea.

Ask meaningful questions: How can I serve today and what can I learn and put to work today? See the wonder in things, and the inspiration will simply lift you up.

Happiness lies in the joy of achievement and the thrill of creative effort.
– Franklin D. Roosevelt

Do You Have a Big Regret and How Does It Settle With You?

At a BnB in the North Carolina mountains, surrounded by what makes me quite content, May 2021

America was not built on fear. America was built on courage, on imagination, and an unbeatable determination to do the job at hand.
– Harry S. Truman

My biggest regret was my biggest challenge, which I've already explained and touch on again here. However, I think the way it turned out has made me stronger and given me many blessings. Let me hurry to add I would rather not confront these "tests" again! Once is plenty; I'm tough enough. I have other things to work on, like getting on with the "Good Life."

Do I have other regrets? Of course. . . .

I wish I'd studied philosophy sooner. – It would have served me well to begin my study of the human condition and life and apply the lessons of the great philosophers, especially the Ancients, occidental and oriental, much earlier, certainly in my 20s. I dabbled but didn't study them until about 15 years ago. The Greats confirm that even the mightiest among us regret not doing something potentially good but a bit frightening, which stops us in our tracks. We never know what could have been. I am proof positive that, with this knowledge and its application, life can be better and better—and certainly good.

The worst is doing something not very honorable that ends up badly, if only because it haunts the conscience for a long time. I was brought up with a Great Depression era mentality: If it wasn't nailed down, it was there for the picking. Not a good lesson, but learn I did, the hard way.

Thank goodness I did begin the study and application of being a good person. What matters is that I continue to study, learn, and try to live this philosophy better and better. I hope by my example and a little prodding, you too study the Greats, ancient and modern.

I wish I had established life goals sooner. – I was so unprepared for life when I was young that I was more apt to make bad decisions than good ones. I wasted a lot of money on this and that idea to begin growing retirement resources.

Although we might begin life wanting to be rich, we gain much more return on investment by being respected. In fact, if we work on being respectable and thus earn respectable acquaintances, the money will come.

I find it's good to be wealthy such that I have some comfort, a little money reliably coming in, respect, worth, and health. I finally paid off my house in 15 years because I bought a much smaller house than I could have had. It's plenty. I have my 2010 Honda Insight Hybrid with just over 240,000 miles on it and may see it to 300,000 before I trade it in on an EV—for cash! I have no bills other than monthly expenses. I am wealthy because I live within my means.

I've realized these life lessons from my study of the Greats, who preach the path to living well with meaning and satisfaction—and from having fought the good fight and won, mostly. It has done much for me, especially as I find from the Greats and from experience that the work of it is never done. That's a good thing, as it means I can continually improve to my last day. Reversals aside, I've put myself on an upward trajectory, not a straight line.

I wish I had known as soon as I had a paying job how investing works as a tool to be free of worrying about money. – When I was growing up, money was a thing to earn and save in a bank account, a quarter or even a penny at a time. I remember Mom would give us a quarter to put toward a savings bond of $25. At $25 she would put it in a bank account. Lesson: Even a quarter adds up—a hold-over lesson of Great Depression, WWII rationing parents. I had an inkling of how it works in my 20s and had a little money in an interest-bearing account, but I got scared, didn't understand it, and withdrew it.

But I did learn, and I want to pass on the lesson to you. No matter how much or how little it is, put at least 10 percent of your gross earnings into an interest-bearing account, e.g., an Exchange Traded Fund (ETF) with the philosophy of "set it and forget it." Learn to live well on the remainder. Each raise goes quickly to paying off debt then into that account—and you will never miss it. But know how it is doing with annual checkups, at least. I find it very informative to peek at the daily close to understand how worldly events affect markets. A Saudi prince makes a speech and the market swings up or down. Why? Learn how money functions, understand trends. But still let it ride. I find it motivating to figure the future value of X amount for Y years at Z interest rate.

Play with your numbers. For example, $400,000 invested at 10% (average stock market interest over time) for 30 years is nearly $7,000,000, and much more if you make monthly contributions. A dollar now really starts accelerating in value at about 15 years. Note also that someone just starting will need probably $6-10,000,000 of income-producing assets just to maintain a middle-class lifestyle. Do not think you can time, or "play" the market. Stay with the bird in the hand.

The goal is to quit working for money in your 50s, with no debt. As an aside and as I've mentioned before, an old colonel told me to "Retire early and retire often." I have retired twice. It turned out to be my best financial advice. I get two pension checks plus Social Security. None would be sustaining alone.

I wish I had understood earlier what happiness is. – The corollary to this is knowing how to put the conditions of happiness in place so that this pleasing condition can occasionally arrive. The fact that it's unexpected and a bit rare makes it all the better. I've found that happiness is rooted in love. So, love with abandon so you may receive love. Yes, risk a heartbreak, which is one of life's worst conditions, but it's one way we know we're human. Know that it's the way of things. Also know that many kinds of love exist: "romantic" love, love of one's children, love of one's parents, platonic love, love of nature, love of country. . . . Plus, there is love of a sport or activity, which can bring happiness. (I just shot 99 at skeet yesterday after nearly two decades of puttering at it. Happy, happy day! As an aside, such happiness is also affirmation that determination and persistence will out.) Sometimes the simplest of things can make us happy, such as baking an award-winning pie. Thus, we are the luckiest of beings.

Say "Yes!" to good and worthy things. It's world changing—
your world—if you do. – JK

I wish I hadn't done so much just to please others. – Working for approval of others never ends—and often they don't appreciate it. Of course I've had to "yes sir" the boss (best, of course if he/she is a good one). But better that I please myself with the improvement of things. If I do what's best for me, it will be the best for others, even though they may not think so. If I lose a job because of it, something better is in store for me if I look for it. As a corollary, ruminating on wrongs done to me is a waste of time.

I regret I did not take more time to get acquainted before I married. – We were in Iran in 1978 and would be moving on to opposite ends of the earth. We felt the pressure to get married quickly, within a matter of weeks from our first meeting. Not the best of reasons, an understatement. With time, we probably wouldn't have gotten married. But that said, we now have you girls, although it appears I have lost Cindy, at least for the time being. Nicole, you are taking the Klopovic name beyond every expectation and way beyond your forebearers. Had I not gotten married when and to whom I did, certainly my beautiful daughters would not exist—and who knows how life would have turned out. Best that I accept fate and move on.

Regrets, oh yes; but I also have learned from these experiences, and thus I have arrived at a good place in life.

It is not the things we do in life that we regret on our death bed.
It is the things we do not. – Randy Pausch

Have You Ever Cut Someone Out of Your Life?

Car camping, Bear Tree Camp, Damascus, Virginia, Summer 2019.
Doing as I please with friends I choose.

Let go of negative people. They only show up to share complaints, problems, disastrous stories, fear, and judgment on others. If somebody is looking for a bin to throw all their trash into, make sure it's not in your mind.
– The Dalai Lama

Cut someone out? Oh yes.

I am the kind of person who expects the natural good in a person and am a bit blind to faults, even when the relationship proves toxic over time. I'm always hopeful about our "kinder angels." When I make a commitment to career, school, or people, I stick it out—sometimes beyond the obvious end, especially with people. It has caused me to accomplish more than I was perhaps destined to do but to hurt more than I should have. I'm getting better.

I am learning that when people are mean, untruthful, manipulative, or hypocritical, I need to cut them loose. It's hard, very hard, for me to do. I don't like negativity, confrontation. I don't want to hurt anyone and especially don't want to be hurt. I try to be a good friend, but cutting loose is many times a point of survival. Life is too, too brief to suffer the loveless and cruel. Of course, there was the divorce.

Family – I remember one instance of a forced "cutting out" that still hurts. Mom, your grandmother, tracked me down at Arizona State University after a few years of enforced estrangement from her. I had to hang up on her before I spoke a word beyond hello for fear of reprisal from your mother, even over a conversation. It hurt both Mom and me deeply. It's impossible to explain, and the story that's told is far from the truth. Regarding the marriage, the truth is I was told "I love you" once in 25 years. I kept a journal during the '90s to shed a little light on how the days passed by immediate documentation, even though it's a gentle telling. I know you will make the right conclusions, Nicole. Let my actions and who I am becoming tell the story of the love of a man for others and of a father for his daughters. That will never die.

Let me shed light on your grandma Klopovic's love. After many years of estrangement, I showed up at the farm quite shattered. The marriage had ended in all but the legalities and perfidious lawyers of three years. Mom welcomed me with open arms, truly open arms, only overjoyed that I had returned. No recriminations, no questions, no harsh words. Just unconditional love and more hugs. What a woman. What she endured. How she rose above it all. Yes, you come from stout and kind stuff. Be proud and be good.

Other Klopovics just don't do family very well. Brother David rebelled and still does. He never got along with Dad and had to leave home. Further, he thought he knew better than anyone and still does. He wasted his life. Coincidentally, he called recently after years of silence to say, "I'm afraid of living and afraid of dying." What a statement on a wasted life. He's diseased, a ward of entitlements, and isolated. I told him he may call at a certain time to relate something good in his life and something good he did for someone. He couldn't. He doesn't communicate, to demonstrate "who's boss." And that's okay. I've also had no communication with brother John and sister Jennifa. Their choice. I tried to reconnect with John after my divorce, but that was short-lived. Again, his choice. Thankfully, I still visit Carolyn and Tom on the farm. A great pleasure. I'm glad to be welcomed and most sincerely love the good hard work I do there and its sense of accomplishment.

Relationships – I have been looking for a good relationship with a woman for a long time, and it now appears to be happening—but I've cast many aside as they have done to me. One woman, very rich, promised splendid things, *really* splendid. She referred to me as her "arm charm." That was deadening. Then she took a swing at me, and that was our last time together. Others have summarily cut me loose. Sometimes mutual, another time out of the blue and into the black.

Acquaintances – In the early 2010s, I met a fellow whom I helped start a company to train police. I never refused any request except to teach, as I was too busy doing his other requests. He professed undying brotherly love, Christian love, as he was "born again." I never asked for a penny. I did let him pay for expenses. I willingly worked for him, from doing a quick task to writing three books and getting legislation passed. All thankless hypocrisy on his part. The moment I would not confer him authorship on my book *Becoming a New Wave Leader* without him writing a page, rather a single paragraph, he summarily cancelled our contract by writing in bold red *Canceled* on each page of it. His "love" was that of a narcissist. It was a greater relief than I imagined to no longer tolerate that relationship.

While we need relationships, they must involve mutual give and take, with few expectations. When truly good, they are life fulfilling if not life giving.

Coincidentally, the *Wall Street Journal* today, January 15, 2023, boasts a headline "The Real Secret of Lifelong Fulfillment." The article is from the directors of the Harvard Study of Adult Development, 85 years running with no end in sight.[15] They give more detail in their book, *The Goodlife: Lessons from the World's Longest Scientific Study of Happiness*. It illuminates what the Ancients knew, that the most important factor in long-term health and happiness is personal connections. Further, good physical relationships, especially long-lasting intimate ones, are the most critical factor to physical and psychological health and satisfying *longevity*.

No one is deserving of love who is incapable of bestowing it upon others.
– Seneca

Thus My Conclusions Regarding Relationships

Don't let anyone detract from your life. – The unworthy lie, cheat, demean, depress, and abuse (in many ways). They are takers not givers; they mean-fully gossip. They never ever stop talking because they simply love the sound of their own voice. They make you feel low and don't care that they do. They're a waste of time, considering the wealth of good people out there to discover. This is one of the reasons the Ancients tell us to keep to a few select people and avoid groups.

Stand up for yourself. – Cutting someone off for cause is standing up for yourself. Resolve to do it, then do it quickly and face to face or with a phone call. Don't hesitate. When done right, it is right. You'll move on with a bounce in your step. Just think of the time saved to do meaningful things, read great books, and make good friends.

Be the friend you wish to have, the one of a lifetime. – That one takes time to find and engender, although it can happen naturally, as it did with me and Marty. Say yes to good, healthy, rewarding experiences with likeminded people.

Don't give up on the search for a life partner. – Find someone with good makings, then work on the relationship. Take the plunge. It's worth the gamble for the remarkable rewards. But don't ignore any red flags.

If you have children, and I hope you do, become lasting friends. – With children, you are in for one of the greatest of loves, for one of the greatest friendships of life. Exemplify what it is to be a good, loving parent and person. Be respectful to get and teach respect. Leave the legacy of a good name from a good, accomplished person.

Do the things with your children that create the ties that bind. – Make memories; you'll be amazed what remains indelible to a child. Call every Sunday. Visit often. Pop in with a homemade apple pie—or carrot cake. Of course, they must help you make one from scratch then have a go at doing it themselves. Have a nice meal together, which you cook together. Establish family events and especially traditions. Connect continuously, especially to share the good stuff of life. Thus, when things go wrong, and they *will*, you will have solid ground on which to confront the problem together. Nothing is so bad that a solid relationship, especially a blood relationship, can't weather and conquer. Give it your best and be satisfied with that.

> *The best thing to spend on your relationship is time, conversation, understanding, and honesty.*
> – Anonymous

What Was Your Biggest Failure and How Has It Affected You?

My logo—a phoenix rising as a symbol of my life

The phoenix must burn to emerge. – Janet Fitch

First, the person who happily reports that they have no failures or regrets is not being candid nor thoughtful about life. This question is about failures, the disastrous versus the regrets and disappointments. Everyone has regrets; how one deals with them matters. I remember Ben Franklin's assertion that we all need time to correct *errata*. Well, if this is good enough for the man who caught lightening in a bottle, well, perhaps I might have an *erratum* or two to work on. In fact, I am compelled to answer with a few.

Maturity – I could have begun maturing earlier into the truths of life by studying philosophy and reading from and about the Greats. This would have to be my biggest failure. "Too soon old, too late smart." I did dabble with philosophical wisdom, but not seriously like I'm doing now. That is, I didn't understand there was more to life than work for pay and being self-centered, which describes me in my 20s. I silently knew I could be #1—then realized how hard it was to get there and even harder to stay there. So I shifted the mindset to working on making #1 sweat. It's a relief, saves a ton of time, and people appreciate you more. I stayed immature in the true meaning of life till my 50s. Then, on my own again, I began an earnest pursuit of "the Good Life." That pursuit reflects throughout these questions and stories.

Money is a concern, which for me has been a regret and a failure. Here, I'll admit money was a failure for the first 50 years of my life. I have wasted so much money. Golly, I "took a flyer" and invested in rare earth metals still in the ground! Huge expensive flop. And I had money wasted *for* me. I was cajoled to buy platinum on margin. Probably the riskiest thing to do. I must hasten to add that I'm doing okay, quite okay, now. It's never too late to live with values but better to start early.

Here are three points of wisdom I've learned from my early failure with money.

Money #1: Know the difference between being rich versus wealthy. – I've wasted a ton of money trying to figure out how to have enough to be secure. That is, not having to work for money yet being able to pay my bills, continue managing wealth building, *and* have fun/make memories.

I have mentioned before, but it bears repeating since the topic requires the repetition, that there's a vast difference between being rich (never enough) and being wealthy by being realistically frugal (just enough). Avoid debt like the plague. Pay yourself first, 10-20 percent of gross, if possible. Put that money, at least monthly, into a managed fund, say of ETFs. Set it and (nearly) forget it, meaning monitor its growth. Remember that the Dow was at 177 when I was born in 1948. It has gone as high as 36,800 two years ago in 2021, even though in 2023 we are in a recession, bank failures and all—the result of easy money—(socialistic, progressive) liberal policies.

Money #2: Experiment with investing. – In finding my way to a rational way to build wealth, I tried things that didn't work out. While under Dad's roof, money was scarce. I would get $3 a week to manage my expenses, which included bus fare and other outlays. On my own, the Air Force started me at $87 a month, and even then, I saved $25 of that. I bought the two lots in Key Largo, which appreciated some and went toward starting married life. I tried selling life insurance on the side—big fizzle. Pay is based on commission and I had only one sale. I put a few dollars in a money market fund, which was a step in the right direction, but I pulled it out of fright and misunderstanding of the long-term compounding strategy. I bought into land where a buddy was building spec Ecco homes. Luckily, I pulled my money on that because I needed money to pay a maxed-out credit card. In my 20s, while in the Air Force in California, I bought a mobile home and a house in Huntington Beach. Both houses did well by luck. After I was married, my new wife got us into rental properties, investing on margin, and living with large credit card maxed balances. All failed spectacularly.

Money #3: Find and employ a wealth-building strategy. – Immediately after the separation, I corrected my *errata*. The first month, I paid off the credit card and have never had a balance since. Then I maxed out retirement account contributions. I bought a frugal house and an even more frugal car. I stuck with a second career. So far so good. I consider myself "wealthy." Wealthy enough to leave you a good name, some hard assets, a little money, a foundation, and bookshelves of good to great books. Oh yes—and a really great (though antique) shotgun and loader, ready for you to shoot your first round of 25 straight.[16]

I stress: Do not let fear of failure hinder you. Act you must. Do not encourage obstacles by being unprepared or foolish. Know they will come, face them with courage, and don't fear them; respect them. In retrospect from my experience, overcoming is a great teacher and strengthens us for the next and the next difficulty. I don't encourage "flying too close to the sun," but sometimes it's necessary to feel the heat of it. Each battle fought will give you more spine. Only by rational action will you become better and accomplish things. Do the best you can to decide a direction, then take it. Reality will determine how to find the way through to a goal, even a noble goal. An action taken may seem like a bad choice, but then time works its magic. Begin as early as you possibly can by living well as the Greeks would have us do. And again . . . it's never too late.

I'd rather regret the things I've done than regret the things I didn't do.
– Lucile Ball

How Did You Lead With Your Heart?

Me at four years, 1953. I would play in the snow till my fingers froze.

Your vision will become clear only when you can look into your own heart.
Who looks outside, dreams: who looks inside, awakes. – Carl Jung

I thought about this question over a few days and even referenced what was written by others. Most say the heart ruled the decision to get married, and so it was for me. I was quite in love; I could tell as I was compelled to run, yes run, nearly everywhere a taxi would not take me, here and there in Tehran. Your mom and I were there complements of our governments. We met, I like to say, behind a bust of Lenin just off Red Square, which is true. We had our first chat there. We were both on a vacation to Russia. She was a vision and obviously intelligent. Being a doctor, she treated most of the travelers for giardia, which we probably got from the Russian water. Her smile, her everything compelled. It was a "whirlwind romance" as I had to visit her in Tehran from the Persian Gulf. She must have felt it too, as we pressed on against some odds, tying the knot in a Middle Eastern country. But the heart can lead one astray.

We experienced contention from the outset, but Cindy arrived within the year—and oh, what a joy. A happy, giggly, squirmy baby. A dream come true. About four years later, you were born, Nicole. "Angel babies," the nurses said, fairly beaming; and they saw a lot of babies. So many good and happy memories with you two. Even to holding you, Cindy, for hours through the night during a fever. You two kept me going out of the love of a father and my dogged determination with commitments. I had said "I do" and meant it. You two are my heart and will be so.

It was my heart and the fact that things were not going to improve that led me, after 25 years, to do the brave thing and take the first step to end the marriage. It was not my dream, and it was difficult for us all.

It's my heart that drives me on to try to leave a legacy, especially of a respected and respectable man who really loves being a father. The love between us will out.

The lesson here is to know when your heart speaks, and when it does, take a big gulp and do it. Without saying yes to my heart, you two would not be here. And you are magic!

Under any circumstance, simply do your best, and you will avoid self-judgement, self-abuse and regret. – Don Miguel Ruiz

Are You Spiritual? If Yes, How So?

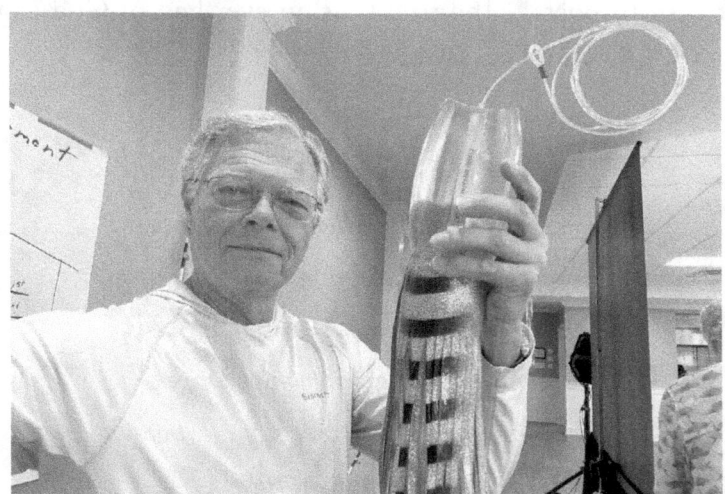

At the NCSU Fishing School—Hattaras, North Carolina, June 2023.
This is a lure for marlins, rare to catch.

Spirituality is recognizing and celebrating that we are all inextricably connected to each other by a power greater than all of us and that our connection to that power and to one another is grounded in love and compassion. Practicing spirituality brings a sense of perspective, meaning and purpose to our lives. – Brené Brown

Yes. This whole memoir is filled with my thinking on spirituality. Becoming spiritual is a matter of continuous lifelong study and work to be good and do good for the common good. I believe there is a Presence, a celestial "Spark," which is completely unfathomable, no matter how many religions and scientists and philosophers claim to know what it is. Still, the brightest among us and from history all come to the conclusion that there is a God. So do I.

I try to deal in essentialities. Essentially, the purpose of life and the purpose of all religions is for a person to become spiritual by living according to natural laws. We are naturally good, and because of our human condition with its ego, we have the capacity to be bad. We work on becoming our best and keeping wickedness at bay. By becoming spiritual, we become "religious" without the baggage, dogma, and questions involved in a particular faith. What matters is that we're on the path to being good, better, our best. The process matters; try, fail, and try again.

We never have nor ever will really know what this spark in the cosmos is. For this we must turn to poets. "The truest vision ever had of God came, perhaps here." (Spinoza)[17] Or, from Wordsworth:

Something

Whose dwelling is the light of setting suns,
And the round ocean, and the living air,
And the blue sky and the mind of man;
A motion and a spirit, which impels
All thinking things, all objects of all thought
And roll through all things.

– Wordsworth[18]

What Makes You Happy and How Does It Do So?

Roadie for a day: Helping Cook BBQ for the Kenny Chesney Road Crew, circa 2005

But in most cases real happiness requires a process and is the distillate of mindful living day after week after month, and even after decades of intention. In other words, as opposed to pleasure, sudden and fleeting, happiness is the fruit of a slow-growing tree.[19]
– Steve Leder

This photo needs a little explanation. It does fit with this question, though. Saying yes matters, then memories happen, and the best are quite unexpected.

Bobby Rupert was in the big-time food business. He catered many a big-name act. We cooked a full grill of BBQ and buckets of hush puppies for the country megastar Kenny Chesney and his road crew of about 125 roughcut fellas. It began the end of the tour party(ing). I recall it took 17 brand new red 18-wheel tractor trailers and three class A RVs to haul all his stuff and people. This was just one of two such caravans to hopscotch him all over the country. Mr. C and select hangers on had a Gulf Stream, no doubt. He has special meals catered and delivered to his door wherever he goes to "keep his figure." I had a plate of that BBQ with Kenny's drummer.

Then I took a break from minding the cooker (tough work) and went to the outdoor arena in Walnut Creek, Raleigh, North Carolina. I sat in the first row, center seat during tune up. Somehow the music from walls of speakers massaged my heart. Yes, my heart shimmied with the band's vibrations, the feeling of great music from a great band. I applauded a number. The band bowed to *me*, the only one in the arena. Happiness found me then because I was ready for it.

Then I stayed for the "End of Tour" party—a party only the wealthy can imagine and professional partiers could have. Yes, he flew in professional partiers! One of the highlights was the serving of the snacks. In came two sets of six courtiers, each carrying a 4x8-foot slabs of wood, exploding with hors d'oeuvres of every tasteful sort, covering two tastefully but very scantily clad, stunning young women from our local universities. Lettuce leaves left essentials for the wondering. I had to ask. So I moved close to the ear of one of the "hors d'oeuvres" and asked, a little naively, "How does it feel?"

"Squishy" was the reply. Bobby later told me that each had to get $5,000 to $10,000 from Mr. Chesney to be a little "Squishy." What an experience—just once.

Mr. Chesney sang backup for a local cover band. I left just as they were filling two plastic yard pools with Jell-O. I still wonder how that proceeded. How many people get to be a roadie, even for a day!

Happiness: a good bank account, a good cook, and a good digestion.
– Jean-Jacques Rousseau

Happiness needs to be defined and deeply considered to understand that it is possible, quite possible, and worth the real work, sometimes even drudgery, of it.

A quick search says it is ". . . an emotional state characterized by feelings of joy, satisfaction, contentment, and fulfillment." Who really achieves all this? It seems improbable as one contemplates it.

I believe happiness itself, as our Founding Fathers wished for us, in fact can't be pursued. One must work continuously, relentlessly, doing those things that are worthwhile; *then* it happens. Yes, it happens when you're possessed with a sense of well-being, feeling that life is good and worth the work, worry, and wonder of it. It's part of the evolution of the human condition. If we were bubbly and giddy all the time, it wouldn't be special. When it captures us, it's that much more a wonder.

Troubles, worries, and catastrophes can mar our happiness, but we must train ourselves to solve them and look beyond them. Happiness is about getting to the end of the day having slain a dragon or two and bested them. It's about knowing that difficulties are worth the toil, as happiness allows us to touch what it is to be human. If we were happy, giddy continuously, it would not be happiness.

Again, if you seek happiness, it will never happen. It arrives of its own time and own volition. However, as the greats would say, we can do whatever nurtures the conditions it demands.

The ancients counsel that happiness is pursuing the Good Life. This is a life of living with—let me say it again—the steadfast intention to be good, do good, for the common good. That, itself, is based on attempting to live with the Cardinal Virtues and character. (For a list of the Cardinal Virtues, see What Makes a Good Person and How Can One Become So?) It matters that we ardently try every day. Study the great ancient philosophers; they had it going on 2,500 years ago. I have a fantasy of having a glass of wine with Cicero, and I have the real joy of a glass with you, Nicole.

Therefore, happiness is a process not a product; thus the path matters. We begin constructing the path to happiness first with ourselves. This is lofty stuff and not meant to discourage but to encourage. Even the great Stoics say they didn't get it right, this thing called life. But they enjoyed the ride. These were not stuffy guys of the stereotype. These guys were fun and fun to be with. They modeled how to live in word and deed and a few written pieces that have survived, thank goodness.

I can say I know when happiness arrives, and it does so more and more. Thus, I count myself most lucky. I realized that we all can be content by living as I describe in these pages. It's not a bad way to pass a lifetime. I can also say I have known happiness more than a little, mainly when my children call me . . .
Dad.

So, to what makes me happy:

You – Children are maddening and magical. Once a parent always a parent. It is happiness to see a baby, your baby, look in your eyes and smile and laugh. Those exhilarating moments will last my lifetime. What a great, great painful and glorious thing it is to be a father. Your troubles are mine. Your triumphs I share. Wonderment!

My child's success – In April of 2022, I met you, Nicole, on the farm by the pond to deliver the oath of office to you. At the "So help me God," you became a captain in the USAF Reserve Medical Corps. This frequent remembrance brings me endless happiness.

Wherever you go, go with your heart. – Confucius

What makes me happy? Your sense of humor, Nic.

Love – Risk finding "the love of your life." Sometimes it works, sometimes not so well. Still, to have someone to share life with is how we evolved—and worth the risk and work of it. Take a chance on love.

Health – It's great to have a good workout and swim a mile. My health enables me to do so much more than I otherwise could. It also gives me a better chance at longevity to enjoy all these things that make me happy.

Friends – Though they can be transitory, distracted, and imperfect, I'm fortunate to have close acquaintances—and to have had that one true friend of a lifetime, Marty. Though he is gone, I hear him even now, as Cicero promised I would.

Conversation – I do love good conversation, which stimulates as it ranges everywhere. Be it with people who complement and nourish you.

There are few things as nourishing as an intimate conversation with another soul.
– Anon

Accomplishment, a job well done – Finishing courses of study—formal, technical, professional, simply of interest. I've enjoyed a great feeling of accomplishment, of happiness, at finishing a project worth doing. It makes me happy to see the evidence of my formal education hanging on the wall in front of me and a few books with my name as author on them sitting on a shelf. Building a house, organizing and landscaping it, brought me satisfaction. I have determination, and each accomplishment brings me more confidence.

Home – The house I built makes a cozy home—my Hobbit Hole, I call it. And it's all paid for now. I am content to meditate under my pergola with the water bubbling and birds singing. The wind through the pines sounds like rivers I have known. I've had a squirrel put his nose on my toe.

A challenge well met – I've been teaching myself to do a flip turn while swimming my Tuesday and Thursday mile followed by a sauna reward. For nearly 25 years, I convinced myself I couldn't flip, but with persistence and determination, I made it possible—and did it.

Travel – So much wonder is about us, manmade and especially natural. Yet, nothing comes remotely close to Mt. Kilimanjaro. Whenever I'm on a trail or in the air, I am dumbfounded, or at least in awe, that pioneers hacked and trudged their way through dense woods and over mountains for a dream. I see a bridge across a gorge and through a mountain and say every time, "How did they do that?" Grand horizons.

Happy Hiker, Muir Woods, circa 2014

Being an American – I've seen much of the world, and I'm so glad to have been born in this wonderful country, let alone to have served it. Believe it or not, knowing I will end up in Arlington makes me smile. Honor.

Working the farm – I really adore being on the farm, especially to put up firewood. It gives me pleasure to see the stack grow under my hand. Accomplishment is happiness. It makes an evening fire that much more entrancing and warmer when fueled by a tired back and perhaps a good cabernet.

So, let's get something straight. People who say they're happy, implying that's true all the livelong day, are being less than candid. The day can be tough, disappointing, with never-ending, grueling work and regrets to boot. I'd get so fed up at the farm hoeing those endless rows of beans or what seemed like miles of sprouting corn and just whack one to oblivion out of sheer frustration. Believe it or not, though, that makes the good times all the sweeter. I actually loved tractor work, endless plowing and disking. It was meditative—the noise, the rumble, the smells of fresh, wormy earth. One can see the accomplishment furrow by furrow. Suffer the work. Man, does a boy learn!

Happiness happens when enough is plenty. – JK

What matters is that our pursuit of life is best served by being involved in worthy things. Accepting challenges, knowing you can figure things out. Getting knocked down to simply get up again. Keeping body, mind, and spirit well. Working on making and keeping respectable people as acquaintances. Working on family.

Never lose focus that, if you prepare for it, happiness arises unexpectedly. Know it, sense it, feel it, relish it in the moment.

Yes, working on the farm was and still is a source of happiness—just not the usual kind.

> ...[Happiness] is a heart-filled thrill we feel when we gather with others
> to celebrate an arrival after a long journey made with deeds of love
> and faith in the meaning of life.[20]
> – Steve Leder

What Is Love and What Does It Mean to You?

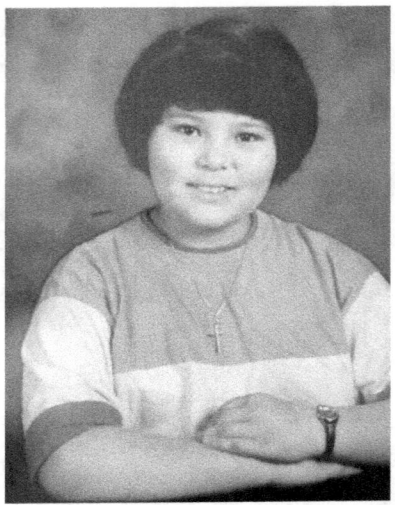

Love personified then and now. Nicole at about eight.

*I shall show you a love potion without a drug, without a herb;
without the incantation of any sorceress: if you want to be loved, love.*
— Seneca

Love in its uniqueness and sublimity makes things worthwhile. We are defined by our being rational and loving. I would go as far as to say, we have a responsibility to love and be loved. Even now as I contemplate this answer, it's magic to me. Even if it's occasionally fraught, love is worth the pursuit. Meaning, risk letting yourself go, as it's wonderful. Love is a gift that comes, if you will, when you give it away—so as Nike proposes, *just do it!*

Love comes in many forms. . . .

Naturally we have love between the sexes—especially when it endures and matures to tender companionship. We also have unconditional love between parents and children, familial love, which can be the best. Then there's platonic, brotherly love—the kind where one soul feels the ups and downs of another. Many of us (and I speak for myself) feel patriotic love of country, exemplified by sacrifice of service. This kind of love can make the heart pulse with pride at seeing our flag.

Love of nature brings appreciation for the sublime beauty of a flower or a honeybee or the cosmos. Spend time in nature to deeply understand the magic of a soundless forest shrouded in mist. Canoe a great river to be surrounded by sculptures that took millions of years to create and the universes they frame; marvel at the inexplicable vastness of it all. Watch bluebirds on the nest in the backyard and get caught up in their timeless work.

Love of music and the arts can sweep us away at a rock concert, compelling us to close our eyes, tap a toe to the beat, and soar. Listening to Leonard Coen's *Halleluiah* is truly transcendent. Love is seeing the Pieta at the Vatican and being brought to tears at its sublimity. It's experiencing *A Midsummer Night's Dream* at Stratford on Avon. Love is appreciating how the Dutch masters can paint three dimensions from two dimensions with a little linseed oil, an egg, and some ground pigments. It's marveling at how Leonardo could capture an enigmatic smile for the ages.

Love is the optimal human trait and thus must be valued in every way.

Unfortunately, love can also bring pain in our worldly state. The pain of suffering with another. The pain of unrequited emotion. The pain of so many disappointments that can cast us into the doom of Mordor.

However, love is also so wonderful that one must surrender to it and work for it. Surrendering means ignoring the possibilities of a broken heart, dreams dashed. The work of it is just that. It may mean getting up in the middle of the night countless times to chase the boogie man away and doing it for years just to see the trusting bliss on a child's face, calm in the knowledge that Dad is there, and nothing is to fear. Be the parent who is simply there, ready, able, willing, smiling. Laugh a lot; children love that. Children are born ready to be loved and love. You, Nic and Cindy, were both born smiling. Love is a tie eternal.

> *There is freedom waiting for you, on the breezes of the sky. And you ask,*
> *'what if I fall?' Oh, but my darling, what if you fly?*
> – Eric Hanson

Realize that the loves I mention above are unique to humans. Other creatures feel deep kinships, largely instinctually. Therein we are truly blessed to be human. Feel the luck at being born with the ability to experience the sublime nature of love.

What is love? Again: It's hearing "Dad."

Nicole on a Serengeti morning on an overlook at Saruni resort, Africa, April 2022

Love means giving a piece of yourself in order to find a peace in yourself.
– Anon[21]

ADVICE

What Life Advice Do You Have to Offer?

The farm made me: I truly look forward to the work. June 11, 2016

*The Stoic regards human lives as interdependent, and finds in this
a source of duty, affection, and solace.*
— Unknown

I wish for you to continuously:

Live with great books. – Thus you will gather the wit and wisdom of the ages. Better yet, you will become more intelligent than your given talents would warrant.

Live well to die well. – This means to be good, do good, for the common good. This leads to satisfaction with yourself and life. Oh, and great, satisfying accomplishments, too.

Live virtuously. – Practice the Cardinal Virtues every day until they become your very breath. Thus, you become honorable.

Live with character. – Simply be humble and introspective. This is the very essence of good leadership and especially of being a good person. Give respect to get respect.

Work on well-being. – Continuously improve body, mind, and zest for life. Thus, you have longevity, which is worthy and truly enjoyable only if you pursue the above with vigor.

Become a good friend. – This to earn the one true friend of a lifetime and surround yourself with those whose company you find interesting and supportive.

Become spiritual. – By all of the above, you will become spiritual in that you will appreciate and live by the laws of nature. Simply, it is natural to be fit, happy, and in awe of that undefinable Spark in the heavens that began it all and continues the work.

Have fun! – Humor is all around you—make it, enjoy it.

These wishes pursued relentlessly are the key to happiness, which comes upon us quietly in uncommon hours. At some point, when you are going about your day, you may realize, "I am happy, yes happy. My goodness!" It will be fleeting, memorable, remarkable, and compel a smile. Golly, I watched bluebirds on the nest this morning. I was happy. If you can finish with your daily trials—some merely the buzz of a mosquito, some that paralyze you with fear and depression—by saying, "Life is good," you will have succeeded.

How long are you going to wait before you demand the best for yourself?
– Epictetus

Travel + adventure + fun + great company = memories of a lifetime!

What Advice Would You Give to a Family Member About to Go to College?

Working four jobs and graduating with honors in Biochemistry as a Certified Physician Associate!

Human wisdom begins with the recognition of one's own ignorance.
— Socrates

Socrates goes further, saying that the unexamined life is not worth living. Ethics, virtue, character are the only things that matter. All else follows well enough. And a good person can never be harmed, because whatever misfortune he may suffer, his virtue will remain intact.

Going to college? Let's see.

For me, practicality matters as much or more than a formal education. Better both together. Yes, I went quite far at the student's desk, yet I still consider practical experience even more important. Formal education teaches *about* work. Practical education teaches one *how* to work—and unlocks the secrets of study. By that, things get done. I am fond of saying, "I can blast a stump and milk a cow." True, and said with pride. And it tells much about me. I say, get your hands dirty.

The question of this section is perhaps *the* question to ask of me, as I was never encouraged to go to college. I didn't know how to study. The thought of failure loomed. I certainly had no example for it. Absolutely no money for it. In defense of the adults in my family, only Dad attended college, but he never finished, which was his pattern—so many things left undone.

Grandpa Ignatz Klopovic was fond of saying in a heavy Croatian accent, "When you go to oonahversity . . . ." Immigrant families came here for a better life, epitomized by "college" for the children, though they knew nothing of what it took because we're from agrarian roots in the old country, Croatia. It took two generations for that to happen. In truth, out of the seven first gen Klopovics, I am the only one I know of who went to "oonahversity." College was a magical aspiration as it meant success and wealth in a country where the "streets are paved with gold." Worth the work and sacrifice. And now you, Nic and Cindy, are the only third gen Klopovics to go to "oonahversity."

He who opens a school door, closes a prison. – Victor Hugo

While education beyond primary and secondary school was talked of around the household, no one ever focused on it. I trembled when bringing my hand-written report card home, as I struggled in school. *Lackluster* is a kind word for it. While Dad let me visit Ohio State University by myself when I was 17, it was a Dad test for my suitability. I'm sure I flunked that one as I was hosted by a frat house. I knew nothing of college and was never encouraged, especially by our high school guidance counselor. I remind you, she was the one who told me to "get a toolbox," or some such enlightening and motivating condemnation. Thank goodness we had the farm and the body shop. They taught me how to work hard and that I was quite capable of figuring things out. And thankfully, I was drawn, I know not by what magic, to the Air Force recruiter.

In the Air Force, I realized I was the captain of my ship of state. I buckled down and did well, very well. I have mentioned my several decades of formal night school, so I won't digress with the retelling.

Education breeds confidence. Confidence breeds hope. Hope breeds peace.
– Confucius

Who would have ever guessed "toolbox boy" would earn a doctorate and be a published, "bestselling"[22] author.

What did I learn from the books shoved my way and the endless hours of biblical proportion studying? How did each step of formal education lead me somewhere impossible to go without it? Let me try to answer by way of (finally) offering the advice requested.

First, know you can do it. – You can get a formal education or almost anything worthwhile with doggedness and direction. So, pursue what is worthy. See that worthy task or goal as the door opener to opportunities never imagined. Realize that learning brings wisdom, which is the key to a worthwhile life. Study is worth that alone.

Many opportunities are not realized until years after they have worked their way into your life. I have done the "impossible." When we were first married, we landed at MacDill AFB, Tampa, Florida. Your mother felt one of the ways to wealth was in rental properties. I learned project management on the farm and in the Air Force. With that alone, I accomplished much of the work rebuilding four rundown houses for rentals. Then I took on the general contracting and much of the work to build two duplexes for rentals.

Following that, I did the general contracting, and much of the scut work again, for our home in Governor's Village near Chapel Hill. It was a "splendid" job according to professional contractors, especially for "toolbox boy." I used a hand-created Program Evaluation and Review technique from school to define a critical timeline so contractors could work in tandem. It allowed me to get the house ready for us, from eliminating the weeds to all the furniture in place, in exactly four months. Pro contractors were taking a year to do the same. The same contractors were betting I would flunk the Certificate of Occupancy last inspection. While I did, all it required was five minutes to pile mulch around the porch to the minimum height for safety.

I can see the last days, 19 contractor vehicles crowding the streets, getting it done. The next thing I applied was real sweat, learned by stacking hay and fixing cars.

I have to add, while my formal education resulted in four "sheepskins," I completed many technical courses and certifications. For example, I got a private pilot and Airframe and Powerplant mechanic license and more. Air Command and Staff College to prepare to be a field grade officer (major) took a year and counted as another master's degree. Then there were professional development classes too numerous to remember. "Just Say Yes!"

Back to getting a formal education. One of the smartest things I did, in retrospect, was finishing with the Air Force. Now, with stoic awareness, I don't have to work for money, a rare, rare privilege. Through the Air Force, I received my education, and education advanced my rank and eventually made it possible for me to have a second career with the Crime Commission. Now, both provide me with a pension. That, Social Security, and my deliberate financial management made this state of my personal affairs become a reality.

Imagine me being a "bestselling" (though not paid) author after being told by high school teachers that I couldn't write. With education, you can do it—and you *can* get education.

Education is progressive discovery of our own ignorance. – Will Durant

Study hard and with intention. – Study every minute you aren't in class or going about the necessities of life. Scope out places to study alone and with like-minded students. Never miss a class. Do assignments well—not necessarily perfectly, but well enough to learn. Sit at the front. Be in class with pen and paper (or a laptop these days), notes, and questions at the ready *before* class starts (teachers notice that). Ask a few good, no great, questions. Sleep and eat well. Exercise every afternoon before a good meal and evening study. Be prepared. Show respect to classmates and the instructor.

Working hard with intention means you approach every quiz or test or final having studied well enough to say, "*Whatever* happens, I have done my best." This establishes the proper confidence to sit for that test and do well. Do well on one, and it sets the pattern for and history of success for those to come. Never have to cram for an exam or any project. Having to cram indicates poor planning, lack of a goal, and a pattern of failing performance. Sit at that test in anticipation of doing well because you are prepared. Prepared means confident of doing your best. Sweat means little if not directed by a good, even noble, goal.

Establish a routine. – Have regular times for sleep, study, exercise, and the duties of the day to maintain health and vigor. Your lifestyle is that of a dedicated student. I scheduled all classes I could during mornings. This allowed me to study all afternoon. I even had designated places to study in proximity to my classes. Always have a book on hand. The day before exams, I studied appropriately, not feverishly, exercised at the regular time, ate a good supper at the regular time, reviewed notes, and went to bed at the same time I go to bed even now. (That's about 10 p.m. for a 6 p.m. rising; I am my own alarm clock.) Good sleep is where lessons, facts, and figures find a place in the brain, mind, and memory. Study enough to be relaxed the day before and confident when you sit for that test. A little nervousness is quite okay; it piques the brain cells. Routine—a set time for the practices and work of the day—is a great mechanical means for getting through the test and life, tough times and tough work.

The direction in which education starts a man will determine his future life. – Plato

Combine formal with practical education. – A formal education alone is a bit sterile. You need to test books and lectures out in the real world. Read, read, read. Travel to exciting places. Investigate interesting things. Accept challenges—especially accept challenges. Observe the successful and unsuccessful; they both teach. Seek a practical education via the "school of hard knocks." Experience tests and refines the processes of thinking and studying for what and how you should best use your time. The classroom plus toolroom plus boardroom plus cruise stateroom is another combination in which the whole is much greater than the sum of the parts. Note that doing nothing correctly is a good use of time, too. It's called relaxation; know how to do it.

I've been asked how I used a doctorate. It goes beyond employing formal education. It was a reach so far that it became life affirming. However, I have to say that the grind of a doctorate was soul killing for the seven years that it required. I actually quit twice, and supervisors brought me back. Thanks be to them. Goodness, I would drive down the freeway yelling all the things I was going to tell the faculty, especially my dissertation reviewers. One in particular wanted a complete rewrite! I answered her questions, and the fact that the other faculty on my review board (who passed me) were eminently qualified, one a Harvard Ph.D., enabled me to make it. I still don't know what that woman's motivations were.

(For a short detour, I think the following quote is especially meaningful and germane.)

> *You educate a man; you educate a man. You educate a woman;*
> *you educate a generation.* – Brigham Young

Now, much later, having that "sheepskin" above my computer screen is most satisfying as the trauma and the work fade with the years. It not only engenders cachet, but it also brings respect. It's rewarding to be called *Doctor* Klopovic. No, it's just plain KOOL. As it is hearing *Major* Klopovic. It helped me survive, if not progress, at the Crime Commission. Then it helped me with the tools for writing and publishing, which have taken me on yet another personal growth path.

Undergrad schooling began my understanding of how to put words together. The master's degrees helped me understand how the public sector worked. The doctorate helped me be persuasive. Practically speaking, it was part of my being able to stay at the Crime Commission. It did not, however, lead to higher paying jobs. That's just the nature of the public sector. And yes, I would do it again. It is rare air and satisfying. It took me years to display my diplomas, now in my study. I gotta admit the array of three degrees surrounding the Doctor of Public Policy diploma is, well, pretty neat. And people are proud of me, especially my children—at least the one who knows me now. (Cindy will come back to me. I will it so. And it will be good. I have my mother's example for enduring.)

> *The next best thing to knowing something is knowing where to find it.*
> – Samuel Johnson

Understand how things work. – Be able to put education and experience to work. Studying Stoicism is a worthy use of time, because I make it lead to action. Ethics and character must be priorities. Concurrently, know how to accumulate money with the goal of retiring from having to work for money. Learn the lessons of noblesse oblige and money as a tool so you can do more for worthy causes that will benefit following generations.

Money is one of the most vexing challenges in a life. It's easily understood, but so few can make money work for them. Learn to live frugally and within your means.

That's the first lesson of money. How much is enough? Not much. The second is to save and invest regularly. Put any raise into your retirement account so you don't miss it. Lifestyle seems to morph to any raise with "essentials." Have one credit card with a low balance and pay it off every month. That type of overall strategy is a good one. It irks me greatly to know the usury interest rate fees on a credit card go to paying executives' six- and seven-figure pay checks. Unconscionable!

Be content with what you do. – This is really tough. Most of life is about grinding out the day. It amazes me to hear so many say they fly through life pursuing their goals and being happy. Life is brutal—but worthy. Choose wisely what you do as you must see it through till its natural end, whether that's completing a project, reaching a goal, or seeing that the effort has become futile and letting it go. Pursue a life of worthy goals, make their achievement happen, and be content.

Recognize opportunities. – Life throws many, if not countless, opportunities at us. But we must be educated, experienced, and knowledgeable enough to recognize them. They'll be at your feet. Have the courage born of successfully meeting challenges to pick them up and run with them.

Never stop learning. – Do what you can to make learning successful, fulfilling, and rewarding. Laziness and failure are wet blankets to the innate spark we all have to know things. I make it a point to read a range of books, even fiction. Try not to be captivated with the frippery of social media and silly entertainment. One can be self-entertained well and productively.

An investment in knowledge pays the best interest. – Benjamin Franklin

Playing the part—or at least one of them

How Do You Face Obstacles Well and Overcome Them?

World-class luthier, Jayne Henderson displays her handmade guitars.
Imagine the years of mistakes it takes to become world class.

Courage is rightly esteemed the first of human qualities because it's the quality which guarantees all others.
– W. L. S. Churchill

Ask yourself questions—learn—adapt—optimize. Dare to do.

Learn to ask Why questions. – Why helps determine direction. Be careful not to get stuck in these analyses as it is a safe place to be: analysis paralysis. No action means no failure. That is, what you learn should contribute to your progress, your moral fiber, your character, your intellect, your well-rounded life, and your worth to society. So, before you embark upon anything big, ask why you should do it and how it will contribute to your life and those about you. If it will be valuable, you can overcome any obstacles you may face with more determination and persistence. Your Why develops a supportive mindset. Choose wisely what you do, then do it with full measure as Seneca advises.

Learn to ask How questions. – Yes, you are obliged, even smart, to also consider the who, what, where, and when of things. This is analysis; necessary, and it's quite safe, even reassuring, to be prepared. However, those questions only get you to the end of the day, not to accomplishment. Thus, they can be endless, looking for that last piece of evidence or confirmation. You must *risk* action, as action is the only confirmation of a decision. Action is the way forward. And in my book, only the how question helps define an action.

Prepare for obstacles. – Life experiences based on troubles are part of the day. In fact, they are the stuff of life in my book, though I hasten to add I could have used fewer troubles. We were meant to struggle and overcome to gain strength. These troubles extend from mere bothers to catastrophes. No one escapes. I know of no one who has not confronted real troubles and won.

These bothers are more than Alaskan tundra mosquitoes—although yup, I've felt the hoards there with Nicole, and I've heard of people being driven mad by mosquitoes. In addition to these daily challenges, tsunami events can and do befall us all. I speak from my own experiences, such as the premature death of friends, foreclosure, firing, marriage failure, alienation of loved ones, auto accidents, and too many near-death experiences. Yet here I am, aiming to reach my 10th decade. It's worth the struggle to see the wonder of tomorrow—truly.

> *Live as if you were to die tomorrow. Learn as if you were to live forever.*
> – Mahatma Gandhi

Believe it or not, we want obstacles, but not foolish endangerments, to help shape us. Don't encourage obstacles, but neither should you eschew them. They are there lurking. In fact, obstacles are the architects of who we were meant to be.

I liken obstacles to the few mountains I have climbed, some with a 35-pound pack. My advice: Get in shape with practice hikes. Have your pack minimally but fully and properly packed. Have your maps and hiking plan, then strike out. . . . You will fall, hard, maybe break your hand as I did. And prepare to get lost! Let the climb be a rhythm of feet, poling, and breathing. It becomes a grand meditation as the miles melt. Enjoy the summit. The accomplishment, the views, the nature, the beauty, the moment. Pick a mountaintop flower to press into your journal. Then spy the next peak, a metaphor again for overcoming who-knows-what toward the next accomplishment. Go ahead, "Take a Hike."[23] Learn to adapt.

Obstacles are the architects of who we were meant to be. – JK

A well-deserved rest after climbing South Mountain, North Carolina

The best view comes after the hardest climb. – Anon

Adapt. – Realize you are capable. Muster your personal resources via self-study and application, and with family and friends. Professionally, people are at their best when inspired by a good leader with a vision and who leads by example. Be that person. One source leads to two, then four, then more. As one source closes, others open. Take care not to lean on external resources for answers too much; you are your best, and sometimes your only, fellow soldier.

Adapting also means preparing. Be about building a worthy, communal, capable, character-based life. These are the strengths that help you meet obstacles head on.

Let us not go over the old ground. Let us rather prepare for what is to come.
– Marcus Tullius Cicero

Optimize. – Optimization is a metaphor for life. In the final analysis, we have limited resources if we consider fleeting time; you must consider how your time is spent. You can buzz round the entire day and most of the night and have done nothing. Always ask yourself, "Is this the best use of my time?"

The Greats observed that the event matters only in that it tests us body, mind, and soul.

Each test has made me stronger, ready for the next thing that slams into me, though I certainly don't encourage such events. Each one has shown me that I can solve things—and know that this self-confidence is success. I have found we are our own worst enemies when it comes to capitulating to "woe is me" moments, even if the day has been good.

Yes, handling obstacles builds true character and helps our progress toward becoming virtuous, as confronting difficulties with a winning attitude is the daily expression of virtues, especially courage.

You're braver than you believe, stronger than you seem, and smarter than you think.
 – Christopher Robin/A. A. Milne

What Makes a Good Person and How Can One Become So?

High school graduation, September '66

Wisdom and humor from Abraham Lincoln:
When I do good, I feel good. When I do bad, I feel bad. That's my religion.
It's not me who can't keep a secret. It's the people I tell that can't.
The best thing about the future is that it comes one day at a time.
I'm a success today because I had a friend who believed in me,
and I didn't have the heart to let him down.
You have to do your own growing no matter how tall your grandfather was.
That some achieve great success is proof to all that others can achieve it as well.

If you want examples of good people, read anything about or by Lincoln. So much progress we Americans have made as people we owe to this man of all ages. Good people are worthy because they work hard on the truths of living well.

They:
- work on earning respect by becoming respectable.
- work on being a good friend and thus earn friendship.
- are calm under pressure and are sought to lead.
- have the determination to overcome and thus accomplish worthy goals, individually and especially collectively.
- are compassionate—the essence of being human but a trait not always developed or realized in unevolved people.
- are humane, e.g., kind, caring, humanitarian, charitable.
- understand the meaning, especially hidden meanings or unintended consequences, in things and others and thus build the conditions for success and especially happiness.
- put process over project and thus are about continually improving day by day, perhaps minute by minute, and strive to be their best selves to the last day.
- understand that true achievement is a result of people reaching for more than the sum of the parts.
- are drawn to good people and thus have good friends and acquaintances.

One must be good to do good, so practice daily, day in and day out. Begin with virtue and character, as nothing else matters if one is corrupt of morals, devoid of concern for others, or physically or mentally debauched. I notice good people are their best seemingly without effort, improving all the time, every day, though I know they're working quite hard at it.

Here are ways we can emulate the best among us:

- *Virtue* – Live with the Cardinal Virtues, defined in everyday practical, doable language.

    o *Justice* – Fairness. Know the difference between right and wrong and do the right thing reflexively, nearly without thinking—even in the middle of the night when no one is watching.

    Is it right to pick up errant trash in a neighbor's yard? Why? Not yours? True, but you are showing personal pride in your community and being helpful and a good neighbor.

o *Wisdom* – Knowledge. Learn to love learning. By learning we discover how words become a book that persuades. Learning is the "secret" to writing, discovery, and rhetoric—especially rhetoric, the honed ability to masterfully explain yourself and compel others to action. I read a great deal, and I try to put into action at least one lesson from every book. If I read a thousand books, that's a thousand ideas from which to build and profit.

To make no mistakes is not in the power of man; but from their errors and mistakes the wise and good learn wisdom for the future. – Plutarch

o *Courage* – Determination. This includes the fortitude to get out of bed in the morning knowing obstacles, small, big, and relentless will confront you. Know you can handle them. Overcoming each obstacle makes you stronger and is how we learn and become.

I write and produce books. It's not fun; just trudging, trudging, trudging. What drives me? The process improves me. And who knows? A life may be changed for the better with the turn of one page. I have known real joy when a young man looked at me and said, "You changed my life." It would be my great honor to change many lives for the better. Well, in fact I have.

o *Temperance* – Restraint. Learn how much is enough. Answer: Not much. Know the difference between being rich, a condition in which accumulation never ends, and being wealthy, in which just enough is a banquet. Temperance applies to everything. It goes way beyond money and things. For example, it's about not speaking intemperately. Once over the lips, something said can't be unsaid. I do try many times a day to make sure a word spoken is true, kind, and necessary. It prevents a lot of groveling.

Three things you cannot recover in life: the WORD after it's said, the MOMENT after it's missed and the TIME after it's gone. . . . – Ziad Abdelnour

- *Character* – Do not react to being wronged. Engaging is being controlled by others.

    o *Humility* – I put this first in pursuing being good. Face it, we all have an ego. Only with humility can we "see" the truths in people and things, and we will never know it all. We must be fair with others. Do the right thing and expect nothing in return.

    I practice saying very little, especially with new acquaintances. Also, I think a big part of humility is having a good sense of humor. True wit is best—and even better when practiced.

    o *Introspection* – Really know thyself. Learn what you are made of. Strengthen strengths and especially correct weaknesses.

    I have tested myself my whole life, and especially now that I'm more aware, I wonder how my behavior affects things. When something goes wrong, I always ask, "What did I do to cause this?" When I get an answer, I ask it again until I unravel the tangled roots of a mishap. I find myself in there somewhere and always find ways to improve. By that, things up the chain of causation get better, too.

- *Building the trilogy of the human condition* – We are a system served best by practicing a lifespan approach. (See the book *Lifespan: Why We Age—and Why We Don't Have To* by David Sinclair and Matthew LaPlante.) Simply put, longevity is a result of our lifespan, the years we live, and health span is how well we do it. It's more than diet and exercise; it's the quality we put into our days. I'm fond of saying we need to live with virtue, character, and well-being (not just wellness). Thus, we approach the day improving each one. Then we can live to a ripe age, still vital and vigorous. Following are my own protocols. I hope they inspire you to develop habits that are appropriate for you. Note that I have treated this topic in some detail previously so the following are more summative.

    o *Body* – This is about working on your physicality. Beware the gimmicks, gurus, and head games that come blasting at us for a quick fix to health and happiness. No self care takes the place of a range of exercises, 150 to 250 minutes a week. Mind your body's biological age, not so much your chronological age, and take care of it appropriately. So if your doctor tells you that your body is one of someone, say, 10 or 20 years younger than your chronological age, you are on the right track. Just remember that the more rigorously you take care of it in the present, the better it will perform for you later in life.

My doc tells me I have the body of someone 10-15 years younger, of which I am proud as it's born of decades of proper sweat. Hence, I can exercise vigorously age appropriately. At the moment, I nurse a finicky lower back, left shoulder, and left knee. Therefore, I do a gentlemanly CrossFit three times a week with modifications. I swim twice a week and do yoga. Attitude is everything. If I am bunged up and in an immobilizing sling, I can still hike. At the very least, and it is rare, I still go to the gym and do a whirlpool, sauna, and cold(ish) shower. I see myself (yes, I see a mental picture of myself) at 95 still going to the gym and doing the exercises I will do.

- *Diet* – Mostly plant based, but a chicken breast or fish fillet is fine. So is a steak, occasionally, just not a side of beef and a two-pound loaded baked potato. (Well, so is a good glass of wine or a shot, *just a shot*, of good double-oaked bourbon—in my case.) Remember my saying:

  A body will not follow a discontented soul.

- *Exercise* – Rigorous, varied, regular. I do what are called Tabata routines. ("Tabata is a high-intensity interval training that consists of eight sets of fast-paced exercises each performed for 20 seconds interspersed with a brief rest of 10 seconds." – Merriam Webster.) I combine variations of these with work on coordination, flexibility, balance, strength, and endurance—in the order of what deteriorates with age so I can delay deterioration as long as possible.

> Make sure your conditioning is age appropriate, so you can exercise till the day you die. Then relax on the patio, perhaps with a book in your lap, after swimming a mile.
>
> o *Mind* – Always be reading. Always be learning. Always be gainfully involved in life and in the company of worthy people. Love learning.
>
> o *Spirit* – Have a reason to get up in the morning. Or better; have a lot of reasons: family, rewarding work, a hobby, for example.
>
> - *Meditate daily* – At least of a morning, and relax with a good novel in the evening to help you drift off.

- Have a philosophy of life, or several! Here are a few to consider:
    - o *Live with Virtue, Strive with Character, Thrive for a lifetime.*
    - o *Aim high, fail often, do well.*
    - o *Obstacles are not in the way, they are the way.*
    - o *The body won't follow a discontented soul.*
    - o *Live long enough to correct errata.*

By that last one, I mean if you are constantly beset by this and that, you just can't concentrate on what's important to a long and fruitful life. For example, it's perfectly acceptable to enjoy a movie in the evening—assuming a good and productive day—but this is hard for me. Worrying about "wasting" the evening dies hard as my consciousness remembers decades of 16-hour days.

These are a few of my suggestions for becoming a good person. Nicole, I know you already *are* a good person, and I'm exceedingly proud of you. Stay at it, and if my thoughts help give you inspiration, so much the better. They are bred from concern that you live long, well, and with consequence. And the same goes for anyone else who may read this.

Ms. Ginny Adams was proprietress of the Lazy Fox Inn, Damascus, Virginia, serving the best breakfast on the Appalachian Trail. She called me the "Apple Pie Guy" because I baked one for and with her in her kitchen. Fun![24]

A slice of handmade Blue Ribbon apple pie is good for the soul. – JK

What Is Good Advice to Live Well and How Do You Do It?

Nothing like a woman in uniform. Captain Nicole Klopovic, ready for duty, Fall 2022

We make a living by what we get, but we make a life by what we give.
— Winston Churchill

Good advice is that which is born of experience and love, especially that which is put to work. The best lives on. It makes a positive difference in lives. Otherwise, it is chin music.

Much of what I write, publish, and say is brimming with pithy sayings about life, mostly from our great thinkers and writers. So, in answer to this question about how to live well, let me offer a few inspirations I use on a regular basis. Some I can directly attribute to others; some I have synthesized from the wisdom I've gained from my readings and my own experience.

Do not even think dishonestly. – Musashi, 1974

The philosophers knew that a dishonest thought leads to a dishonest word, then a dishonest deed, then a dishonest character, and finally a dishonest reputation. Then, all is lost. Ruin.

Write something worth reading or do something worth writing. – Benjamin Franklin

We all need to become "Franklinophiles." His thoughts are examples of practicality applicable to us all. His genius of many dimensions is in his ability to "speak" to the common man (and woman) throughout the ages. He must be one of the top 100 most significant people in all of history. His books and Churchill's fill a good chunk of my bookcase.

Per Franklin's advice, become a lover of books—good books. Learn at least one actionable thing from each book and do it. It's another way to grow and progress.

Eighteen and headed to the Air Force, May '66 (Can you spot the anomaly in this photo?)

Make sure what you do is simple, suitable, and sustainable. – JK

Simple does not mean simplistic nor necessarily easy. Suitable means appropriate to you as a person, those involved, and the situation. Sustainable means to aim in your endeavors for a beneficial lasting effect, if possible. At least pursue something till it's finished or reaches its natural end. (I stress this in my Capacity Building series for developing public programs.) That said, know when the horse has died and move on.

Learn to ask Why and then How. – JK

Nothing happens until something moves. – Einstein

*If no mistake have you made, yet losing you are,
a different game you should play.* – Yoda

As previously mentioned, asking *Why* determines if an endeavor is worthy. Asking *How* properly compels action. Yes, that action may be marked by frustration, failures big and small, disappointments, setbacks—you get it. However, start with a positive mindset: Expect the best and affirm that your endeavor will happen with ease and whatever you need will fall into place. If you encounter undue obstacles, reevaluate your Hows, which may include how to overcome those obstacles. *Where there's a will, there's a way,* as the saying goes. Ensure your *Why* is worthy, then consider your critical *Hows.*

Be respectable so you attract respectable people. – JK

Most who take your time are not worthy of your time. – JK

Learn to discern character and associate with good people or move on immediately. Develop supportive, positive relationships—and if you can, a long-lasting one.

The Harvard study on aging, 85 years and running, determined that having healthy relationships—especially one long-lasting one—is the overriding factor in determining longevity.[25] This very human propensity matters more than diet, exercise, and healthy living, which of course help, but they rest on good relationships.

Our lives are measured in hours. – JK

Learn the lessons of the greats as soon as you can. Learn the five ways of spending your time: personal maintenance, working, resting, relaxing, and leisure. Remove wastes of time. I wish there were no such thing as streaming, as I am unable to resist the lure. That said, I can include it in the category of relaxing—and at least watch inspiring, fun, or educational programs or movies.

> *Wherever you go, go with your heart.* – Confucius

When you go with your heart, you live with love, and living with love ensures that you're living well.

> *Know when enough is a banquet.* – Aesop

Then you are wealthy. Then you are content. Then you enjoy life.

> *Think before you speak. Is it brief, true, necessary, and kind?*
> – Bernard Meltzer modified by JK

Try never to speak out of anger, frustration, or ill intentions. Calm down, and if your rational moment dictates, then speak. You will find you have little to say. What you do say will be quite persuasive.

What saying captures what I am trying to relate to you about living well? It would have to be what I reiterate throughout:

> *Be good, do good, for the common good.* – Attributed to St. Thomas Aquinas

The sooner you begin the study of philosophy, the sooner you can become this person who lives well. Your work is never done—and that is wonderful. Tough? Yes. But this path promises you'll become better and better, your best, to your final earthly day. Your example lives on in those around you and in many you will never know, but who think of you kindly. Then you will have lived well. That is energizing.

> *In one drop of water are found all the secrets of all the oceans; in one aspect of You are found all the aspects of existence.* – Kahlil Gibran

How Does Good Financial Advice Work?

Names on memorial wall near Ellis Island

My sister Carolyn got our Mom's name engraved for a reasonable donation, quite significant for what it represents. The Klopoviches began here in America—yes, Klopovich with an *h*, which was dropped by the immigration officer.

When prosperity comes, do not use all of it. – Confucius

The world is rife with tragic stories of generations of hard fought and well won wealth gone literally with a roll of the dice. Then there's the story of a woman taking in laundry who becomes a six-figure benefactor to a big-name university.

Building wealth is mechanical. Have a plan and stick to it. Here's a little motivation: In your lifetime, you will need a healthy seven-figure income to support a modest lifestyle without exhausting your nest egg. This is not a bridge too far. Even on a modest income, resolute, regular, required investment will get you there. Just think: Investing $1,000 in the Berkshire Hathaway IPO (Warren Buffet) in 1964 was worth $26.6 *million* in 2018, *before* this latest run.

Plan on at least 40 years of living without having to work for money. Those years can and will be your most productive and *rewarding*. Much more so when you are no longer concerned with where a buck is coming from. (Did you know that a deer skin, a buck, was sold for a dollar back in pioneer days? I love little historical facts.) This type of long-term view also teaches the value of a dollar, how it can grow, how to keep it and especially what good you can do with it.

Reserve a bookshelf for books on wealth building. – First, get *The Simple Path to Wealth* (and don't miss chapter 32).[26] If it isn't in print, it's on my bookshelf with other wealth-building books on minding your money. Read it. Reread it. Dog-ear the pages and read it again. Then act, act, act accordingly.

I may dwell on the correct relationship with money, but in the end, you must make your own decisions to achieve financial independence. That comes of being aware of the state of the world and your world with a daily newspaper. Be informed, generally and specifically, especially about how money works, and how to accumulate it. Read about and study financial management. Refer to my books on money, banking, and investing.

Listen to the voice of experience. – I had no example for making money work. The immediate generations before me lived through World War I, the Great Depression, WWII with draconian rationing, then lengthy recessions. Investment advice was to scrimp and save pennies and nickels. My grandma's stairs to the cramped bedrooms above where eight people slept were caving in with used cottage cheese containers, balls of string, bags, and scraps—'most anything that could not be eaten and *must* be saved as it was "useful." One worked until death or was a burden on the family until death. Thus, my lessons are formed from brutal experiences generations in the making. Yours need not be; your world is much different. You can be well, financially secure, and full of potential beyond 100! I have wasted so much money in my day trying to learn the lessons of wealth building. Learn from my mistakes.

Morals first. – The prelude to wealth building, which runs throughout this memoir and my other writings, is that one must first be in the process of becoming a moral person based on practicing the Cardinal Virtues and growing your character. This is a minute-to-minute practice so that being good is your natural reaction to life. It's great to earn respect and friendship and watch a nest egg prosper. While there are countless people who are quite powerful, rich to extravagance, and "have it all," they can have it, as it comes at remarkable cost to so many. In my book, bad morals and bad character mean no money that's worth it.

Work on being good, then better and better. – Money does not matter if your hand, head, and heart are not continuously evolving upward, forward. This is due to merely being habitual about the right things.

Start early. – It's a great idea to learn to put aside at least 10 percent of your gross income, even if you do cat sitting as a youngster. I remember I matched those sums of yours to total $1,000, which was your nest egg. The younger the better to learn so many essentials such as values, frugality, the magic of compounding, and saving for what is meaningful.

Continuously study. – No apologies for repetition. I can't seem to get away from books, but bear with me. Plan a bookshelf, a library. Perhaps one of my fondest desires is that you ravage my library. Oh, that you should take them all to begin your own libraries! Thus you are continually learning, proving a path, building a knowledge base to pass forward.

When you have a love affair with books, you are never alone, you are never without wonder, you never lack for conversation, you never stop "traveling." Even if you can't read some day, someone, some device can read to you. – JK

Organize your many volumes by areas of pursuit. Begin with philosophy, for sure. Then label shelves for Health and Wellness and Wealth Building. Then. at least, label for History, Biographies, Historical Fiction, Travelogues, Fiction, ...

There is nothing like having dinner with Churchill or sitting in the stoa (portico) at the feet of Seneca.

Make books mark your path through life. They can be a big part of your legacy. – JK

See it; do it. – Visualize your growing financial worth, act on it diligently, and it will happen. You can do this with a single fund.[27] I'm in Schwab, a legacy money manager from USAA.[28] Vanguard bears close consideration, too. For those just starting out: Invest a couple of bucks when you're a teen. Certainly, an investment vehicle must be in place when you get your first real job.

Set it and forget it. – One lesson for sure: You can't outguess the market. Second lesson: The market continually rises over time. I remind you again that, when I was born, the Dow was at 177, and now it has approached 37,000!! In less than this lifetime. *Set it* means start with the intention of continuous monthly infusion. *Forget it* means staying the course. And get semiannual briefings from your money manager and call as needed. Monitor the vicissitudes of your money to witness the ups and downs with aplomb. Dream of financial independence. Then make it work for you. Again, money is a tool, way more than what it buys.

Be conservative. – This is the best policy for money management (and not a bad way to go politically, too). I make this point to note that this our greatest country, the greatest in all of history, has been careening to socialism. Free this, that, and the other; money unearned yet "entitled." Politicians taking advantage of a crisis saw COVID as an excuse to spend trillions! All borrowed. All but the dregs of the expenditures to "buy" votes. And they want more! Deficits and debt balloon, and the government has to borrow more to pay interest on that debt. The Fed must crank up interest rates to cure the manufactured inflation. Then banks fail—panic. The Fed must stop controlling inflation to fight banking collapses. The greatest problem is that no politician wants to address the careening expenses of entitlements. There will be a reckoning. Extreme measures, cutting benefits, more taxes, means testing, and more will be necessary to stop a collapse. Depression by any definition. Be conservative. Vote conservative.

National recession, the path to depression, looms. Yet people expect and get more. Let's not mention WWIII between Ukraine and Russia, with Chinese hegemony worldwide, Islamic states rushing headlong to build nukes, and the collapse of the misbegotten green and woke agendas. Only the prepared will weather world events. Yet this is the course of history; civilizations rise on democracy, fall on totalitarianism. You are your own best counsel for health, security, and wealth.

*Wealth is the **topic**.* – It is impossible to be rich. There's always some other bauble that's bigger, better, bouncier, brighter than the one you have. P.S.: The bouncy thing goes as flat as your right rear tire with a 16d nail through it, usually when a tire shop is 200 miles away and the spare was never checked. Then that nail pesters your thoughts for years. Wealth endures in the right hands—yours.

*Wealth is the **plan**.* – If you don't have a plan, you will get nowhere. It begins with the habit of saving and investing conservatively for the long haul. Treat this growing pot of money as if it doesn't exist. It will then take care of you. The only exceptions I see are to educate a *worthy* child or to preserve life, if and when necessary.

*Wealth is the **goal**.* – This means *financial independence.* No credit card balance. Pay your monthly bills and be pleased, very pleased at the little pot-o'-gold remaining in the check book to do as you please. Retire on your terms. No more hoppin' to da man. Make memories, be a philanthropist, host a lovely dinner party. It does not take piles of money when you know how little the "good life" takes.

*Leisure is the **aim**.* – This manner of money management will leave you with the lengthiest paid for retirement possible to be and do what you were meant to be and do. You will have leisure time to make a mark on those around you and pursue happiness. I know, as I am trying to do that now with growing success. Best of all, you will have a tidy sum to leave to the next generation. Again, it is legacy.

Mitigate then remove one of life's biggest stressors. – Having a goal of financial independence pleases the mind in two ways. First, it's fun to watch your finances grow. As I experienced cutting wood on the farm, you can see that "pile of logs" stacking up under your hand. You can anticipate then enjoy remarkable, productive years beyond working for money. And when it happens—whoa!—yes, when it happens, it's like the gates of Narnia open for you. Satisfaction almost unmeasurable. How fun it is to go to a nice restaurant and not calculate the tip to the farthing.

My second try at wealth building didn't begin in earnest until I was 53, and then I started over from insolvency. Just know that this stuff works; it's working for me. These tips, truths, and tactics were born from real experience. Nic, I continue to learn by watching and participating in your path to financial independence.

I was on the wealth path the first time when I came to family life in 1978 with $93,000, real estate, and savings. I was learning to make money work for me; but . . . it was all wasted and I was facing three foreclosures in three years. Then I lived paycheck to paycheck for 25 years, with credit cards maxed and getting more cards to pay off others. I did squirrel away a bit—a 401(k) with only about $50k—by 1999. Then on my own—painfully, painfully on my own—I paid off the house in about 15 years, had no long-term debt, no credit card debt, and a little money saved. Thus, I could and did retire at 66, never having to work for money again.

Another intelligent financial decision I made was fully retiring twice. My smartest move was to stay in the Air Force against all odds. Now it is my biggest check and overall best secure source of wealth, considering the health care. While I worked for my military retirement, it's another great relief to be able to see whatever health care pro I wish, when I wish, for what I wish. Oh—I do have a copay for dental exams and a new set of glasses every 10 years or so.

I am second generation Croatian, and the first to retire to do as I please—and be able to leave you, Nic, seed money to grow so you can retire early and give back. Act on these simple lessons: less is more, save/invest early and continuously, and learn to live well. You will be rewarded beyond imagining. I won't wish you "luck," because I know you are absorbing this wisdom and you work as hard or harder than most other people. I wish you triumph over obstacles and a Good Life that's long and hearty with significance and legacy. I do love you as only a father can.

We are what we repeatedly do. Excellence then is not an act, but a habit.
– Will Durant

REMEMBRANCE

How Do You Wish to Be Remembered?

THE way to do shots: Maple syrup hot off the evaporator pan
with my Amish friends and neighbors

You can't stop the snow, but you can learn to snowboard. – JK

I wish to be remembered with respect and fondness.

Remember me well as one who tried to do things that matter. What I leave has been and is a driving force for me. My path through life has been quite bumpy, but I know I have made a positive difference in many lives.

I want to be remembered as one who had a great formal education as a result of nearly 30 years of night school, even though no one thought I was college material. I have also learned by traveling widely and have been through the school of hard knocks, my real education. In many ways, I am self-educated. I leave a few books I have authored, even though in high school I was told I couldn't write. I hope I can be an inspiration to those who may not think they can be successful. Yes, you can.

I have chronicled my memories and adventures in photo journals. They relate a love of the world, the people in it, and the countless ways to see and experience being in the world. I also leave this memoir of questions and answers, experiences, and a little wisdom, which I hope leaves many good memories and a little advice to you two, Cindy and Nicole, and to anyone else who cares to read it.

You will see me in my library. My hope is that you keep these volumes for your own edification and pleasure. Know they track my interests and travels.

I also leave a Donor Advised Fund: The Nicole and James Klopovic Charitable Foundation. Whosoever inherits it is tasked to first grow it, do good things with it over the years, and see that it continues to grow beyond the granting. As I have mentioned, its guiding words are to *"Fund permanent answers to permanent problems at the local level of government."* This is by using my take on capacity building, the infrastructure of delivering a local service. Local governments are where good things are possible. Your instruction manuals will be four of my books on the same. At this writing, I have all four drafted as part of my dissertation and one of them published—*Decriminalizing Mental Illness: A Practical Model for Building Sustainable Crisis Intervention Teams.* After this memoir, I plan to produce the remaining three. See the list of titles under *If You Could Have as Much Money As You Wanted, How Would You Spend It?* Wish me the fuel in my writing/publishing tank.

I tried to be a good, though imperfect, example. It took me decades to arrive at this stage of life—by living a life worth living via reading, learning, traveling, making friends, making a difference. I have tried to earn the respect of respectable people and be a person you admire. Thus, I endeavor to live with virtue and character and work on well-being as an example to you. Tough . . . but doable.

Imagine me in my "uniform" of the day—light blue Simms long-sleeve casting shirt, Tommy John jamma bottoms—in my Churchill recliner by the craftsman cherry side table with that Japanese table lamp. Oh yes, and in my grey house coat and my Ugg Australian Marino slippers with a book on my lap desk taking me to other worlds, chatting with Franklin, strolling with Seneca and Cicero, or boating on the Mississippi with Twain. I hope I'll find books, tons of books, in heaven.

Remember me laughing. Gadzooks, I love to laugh!

Leaving ought not to be painful, if your soul has accomplished what it was intended on this earth to do.[29]
– Steve Leder

What Will Your Epitaph Say?

He Loved—He Laughed.
He Tried—He Failed.
He Did Well.

What Will Your Final Blessing Be?

At a DC Conference, February 2020, with my book *Decriminalizing Mental Illness*

Be happy again. Forgive the worst of me and hold the best of me in your hearts.[30]
– Steve Leder

Know that you were loved, are loved, and will be loved, even from beyond the grave as only a father—your dad—can love. This love is *true* enduring love. Pass it along. After I'm gone, tell me about how life is for you. I suspect that if you listen intently, you will hear me answer you with love and, if appropriate, laughter. The trials, love, and remembrances remain.

You must know that you both have been *the* driving force in my life, even from boyhood to this day, and eventually at Arlington. You have been with me working the farm, putting up hay all day, too tired to eat. You were there as I joined the Air Force, where I learned I could do college, and were beside me for 30 years of night school. You waited at home as I worked menial jobs to make ends meet in the 90s. Ah, I remember letting you, Nic, "drive" the Bobcat loader at a nursing home construction site. And you, Cindy, on the bicycle Kiddy Carrier, yelling with peals of laughter, "Faster Daddy, faster!" You both made *two* careers happen against so many odds. You were with me as I worked to make my last years ones you would respect.

Blessings? They come in many wishes for you:

I wish you *strength of constitution*. Be moral, of good character, physically and mentally fit, and be humane—a good, even revered, member of the community. Study the Greats so you may learn then continuously build virtue and character and thus grow to be your best to your last day.

I wish you a *life well lived*. Be the example you can be for those around you and who will follow you. You were meant to follow the natural laws to be good, do good, for the common good and lead accordingly. You both inherit the family name; I did my best to make it worthy of you.

I wish you a *good day*. Hard, productive work rewarded by more of it because it's so satisfying as you solve and build things. A good day also includes a great book, music, good food (preferably which you cook), and a good wine of your choice to go with it. May your day include beauty, that which is natural and that which you create in your homes. Beauty is calming. A good day also includes those things you personally enjoy that lift you up and enhance your happiness. And again, I wish you a few good acquaintances and one dear friend to share your days as well as a significant other to share your life. I want you to know I still believe in marriage based on love and understanding such that it matures as we age into something perhaps less intense but still comforting, uplifting, and supportive.

I wish you to *find interest in life*. Be interested in the various dimensions of being alive in this greatest country in the march of civilizations. Read. Study. Learn. Do. Travel. Write. Cook. Make music. Play. Make memories. Be joyful. And love. These are the best privileges of being human. They all take glorious work.

I wish you *success*. It is said, and it's true, that 90 percent of success is showing up. How much better if you show up prepared, willing to work hard with a smile (and perhaps even a witty comment), goal oriented, accepting earned leadership, leading by example, and ready to achieve more than the sum of the parts. With this, you can only win in the end. Humbly assume your rewards.

I wish you *patriotism*. Do your part to continue the family's contribution to this experiment in living and progressing together, equitably. Thus earn your dreams in this wonderful country of opportunity that you seize vigorously with heart, head, and hands.

I wish you *respect*. Work hard to be respectable so you may earn the company of likeminded people. Frolic with the best of them, discuss good books with them, and walk away from those not worthy of respect.

I wish you *health*. Take care of yourself—body, mind, and soul. These are your natural vehicles at the ready to carry you through the muck to the wonders of life and the natural world to prosperity and a ready smile.

I wish you *fearlessness*. Do not fear obstacles as the day breaks. You are made of the stuff that conquers troubles and celebrates wonders. Remember Churchill's you are not "made of sugar candy."

I wish you *interest in being alive*. I think endlessly about the indescribable wonderment of life. From a whale to a titmouse. From the first fire to Mars. From earth to flight. And wonderful humanity. People are basically, naturally good and do good. This is the best, no, the only defense against wickedness.

I wish you a *good book* by your side. What a blessing should you find a few titles from my library that are meaningful to you and from which you learn. Always learn. Let them be the start of your own libraries. See me as you read, and you will not be alone . . . ever.

I wish you *longevity*. Plan well and work toward having many years to become what you were meant to be and so your full life reflects vitality and vigor. Shoot for 100 great years! Then you must shoot 100 at skeet (smile). Or excel at what *you* enjoy most. It's worth it to live long and well and prosper. Again, you never know: The next day may be the best day of your life. So many wonders.

Oh, and when you were born! You may have heard said that the joys of life "floated me off the ground." It's true. Hear it now. You were there from your first blue breath, you were next to me through indescribable struggles, helping me to get up in the morning, to survive, then thrive. How could I fail? Now, as we consider your lives without me physically, hear me, I will speak to you. See me, I will be there. I wish you to be as proud of me as I am of you. I did my best.

Again . . .

There is nothing that matters more in the end than love.[31]
– Steve Leder (Ditto – JK/Dad)

I WISH YOU HAPPY TRAILS!

EPILOGUE

My Legacy

One of the best things we can do for subsequent generations is to pass on the legacy of a good name, meaningful experiences, and especially what we have learned about living. These remembrances are best served in written form. Like history, much of what one leaves doesn't exist unless it's penned. Memories are faulty, fade, and are far gone in a generation or two. Keep them alive. One can do much to be remembered well and fondly—and hopefully leave inspiration for those whose lives will follow.

This goes way beyond just estate planning. For example, I have left a journal, written a memoir, compiled a photo journal, begun a small charitable foundation, written books, and left an ethical will. *Someone someday* may find *something* useful, if not interesting or amusing, in it all. I hope to even save someone from making the mistakes I have made. This alone would make it worth the effort.

You will find my rough-draft journal, which I kept largely in the 1990s, in my study closet. It's in three, three-ring binders. They are for both you, Nic, and Cindy.

You are holding a *memoir*. Thank you for reading this far.

You'll also find my *photo journals* in three-ring binders—nine volumes and counting, begun around 2000, which works out to about one binder for every two years.

I have grand hopes for The Nicole and James Klopovic Charitable Foundation. I have planted the mustard seed. I plan that it is accompanied by a four-volume set on Capacity Building, explaining how to do granting that works to build *permanent answers to permanent problems,* the tagline to the Foundation. The focus is at the local level of government where the action occurs and progress is made. That's where people define their problems, develop their answers, and commit their sweat.

My lesson of learning, especially self-study, is to *read* something worthy, *do* something worthy, then *write* something worthy.

The remaining Capacity Building books will be accompanied by my books already published—six thus far (see list below). It's an eclectic bunch but worth a read at least once to see where I have traveled with the written word.

1. *Becoming a New Wave Leader: Principles and Practices to Live and Lead Well* (2021)
2. *Your Moral Compass: A Practical Guide for New Wave Leaders* (2020)
3. Volume II of the Capacity Building Series. *Decriminalizing Mental Illness: A Practical Model for Building Sustainable Crisis Intervention Teams* (2019)
4. *Little Stories: A Legacy of Learning, Laughing and Loving* (2019) (About my true friend Marty)
5. *The Honest Backpacker: A Practical Guide for the Rookie Adventurer over 50* (2017)
6. *Effective Program Practices for At-Risk Youth: A Continuum of Community-Based Programs* (2003)

Thus, I am creating my legacy, largely inspired and motivated by my two beautiful daughters as well as the sincere desire to be of service to others.

Last Words in Summary: My Ethical Will

Wisdom begins in wonder.
– Socrates

Here I wish to reiterate my fond feelings, wishes, and hopes for you both.

I love being your Dad. I love hearing "Dad." My life was, is, and will be all about having you, Nicole and Cindy, magical that you are. Bring to the fore fond memories, as I do.

Sometimes you will never know the value of a moment until it becomes a memory.
– Dr. Seuss

Find someone to love for a lifetime. – May he be of good character and a sharing, loving nature, unafraid of hard work. You will know when he arrives; keep your arms and heart open so he may know you and what you are. Lifelong companionship is the true foundation of longevity and happiness. Then all the other things I tried to convey here can happen well enough. Together, the good times are all that much better beyond the hubbub of the day.

Love as you have the natural capability to do. – Recognize that love usually starts with a bang. It's natural and instinctual. Ensure and enjoy that it be true intimacy in all its dimensions. Love survives the routine of work, life, and children, then matures into something else. It becomes the companionship of caring, sharing, growing old together to laugh at the aches and pains running top to bottom, usually in tandem. Expect to forget glasses at your fingertips and still remember minute details from a lifetime ago.

Laugh as I have heard you laugh. – Oh yes, life is so serious. And if you peek around the day, it is wildly funny, too. Oh, I love to laugh, and I know you do, too.

Recall with me the moments we laughed till we couldn't breathe. – JK

Find and earn that one true friend. – This individual is a remarkable gift of joy. Choose friends wisely. The respect you show is the respect you earn. The majority who pass by are merely acquaintances; gather them sparingly. Among them, I wish for you to have that one true friend who viscerally feels what you feel and fears not to tell you truths.

Meet obstacles well; they will make you. – Tough times come and go; know that you have the fortitude to conquer them and thrive.

Life is good, live it. – Life is very good, even magical indeed—especially with worthy children in it. Take the plunge and do your best. You will not be alone as I will be there in person, then in memory, with a smile and a baritone voice you will not forget and will actually hear when you need it most.

Remember that the remains of the day are the pleasant, sometimes mystical moments of being alive, humane, and human. I get so much pleasure sitting on my newly built patio under the cedar pergola I designed and finished. Better with a sip of good double-oaked bourbon and a book, a gentle breeze, the fountain bubbling, and the birds singing and bluebirds on the nest just for me . . . and you. Have a seat.

> *Marvel, truly marvel, at a flower, a bird, a tree, a mountaintop. Goodness!*
> *Roll in the snow and bathe in a natural hot spring.* – JK

Nature is the gateway to so much more; get out in it. – Get into nature, even if it's your own backyard sanctuary. River raft the Middle Fork of the Salmon River, canoe the Rio Grande and the Grande Ronde; you *will* see me there. The wonders of nature will help you feel small, humble, human, and euphoric about life. Here I am compelled to pause as tears of joy overtake me.

Be optimistic. – Think of what humanity has accomplished. Gracious—we just may colonize other planets. Oh, the things you will see and do. Marvel at the works of man. From cave paintings to the Pietà and a Rembrandt to the transcontinental railroad built with pick, shovel, mules, a few sticks of dynamite, and "foreign" labor. My word! Crews of the Central Pacific Railroad, 90 percent Chinese and the rest Irish, laid 10 *miles* and 56 feet of track in a *day!*

*You're off to great places! Today is your day! Your mountain is waiting.
So . . . get on your way!* – Dr. Seuss

Appreciate the genius of art. – Sing "Hallelujah" with Leonard Cohen, then sing it with me. Hear me singing "Sixteen Tons" in a deep, deep round base voice. And gee whiz, I do love a rock concert. Learn to play a great guitar and teach your children, too.

Cultivate hobbies besides reading. – Golly, I do hope it's skeet. You will have a good Krieghoff with which to do it. Wear the nickel finish off the action and hit 100 for me.

Become spiritual, no matter your path. – If you choose an organized religion, know that it's an attempt to help people be good. If you do it by self-study and application of philosophy, well and good. I wish for you to reach for being good and doing good for the common good. Thus, you learn to live, strive, and thrive.

Make time for family. – Build and maintain family rituals. Have at least Saturday or Sunday dinner together. Teach the children to cook. There's nothing like a first PB&J, oozing jam and peanut butter, constructed by a five-year-old. You have cooking in your genes; find it, revel in it. Good times are the insurance that keeps family together when things go wrong.

Get quickly past worrying and on to achieving. – I can't stop you from worrying. I'm my own worst enemy in that department. One truth I know, though, is that quite quickly one forgets what all the fuss was about. As if to make my point, my computer crashed . . . again. Couldn't figure it out. Called tech help, and it was a matter of unplugging the dock and plugging it back in. Egads. Seems Google is busy crashing stuff again. *But,* I maintained my cool, this time: I'm learning.

*Even the most trying of times look quite frivolous with the morning sun
and bluebirds on the nest in the backyard.* – JK

Be of action. – Yes, plan then *do*. See worthy things then make them happen.

Take time for leisure. – With all your doing, set aside time for leisure. It will define you and give you up to thinking, reading, relaxing, and becoming better.

See the blessings all about you. – Meditate daily and learn to count the wonders of living in a free country where you can be who you were meant to be. Miracles are everywhere; count them daily. They are the bullwork against the doom and gloom pounding us in waves. Bah! Pick up Mark Twain, raft the Mississippi with Huck and Jim, and giggle, guffaw, and laugh out loud with the master jokester.

Don't lose your faith in your fellow humans, but use discretion. – Work on respect and thus you will find the worthy. Just note when someone brings you down or, horrors, wastes your time. Run as if your life depended on it, because it does. Learn from the experience.

Make time well spent, often. – The older I get, the more I see the magic of time well spent and the tragedy of it wasted. I wish for you a productive day with worthy work, laughter, family (a giggling infant is surreal, and you gave me that gift of gifts), gratitude, and a prize-winning apple pie.

Take me with you wherever you go, whatever you do, whenever you wish. I will be there.

*I wish for you to know that I am so proud of you—
and that you are loved, loved, loved.*

DAD

Bibliography

Cicero Selected Works. Trans. Michael Grant. London: Penguin Books, 1960.

Cicero: On Living and Dying Well. Trans. Thomas Habinek. London, Penguin Books, 2012.

Collins, J. L. *The Simple Path to Wealth: Your Road Map to Financial Independence and a Rich, Free Life.* JL Collins, 2016. See www.jlcollinsnh.com.

Durant, W. & A. *The Lessons of History.* New York: Simon & Schuster Paperbacks, 1968.

Durant, W. *The Story of Philosophy.* New York: Simon & Schuster Paperbacks, 2005 (first published in 1926).

Farnsworth, W. *The Practicing Stoic: A Philosophical Users Manual.* Jeffrey, New Hampshire: David R. Godine, Publisher, 2018.

Leder, S. *For You When I Am Gone: Twelve Essential Questions to Tell a Life Story.* New York: Avery, an imprint of Penguin Random House, LLC, 2022.

Musashi, M. *A Book of Five Rings.* Trans. by Victor Harris. Woodstock, New York: The Overlook Press, 1974.

Seneca. *Seneca Six Pack: Six Essential Texts.* Trans. by various authors. Los Angeles, California: Enhanced Media Publishing, 2016.

Sinclair, David A. & Matthew D. LaPlante. *Lifespan: Why We Age—and Why We Don't Have To.* New York: Atria Books, 2019.

Endnotes

[1] Steve Leder, *For You When I Am Gone: Twelve Essential Questions to Tell a Life Story.* New York: Avery, an imprint of Penguin Random House, LLC, 2022, p. 196.

[2] D. Armitage & M. McQuery, *Big Ideas for Little Philosophers.* R. Rosenthal, illustrator. New York: G. P. Putnam's Sons, an imprint of the Penguin Group, Oct. 2020.

[3] *When Harry Met Sally* is a famous movie of 1989. You (Nic) and I went to the legendary Katz Deli in Brooklyn. It's a famous Jewish eatery known for its six-inch, piled-high, corned beef-and-rye sandwiches with a full meal of pickles dressing the stack. The "cutters," who had to work at Katz for 10 years before they could make a first sandwich, were all from the Dominicans. You bowled them over as you ordered in Spanish. We got our meals and wandered the place to find a seat. The cutters massed in a little knot, jib jabbering, when one pointed to the ceiling to a sign and an arrow pointing downward to our little table, reading "This is where Harry Met Sally." What a memory in a memorable longweekend. We went back the next morning for knishes and bagels to die for.

[4] My reading takes me far and wide, with some concentrations. One is understanding money. Way at the back of one such read, *The Simple Path to Wealth*, J. L. Collins devoted a few, really few, words to the fact that anyone can be aphilanthropist. So you and I are, Nicole.

[5] "Billy" is what my friend Marty's momma called him and how he was known. Recent friends called him Don. I havealways called him Marty as that was his Air Force nickname. We had our nicknames embroidered on our hats, and Iwas "Klop." No one knew my first name for 18 months!

[6] Under Marty's coaching I put three rounds in the circumference of a quarter. He was so meticulous he would fire a number of rounds and select the shells that were the most accurate. He hand loaded four select bullets. Why four? Because that was the limit for the year. He never missed. He could choose the vertebra he wanted to hit. Instantlydone. Most humane. Not a edible scrap of the deer was wasted.

[7] *Cicero: On Living and Dying Well.* Trans. Thomas Habinek. London, Penguin Books, 2012, p. 83.

[8] Mine was the biggest fish on the party boat off Key Largo, Florida. It's customary to throw a dollar or two in a pot, and whoever gets the biggest fish wins the pot. I wasn't in the big fish pool, though, because the tail of my king mackerel was broken by a barracuda. However, we ate off that fish for much of the trip by taking steaks to restaurants for prep and service.

[9] W. Farnsworth, *The Practicing Stoic, On Interdependence and Service.* Jeffrey, New Hampshire: David R. Godine, Publisher, 2018, p. 219.

[10] David A. Sinclair & Matthew D. LaPlante, *Lifespan: Why We Age—and Why We Don't Have To.* New York: Atria Books, 2019.

[11] The Harvard Study of Adult Development and now The Harvard Second Generation Study point to the fact that having someone to love into old age is the greatest factor in determining longevity and happiness. *https://www.adultdevelopmentstudy.org/*

[12] Op. Cit., Sinclair & LaPlante, *Lifespan.*

[13] Op. Cit., Leder, *For You When I Am Gone,* pp. 97-98.

[14] "TROSA is an innovative, multi-year residential program that empowers people with substance use disorders to be productive, recovering individuals by providing comprehensive treatment, experiential vocational training, education, and continuing care." TROSA is located in both Durham and Winston-Salem, North Carolina. *https://www.trosainc.org*

[15] Op. Cit., Harvard Study of Adult Development, *https://www.adultdevelopmentstudy.org/.*

[16] There are 25 rounds in a box of shotgun shells. There are 25 shots in a round of skeet. What a coincidence. The idea is to go 25 straight and then the craziness starts. Next you want to do 100 straight. Then 100 straight in all four gauges: 410, 28, 20 and 12. That's a 4x4. Then do 25 straight with doubles (don't ask). To do that, you have to practice about 30,000 rounds a year and go to at least 10 tournaments to register your scores. Shoot, load, sleep, eat, repeat. No life. The kids and wife disappear while you're shooting the USA Open. Then, if you're lucky, you get a belt buckle and a hamburger and fries. So you go through D - C - B - A, AA, AAA classes. Now you're cookin'. You've also gone through at least two divorces and drive a klunker to keep in powder and shot. Your kids drop out of college the first year— no $$. But ya gotta have more. Ha ha, you've arrived . . . the looney bin. See why I shoot only one gauge and no tournaments? Most happy as a C shooter.

[17] B. Spinoza, *Ethics,* Everyman ed., Intro, p. xxii (note) as referred to by Durant in *The Story of Philosophy.*

[18] Will Durant, *The Story of Philosophy.* New York: Simon and Schuster Paperback, original copyright 1929, renewed 1961, p. 131.

[19] Op. Cit., Leder, *For You When I Am Gone,* p. 66.

[20] Ibid., p. 68.

[21] Ibid., p. 135.

[22] Publishers set a low bar for the designation "bestseller," as it's good for sales. They never told me, but I suspect, guess, that my first book, *Effective Practices for At-Risk Youth,* sold about 4,000 copies. Not bad. Authors are the last to be paid from the crumbs. Many books sell just a few copies as promotion is quite difficult.

[23] J. Klopovic and N. Klopovic, *The Honest Backpacker: A Practical Guide for the Rookie Adventurer over 50*. Morrisville, North Carolina: Affinitas Publishing, 2017.

[24] Still serving another legendary breakfast for guests, Ms. Ginny died at 95 by slipping on a carpet and hitting her head. I treasure the picture of the two of us next to "her" Laurel Creek.

[25] Op. Cit., Harvard Study of Adult Development, *https://www.adultdevelopment-study.org/.*

[26] J. L. Collins, *The Simple Path to Wealth: Your Road Map to Financial Independence and a Rich, Free Life.* JL Collins, 2016. www.jlcollinsnh.com

[27] Ibid.

[28] USAA insurance is available only for current members of the military, veterans, and their families.

[29] Op. Cit., Leder, *For You When I Am Gone,* p. 165.

[30] Ibid., p. 197.

[31] Ibid., p. 196.

www.ingramcontent.com/pod-product-compliance
Lightning Source LLC
Chambersburg PA
CBHW060537010526
44119CB00006B/181